THE SCIENCE OF CHANGE

Elizabeth
Thank You For
Coming To the Event
And Best of Luck!
11-7-13

THE SCIENCE OF CHANGE

BASICS BEHIND WHY CHANGE SUCCEEDS AND FAILS

TOM SOMODI

The Science of Change:
Basics Behind Why Change Succeeds and Fails

Copyright © 2013 by Thomas James Somodi

International Standard Book Number: 978-0-9897589-0-1
Library of Congress Catalog Number: 2013949381

All rights reserved. No part of this book may be reproduced in any form or by any electronic means, including information storage and retrieval systems, without written permission from the author, except by a reviewer who may quote brief passages in a review.

Disclaimer. The author and publisher make no promises, warranties, or representations as to the contents of this book. This book contains general information, and its contents may not apply to any particular circumstance.

MANUFACTURED IN THE UNITED STATES OF AMERICA

PRODUCED BY ADAMS PRESS, CHICAGO, ILLINOIS

CHANGE SCIENCE INSTITUTE, LLC
WWW.CHANGESCIENCEINSTITUTE.COM

PRINTED ON RECYCLED/RECYCLABLE PAPER

To my wife

Nancy

who was continually there with me through all the hurdles, time commitments, and anxiety.

Nancy has brought a new meaning to the definition of support.

TABLE OF CONTENTS

List of Figures XV

Introduction 1
   Commitment—or Lack of 5
   From Methodology to Science 9

Chapter One | Change Science Overview 13
   The Definition of Change 19
   The Elements of Change 21
   Environments 29
   Types of Change 31

Chapter Two | Change Science Principles 37
   The Environmental Override Principle 40
   The Change/Time Continuum Principle 43
   The Chain of Events Principle and Perpetuating Change 47
   Change Science Principle of Simultaneous Change 55
   Significance of Change Science Principles 58

Chapter Three | Change Dynamics 61
   Defined Processes and Change Dynamics 64
   Defined Implementations and Change Dynamics 66
   Environments and Change Dynamics 74

    Relevant Environment and Conditions............................ 75
  Change Dynamics Profiles and Analysis............................ 80
    Change Dynamics Profile 82
    Change Dynamics Analysis.. 86

CHAPTER FOUR | ENVIRONMENTS PART I: STRUCTURAL NATURE OF ENVIRONMENTS 89

What Is an Environment?... 92
Selection of an Environment 93
  Rules for Selecting an Environment................................. 95
    Primary and Secondary Environments 101
Types of Environments... 103
Conditions 106
  Classifications of Conditions 106
    Relevant Conditions 106
    Classification of Conditions Based Upon
      Underlying Origin 109
      Constant Conditions 110
      Dominant Conditions 111
  Environments Versus Conditions................................... 112
  Transition into Environmental Dynamics...................... 115

CHAPTER FIVE | ENVIRONMENTS PART II: ENVIRONMENTAL DYNAMICS 117

Environmental Adjustments 120
  Relevancy 124
Relativity... 126
Inter-environmental Influence 128
  Change Dispersion 132
    Observation and Change Dispersion........................ 136
    Change Dispersion Dynamics.................................. 139
      Butterfly Effect.. 145
Beyond Environments 148

Chapter Six | Defined Change 149
Definitions and Concepts Revisited 152
Definition of Change and Defined Change 153
Types of Change 153
Conscious Versus Unconscious Cognitive Influence ... 155
Cognitive Influence and Organizations and Society ... 157
The Evolution of Society and Repeatable Change 159
Anxiety and Frustration Associated with Change 162
Answering the Pertinent Questions 167

Chapter Seven | Defined Processes Part I: Structural Nature of Defined Processes 171
Definition of a Defined Process 174
Process Factors 177
Process Maps 178
Importance of Determining Appropriate Process Factors 184
Three Additional Underlying Aspects of Defined Processes 187
Interrelationship of Defined Processes to Other Defined Processes and Defined Implementations 188
Defined Processes Versus Defined Implementations ... 189
Multidimensional Aspects of Defined Processes and the Hierarchy of Change 193
Constant Conditions and Relevancy 194
Beginning and Ending Points of a Defined Process 196
Single Defined Process and Single Defined Implementation 202
Long Defined Process and Short Defined Implementation 202
Short Defined Process and Long Defined Implementation 203
Lack of a Continuous Execution Cycle 204

Chapter Eight | Defined Processes Part II: Selection of Defined Processes 211

Process Selection Considerations 213
   Reasons a Defined Process Can Fail 214
   Validity, Efficiency, Effectiveness, and Reliability 218
      Validity 218
      Efficiency 219
      Effectiveness 221
      Reliability 223
Final Selection of a Defined Process 224
   Selecting a Defined Process That Explains Why a Certain Defined Change Has Already Occurred 224
   Selecting a Defined Process to Explain a Defined Change That We Expect to Occur in the Future 232
   Selecting a Defined Process That Will Yield an Effective Desired Defined Change That We Want to Obtain 240
Testing One, Two, Three 246

Chapter Nine | Defined Implementations 249

Key Points of Defined Implementations 253
Basics of an Implementation Plan 255
Implementation Selection Considerations 257
   Reasons a Defined Implementation Can Fail 258
   Tiered Implementation Processes 260
   Validity, Efficiency, Effectiveness, Reliability, and Process Stacking 264
      Validity, Efficiency, Effectiveness, and Reliability Associated with the Specific Structural Nature of a Defined Implementation 265
      Impact Associated with Process Stacking 266
   Selection of a Defined Implementation and Implementation Plan 269

Selecting a Defined Implementation That Explains
    Why a Certain Primary Defined Process Has
    Already Occurred 270
  Selecting a Defined Implementation to Obtain the
    Execution of a Future Desired Primary
    Defined Process 273

CHAPTER TEN | SYSTEMS 297
  Definition of a System 300
    Other Characteristics of a System 305
    Types of Systems 306
  Reasons for Using a System 308
    Systems and Our Ability to Obtain Change 308
    Systems and Overall Defined Change Versus
      a Defined Change 312
    Systems and Our Ability to Standardize 315
    Systems and Our Ability to Control Change 315
    Systems and Continuous Improvement 317
    Systems and Our Ability to Capture Experience
      and Knowledge 318
  Discrete and Repeatable Systems 319
    Discrete Systems 320
    Repeatable Systems 322
    Potential Disadvantages of Repeatable Systems 323
    Favorable Characteristics to Look for in a
      Repeatable System 325
    Repeatable Versus Repetitive 328
  Development and Implementation of a System 328
  Evaluation and Selection of a System 333

CHAPTER ELEVEN | RISK DYNAMICS PART I:
  STRUCTURAL NATURE OF RISK 337
  Definition of Risk 342

Risk Factors 343
   Fundamental Versus Tactical 345
   Levels of Risk Factors 346
      Primary Level Risk Factors 347
         Validity of a Defined Change 347
         Validity of a Defined Process and/or
            Defined Implementation 349
         Validity of the Primary Environment 351
         Environmental Override 352
      Secondary Risk Factors 353
         Time Intervals 353
         Conflicting Relevant Conditions 356
         Complexity 357

**CHAPTER TWELVE | RISK DYNAMICS PART II:
CONCEPTS AND TOOLS TO CONTROL RISK** **365**
   Significance and Probability 368
      Significance 368
         The Global Perspective of Significance 369
         Micro Perspective of Significance 370
      Probability 371
   Controllable and Uncontrollable Risk—Eliminate
      and Mitigate 372
      Controllable Risk 373
         Definition 373
         Functionality Trade-off 373
         Elimination of Controllable Risk 374
      Uncontrollable Risk 375
         Mitigation of Uncontrollable Risk 376
      Eliminate and Mitigate 377
   Disconnect Analysis 378
   Energy/Effort Hump Theory 392
   Time Interval Considerations 398

Control, Monitoring, and Adjustment Points 406
Validity Testing 408
Final Thoughts 410

Epilogue | What We Have Discovered 411

Glossary 417

Index 441

FIGURES

1-1a	Defined Change of Burning a Piece of Paper	22
1-1b	Defined Process of Combustion	24
1-1c	Defined Implementation of Lighting Match and Holding It to the Paper	25
1-1d	Change Elements Associated with Defined Change of Burning a Piece of Paper	28
1-2	Different Types of Environments	30
2-1	Change Science Change/Time Continuum Principle	45
2-2	Time/Change Continuum and Chain of Events Principles	50
2-3	Example of Watering Your Garden	53
3-1	Execution of a Process in the Chain of Events	65
3-2	Defined Change = Change in Environmental Conditions Resulting from Execution of a Process	66
3-3	Change in Environmental Conditions Resulting from the Execution of a Defined Implementation with the Objective = Execution of Process 1	70
3-4	Implementation of a Process in a Chain of Events	72
3-5	The Chain of Events for a Given Environment XYZ	77

5-1	Structural Dynamics of Internal and External Environmental Conditions	122
5-2	Speed of Light Versus Sound Across Multiple Environments	130
5-3	Example of an Environment with a Single Epicenter	143
5-4	Examples of Different Types of Change Dispersion	144
5-5	Different Types of Change Dispersion Along Multiple Points on the Change/Time Continuum	144
5-6	Different Types of Change Dispersion Along Multiple Points on the Change/Time Continuum Across Multiple Environments	145
5-7	Single Grain of Sand	147
7-1	Hierarchy of Change—Levels of Change Occurring Simultaneously in the Known Universe	193
7-2	Single Defined Process and Single Defined Implementation	207
7-3	Long Defined Process and Short Defined Implementation	208
7-4	Short Defined Process and Long Defined Implementation	209
7-5	Lack of a Continuous Execution Cycle	210
9-1	Example of Tiered Implementation Referencing	263
9-2	Summary of Possible Implementation Scenarios	276
9-3	Change Dynamics Profile	280
9-4	Change Dynamics Profile—Primary Environment Condition Considerations	285
9-5	Change Dynamics Profile—Possible Strategies	286

9-6	Change Dynamics Profile—Triggering Event Considerations	288
9-7	Alternative Defined—Implementations	289
10-1	A System Producing Overall Defined Change	303
10-2	A System Producing Overall Defined Change 6 with a Subsystem Producing a Component Defined Change 2	304
12-1	Risk Assessment	372
12-2	Bonfire Example of Steps Included in a Disconnect Analysis	385
12-3	Energy/Effort Hump Theory	394
12-4	Time Interval Scenario Analysis	400

Introduction

My progression and my passion!

Tom Somodi

If you are like me, there have been times in your life when you have been frustrated or anxious dealing with some sort of change. Maybe it was the anxiety you experienced when learning to drive so that you could change from relying on others to drive you around to having the ability to go places on your own. Or maybe it was the change you experienced when you graduated from high school and you had to cope with the life changing experience of being separated from the ones you love. Then again, maybe it was the change you had to participate in at work or the diet you failed at or the move you had to make from one house to a new house.

But wait, I am sure you have learned to deal with all that change in your life by reading the numerous books and articles written by all those experts who tell you how easy it is if you just do this or just do that. What the heck, your life of dealing with change becomes a piece of cake once you hear that expert talk about change management on your favorite talk show. If these statements are, in fact, true for you, then there is probably not much benefit in your reading the rest of this book.

However, I would strongly suggest you continue to read on if your success at dealing with the change in your life, whether personal or business, has been mixed at best:

- no matter what experts you read or listen to, or
- no matter how hard you try to make something happen, or
- no matter how committed you are to making a change work out the way you want it to.

It is my objective to help you develop a deeper, more scientific understanding of change.

This new understanding is not intended to be just one more false claim that the change you want can be guaranteed. Instead, it is intended to help you better deal with the change in your life through a pragmatic comprehension of the dynamics of change. As you reach a realization of just how change really works and the fact that change cannot be guaranteed, you should be able to reduce the amount of frustration and anxiety you experience when dealing with change.

Nevertheless, while change cannot be guaranteed, all is not necessarily lost. This book will help you develop an insight into how to improve the possibility of obtaining the change you are striving for in your life. In addition, you will be able to develop an understanding of how to positively adjust your strategies when dealing with change that is not occurring the way you had planned.

My career has taken me around the world and has involved hundreds, if not thousands, of systems implementations, process improvement projects, and change management assignments. At a personal level, I, like everyone else, have struggled with my share of challenges associated with the change that occurs in our everyday lives. Needless to say, my exposure to dealing with change has, if anything, been more extensive than that of most people and maybe could even be considered on the excessive side of the equation.

Early on in my career I was schooled by some of the best in traditional system implementation methodologies and what was soon to become popularized as change management techniques. Training and interactions with the likes of IBM consultants and purveyors of other major software and hardware systems, along with studying the works of numerous self-help authors, have been commonplace and continuous over my lifetime. To say the least, I have been well indoctrinated into the methods, critical success factors, and pitfalls of system implementations and change management.

Then something happened to me that would forever change my life and my perspective about change. I began to struggle with the rationale used by many purveyors of change management as to why change fails when in their opinion, it should have been successful.

This challenge came about as I was trying to develop a better understanding as to why certain change fails even though everything points to the fact that it should succeed. As you would expect, in both our personal lives and in business, change is not always successful. Even authors and consultants proposing to have the number one methodology for successful change have their share of failures and under-realization of benefits. But while the list of reasons for failure can be lengthy, there is one explanation of why change fails or, more specifically, why a specific change methodology that appears to be more prevalent than any other fails. That explanation is "lack of commitment."

COMMITMENT—OR LACK OF

Commitment is supposed to be the sure-fire way to successful change. It is a proven requirement. In your personal life, I am sure you have read this, heard it on the radio, seen it on TV, attended classes on it, and maybe even paid professionals to obtain it. Just add some time, a little money, and, most of all, commitment, and you just cannot fail. By the way, if you do fail, it is almost certain that you really did not have the true commitment necessary to succeed. After all, the methodology used has been proven to work. Look closely at what many of the self-help, how-to, and self-proclaimed experts write or say. You will almost always find the section on how, "if you want to truly be successful, you must stay committed to the plan, the course, the theory, or the conviction."

Sometimes in your heart of hearts you know you are not truly committed to wanting to change so this lack of commitment theory makes sense. However, there are other times that this just does not make any sense, and you become frustrated at these comments.

Because weight loss is a common goal for many, I will use this as the example. You want to have a change in your life by losing weight. You buy and read the books, follow the recipes, increase your exercise, and take all the vitamins suggested—all without obtaining the desired change. On top of all that, someone comes along and tells you that you are failing because of a lack of commitment. At that point in time (after you smack the other person), you say to yourself, "What is up?"

Of course, you are not perfect, but you are definitely committed. Can a lack of commitment truly be the reason for failure to change? Where is the logic in that?

Likewise, think of the executives or managers who have authorized and supported the implementation of a change initiative. You can hear them say, "I have committed some of my best staff to the project, hired a reputable consulting firm, and purchased some of the most sophisticated software available, and yet you tell me the implementation of the new system to derive the required change has failed because of a lack of my commitment. What is up?

"Of course, I may not have been perfect, but I was definitely committed. Can a lack of commitment truly be the reason for failure to change? Where is the logic in that?"

You might ask, if the lack of commitment argument is so frequently illogical, why do we accept it as a legitimate explanation? If you think about it a second, the reality is that this claim often exists in the context of one of the following:

1. The claim is made by individuals or organizations with a great deal of credibility—highly paid professionals or very successful writers and consultants. While not 100 percent successful, they almost always have a record of solid training, experience, and success. Remember, if you are not successful, these experts remind you that it was due to lack of commitment or understanding on your part. This not only sounds very logical given their expertise, but under closer examination it is a closed loop argument in their favor. They cannot lose. If you succeed, it was because you were committed to their methodology, which is the best methodology around. On the other hand, if you fail, they warned you up front that it would be due to a lack of commitment because the methodology is a proven one. How can you argue with all of that?
2. As individuals we often ignore this emphasis on a lack of commitment because it helps us rationalize our failure. In the beginning of the process, we assume our commitment and conviction are very strong and, therefore, this will not be an issue for us. There are countless studies that show humans by nature tend to be overly optimistic. For example, in one study of MBA students, more than 50 percent of the students felt their performance would be in the top 20 percent of the class even though they all knew that in reality only 20

percent can fall into this category (Thaler, Richard R., and Cass R. Sunstein. 2009. *Nudge*. New York: Penguin Books, 31–32). So when failure does occur, there is an inherent willingness to accept lack of commitment as the reason under the context that this would be an acceptable excuse by others. Rather than challenging the validity of the notion of a lack of commitment, it is easy to rationalize that we were not able to be committed because of other demands in our lives or the actions of others, thereby creating a buy-in to the concept of a lack of commitment.

3. The claim is made to individuals and organizations that are often desperate for success. They have tried several times to personally lose weight or to improve the performance of their organization, all with limited or no success. Again, lack of commitment can sound like a very logical common denominator given that other individuals and organizations have been successful.

4. Finally, the claims are often reinforced by someone that has personal credibility. Therefore, if you fail, then you must have done something wrong. Do the following examples sound familiar?

    - "Looks like you have lost some weight?"
      "Yes, I went on the XYZ diet a couple of months ago and lost 15 pounds."
      "Maybe I should try that. Where do I get the information?"
    - "We have really been struggling to increase our output."
      "We had the same problem, and then we hired XYZ Consultants who helped us make it happen."
      "What is XYZ's phone number, I think I will give them a call."

If you fail under these circumstances, it much easier to accept a difference in commitment than to spend the time trying to analyze what other conditions or factors may have been different between you and the person giving you the reference.

Even though I can understand why experts use this reasoning and why people in turn accept this reasoning, I struggled with the concept of a lack of commitment. In the end, it was still the lack of logic that often surrounds the use of the term "lack of commitment" that awoke in me a passion to increase my understanding about the dynamics of change. Although there is obviously a tremendous number of reasons as to why change fails, it was the lack of commitment argument that had the greatest influence on me and on my quest toward a better understanding as to what change was really all about. So from that point on, as I continued to be exposed to and involved with change initiatives, my focus went beyond the success and failure of any given initiative. Instead, I began to develop what I viewed as a broader picture of the dynamics surrounding change.

FROM METHODOLOGY TO SCIENCE

This focus led me to new perspectives on the dynamics of change and on how to increase the odds for successful change. It is important to note that unlike many who claim to have sure-fire methodologies to guarantee change, I recognize that change cannot always be guaranteed. However, I also came to realize that an understanding of the science of change can help increase the chances of obtaining a desired change. In addition, the concepts associated with the science of change can help us better understand why a change does not occur. This in turn, can enhance our ability to know when to move on or how to compensate in order to increase our odds for successful change the next time around.

As you might guess, this was a gradual progression for me. I went from observation, to the developing and testing of different concepts, methodologies, and approaches. This lead to finally reaching a solidification of the concepts that I have been fine-tuning and expanding upon ever since. Along the way I developed training materials and held training exercises that, of course, eventually led me to the desire to write a book about what methodologies to use to increase your chances for obtaining successful change.

So there was my new mission. Write a book that would describe my many discoveries about change management. The book could provide approaches and methodologies that could be used in both business and in our personal lives to increase our chances of obtaining the desired change we are searching for. However, as I was writing this new next bestseller, I came to a new epiphany. Halfway through the completion of my book I realized I was following the same path as all those who preceded me. It was a path that focused on the "how to" and on "methodologies" with just enough reach into a true understanding of change as was required to support my ideology. Bottom line, I realized that I was writing what needs to be my second book and that a new first book was required: a first book focused on change itself, a book on the science of change.

I came to understand that if we are ever going to be able to truly harness change to our benefit as individuals or as society as a whole, we must stop looking at it in the form of disjointed disconnected concepts, methodologies, and strategies. It is time to look at *change as a science* with definitions, principles, and theories that can be challenged through discussion, experimentation, logic, and mathematics. Change science is a science that is universal, bidirectionally interacting with other sciences: physical and social.

The study of change as a science can be used to explain and explore possible solutions and answers to open questions haunting us in other disciplines. Such as, "What is the definition of complexity?" and "How do we understand the dynamics associated with the laws of science, economics, human interaction, problem solving, and cognitive thinking?"

So the definitions, principles, and theories presented in this book, my first book, are intended to be a foundation to use in building the science of change. They are concepts aimed at driving further study and development for change as a science. These concepts are also a basis for the recognition and promotion of change as a science along with all the benefits that can be derived therefrom.

Much that is discussed about change is too often superficial and makes the assumption that everyone is automatically using the same language and a consistent set of definitions (come on, who does not know what change is?). In reality, change needs to be approached like any other science. Just like in mathematics, physics, and other sciences, you need clear definitions with mapped out principles and interrelationships that build on each other. You need to show how these definitions and principles are supported in reality and are incorporated in the day-to-day environment and society we live in.

Using change science, we will once and for all have an ability to formally evaluate and challenge the claims, concepts, theories, and methodologies promoted in the marketplace. We will no longer need to accept claims that change concepts and methodologies are legitimate or even relevant at face value. Instead, we will be able to evaluate them using assessment tools based on substance and discipline.

So follow me through the rest of this book as I continue to search beyond the illogical notion of a lack of commitment and into the new frontier of *change as a science!*

CHAPTER ONE

Change Science Overview

*In the beginning there was chaos. And chaos led to change.
And change led to chaos. And so the cycle goes!*

Tom Somodi

I want you to think a second about your exposure to the concept of change. If you are like many of us, you will probably not think about change in a context of something you experience as much as think about change as something you must acquire or work at to obtain. You have been told that if you want change then you must "do this," "act like that," "proceed in this manner," or "follow that path." Change is discussed and consulted over ad nauseam. Change management, project management, opportunity management, and change agents are all hot topics and give you the impression that you must manage something or execute a special process if you want to obtain change.

Now I want you to stop and specifically think about change in the context of what you have experienced and are experiencing right this very second. I hope you will recognize that change is not strictly something you need to obtain or a strategy to follow but is, in fact, something that you are constantly experiencing. Change is not just some method or procedure to execute but an integral, if not a driving, force behind all that exists and all that is happening around us. We need to recognize that change is so universally occurring and integral to all that is around us that if we really want to understand it, we must move beyond the concept of change as we have come to know it and to recognize it as a science.

Only by classifying change in the same context as such sciences such as physics, chemistry, and biology will we truly be able to explore it, understand it, and hopefully better harness it to provide benefit in the daily lives that we lead. By viewing change as a science, we will establish definitions and principles for change that can be challenged, validated, and expanded upon. Like other sciences, these definitions, principles and concepts will give us the ability to use the science of change to better understand the world we live in. This newfound knowledge and understanding can then be used as a basis for improving the possibility of obtaining a desired change.

So why look at change as a science now? Why has no one promoted change as a science prior to this? I am not sure I have the true answer to those questions. I can theorize that change is so universal in nature that it has been, and currently continues to be, discounted and ignored. Change is so fundamental that it is not recognized for the all-encompassing effects it has on everything that exists. Change is just accepted as a given and, therefore, the ability to strongly connect the dots to a science of underlying definitions, principles, and theory has not taken place. Obviously, there are an endless number of concepts and discussions about change, but not the recognition that these concepts and discussions could be distilled down into a true science.

I can also see how over the years the evolution of the concepts associated with change management and the attempts to figure out how to control or execute change in business and our personal life have perpetuated a focus on change as something to obtain or a strategy to execute. Let's face it, change in this context is much easier to leverage off of and promote. Not only does it give hope (that is, I can obtain the change I desire if I just do X), but it also becomes a basis for the lucrative self-help and change management industry. When you start to establish change as a science, then you begin to create an opportunity to scientifically assess these existing concepts and promoted methodologies. Change agents begin to be replaced with change scientists, or, at the least, there is recognition that change agents perform a much more limited role in the field of change.

You will also see that change science begins to challenge the notions on how change can be controlled or managed. We begin to recognize that the best we might be able to do is influence the ability to obtain a desired change. You will come to understand that it is difficult, if not impossible, to guarantee a specific desired change. It might be possible to assume that under the right conditions a specific process will work. However, we will learn that the actual success of that process is dependent upon the laws associated with change science. Therefore, while change might have a high degree of probable success, it rarely, if ever, can be absolutely guaranteed to be successful. In the world of change science, change management does not go away but becomes recognized as nothing more than trying to manage a given strategy or process. However, even when you use change management techniques, the probability of success will still be dependent on the underlying principles associated with change science.

Many of you will come to realize that certain of the concepts discussed in this book are similar to, or have a basis in, concepts developed and promoted in other sciences and disciplines. For example, those of you schooled in physics will see many parallel concepts to those found in physics. However, conceptual overlaps and duplication are not unusual among various scientific disciplines. So it should be no surprise and, if anything, reassuring that these overlapping concepts exist and that the science of change contains these connections to other sciences and disciplines.

It should be noted that I am not a physicist or a trained scientist. However, my expertise in change has given me an insight capable of creating an initial scientific basis for change. I have also created a personal goal for the promotion of further research, education, and training for the advancement of change as a science. Through these efforts, it is my hope that improvements in the linkage between change science and other disciplines can be used to further broaden the principles, concepts, and methodologies associated with the science of change. Most importantly, in the end, the overriding objective will be to empower ordinary people with concepts and a science that enhance their ability to understand the change that surrounds them.

I would hope by now you recognize that change is, in fact, not something to obtain but is all around us and a part of everything associated with the universe (both known and unknown) we live in. Therefore, it is finally time to move on and establish a scientific basis for change. That is what we will be focusing on in the rest of this book. What are the definitions, elements, principles, and theories we can use as a basis to launch the science of change? What are the concepts that represent a starting point for a future progression of expanded ideas and challenges related to the science of change? I will begin in this chapter with an initial overview of some of the definitions, elements, and principles that I feel represent a starting point in the science of change. In future chapters, I will expand on these concepts, establishing additional principles and using everyday examples to help solidify our understanding of change as a science. I hope that through this process you will not only develop a deeper understanding of change as a science but that you will learn how to use this understanding to better cope and positively leverage off of the constant change occurring in your life.

Before we start, I should highlight here that from this point forward I will italicize terms associated with change science on their first occurrence. These italicized terms will also appear in the Glossary that has been assembled in the back of the book. The Glossary will provide us a quick reference and will help us begin to recognize change science as a true scientific discipline.

THE DEFINITION OF CHANGE

We begin our journey into the world of change science by defining what change is:

> The definition of *change* is the transformation or alteration of the current state of being (or state) to a different state of being as it relates to a person, place, or thing or as it relates to the interrelationships between persons, places, or things.

Thus, every time something, (whether it be a person or a thing) moves from one position to another position, transforms into something else (for example, gasoline becoming carbon monoxide in your automotive engine or the food you eat being digested in your stomach), or is somehow modified (for example, ice melting into water), you have change. While you might need to read the definition a couple of times to understand it, the definition of change is really pretty simple. Yet the implications are enormous! You should now realize that all that we know and all that we experience are, in fact, based on change. I realize this is a very bold statement so let's look at it more closely.

As already stated, change is all around us, constantly and continuously occurring on a universal basis. From the motion that is taking place at the subatomic level to the movement of the stars in the sky and from the thoughts that are generated from the firing of the neurons in your brain to the freezing and melting of water at the North Pole, we are constantly observing and experiencing change. The definition of change reinforces that all other sciences exist because of change. Physics to chemistry to behavioral science all depend on change as an underlying requirement. You cannot have motion in physics or chemical reactions in chemistry without having change. Nor would the study of people's actions or their interrelationships with each other in behavioral science be possible without the underlying concepts associated with change.

The definition of change also highlights how the amount of change that is occurring every second, even millisecond, around us is almost scary, even incomprehensible. The extent to which change is taking place and the dynamics surrounding change give the impression that the ability to truly understand change, much less harness change, might be totally impractical or even impossible. It might be this overwhelming feeling of complexity that to date has driven society's inability to fully deal with all the change around us.

However, by building off of the definition of change with the establishment of some additional basic principles and concepts, we can harness a better understanding of change. Plus, these principles and concepts will not only improve our understanding of change, but will also allow us to enhance our everyday lives when dealing with change. We will in fact, be able to improve our potential to obtain the desired change that has so often been elusive.

I also think that many of you will be surprised at how simple some of these principles and concepts surrounding change science are to understand. That is not to say understanding them will be a slam dunk, but you will not have to be a scientific genius to develop a sufficient level of understanding to make them useful to you in your everyday life. Some of the most complex issues we deal with everyday are often based on some very simple concepts. For example, when you look at the complexity of the weather, it is hard to believe that much of it can be explained by the simple law of thermodynamics or that the complexity of the tides can be so easily explained by the gravitational pull of our moon.

So let's move on and explore the elements that make up change.

THE ELEMENTS OF CHANGE

The next step in our journey into change science takes us beyond a strong definition and into an understanding of the elements that make up change. There are three basic elements associated with change:

1. *Defined change* is the first element of change and represents an identification/definition of the exact change you want to obtain or examine.

    It is important to clearly identify and define the specific change in the state of being that you wish to obtain or examine. Keep in mind that you not only must clearly define if the change is associated with a person, place, or thing or the interrelationship between persons, places, or things but also must describe the current state of being and the state of being that will exist after the change occurs. Some examples of a defined change include:

    - The motion of a person or object from one location (the beginning state of being) to another location (the ending state of being). This could include a person walking from point A to point B, a ball rolling down a hill, or the movement of an electron around the nucleus of an atom.
    - The modification of a person or object such as the sculpting of a statute (the ending state of being) out of a block of stone (the beginning state of being) or the change in a person's appearance from before a haircut to after a haircut.

Chapter One

- The transformation from one substance to another substance such as creating whipped cream (the ending state of being) from cream (the beginning state of being) or the transformation of carbon dioxide into sugars using sunlight through the photosynthesis that occurs in plants.
- The change in the interrelationship between things such as the change in the interrelationship of air outside a bicycle tire (beginning state of being) to the air inside of the bicycle tire (ending state of being) after the tire has been inflated.

Figure 1-1a is a graphical depiction of our first element of change representing the burning of a piece of paper. It shows a defined change with a beginning state of being of a piece of paper fully intact and an ending state of being represented by a pile of ashes created from the burning of the paper.

Figure 1-1a
Defined Change of Burning a Piece of Paper

A Defined Change = the <u>specific</u> change under consideration out of all the possible change that exist

Of course, with so much change constantly occurring around us the examples are endless. And it is exactly this magnitude in the amount of change occurring around us that makes it critical to clearly define the change that we are interested in obtaining or examining. That is why the first element of change is to define the change so that there is no confusion as to what the next two elements of change are associated with.

2. *Defined process* is the second element of change and represents the identification/definition of the exact process that was used or will be used to obtain the defined change under examination.

   In order to move from one state of being to another state of being, a process must occur. Definition of this process includes an identification of any factors that will be required, including the sequence of activities and actions that need to take place, in order to move from the beginning state of being to the ending state of being associated with the defined change.

   Note that in change science we will use the term *process factors* when referring to the specific variables, elements, activities, or other types of factors necessary for a specific process to occur.

   These process factors can include anything from a specific amount of a chemical or other substance to a certain amount of sunlight to a certain range of temperature. But in every case, process factors need to be all-inclusive when establishing the defined process that will be used to obtain the defined change.

   It is also very important to recognize that there can be more than one process to select from as the defined process to use for a given defined change. For example, if someone wants to move from location A to location B, he or she might be able to choose from various processes including running, walking, or driving between the locations. Any one of these individual processes could be selected as the defined process to achieve the defined change of moving from location A to location B.

   As depicted in Figure 1-1b, a defined process of "combustion" can be used in our example of burning a piece of paper.

The defined process of combustion allows us to move from the beginning state of being to the ending state of being for the defined change of burning a piece of paper.

Figure 1-1b
Defined Process of Combustion

A Defined Process = the <u>specific</u> process used to obtain the defined change out of all the possible processes that exist.

3. *Defined implementation* is the third element of change and represents what conditions must exist in order that the actual execution/implementation of the defined process can take place and how those conditions will be obtained.

Just knowing what defined process is required to obtain the defined change is not enough if the defined process is never implemented. A defined process can be 100 percent accurate; but if it is not implemented, then the defined change will never take place. Lack of defined process execution results in a lack of defined change. This can be a somewhat difficult concept to understand, and we will explore it in much more detail later in this book. For now the following examples might help:

- Let's say the defined change is to boil water. So the existing state of a pot of water is 70 degrees Fahrenheit, and the desired state is 212 degrees Fahrenheit. The defined process is to use a gas burner on a kitchen stove that is turned on high to increase the heat of the water in the pot from the existing state (70 degrees) to the desired end state (212 degrees). However, just having the pot of water in the same room with a stove that has the gas burner turned on high will not be enough to obtain the defined change. It is not until the pot of water is placed onto the gas burner on the stove (the defined implementation) that the defined process can actually take place and the desired end state can be obtained.

- What about our example of burning a piece of paper (the defined change) using combustion (the defined process). Just having a box of matches sitting on a table next to a piece of paper will not be enough to obtain the defined change. As depicted in Figure 1-1c, it is not until a match is ignited and placed to the paper that the defined process is implemented and there is the ability to obtain the defined change from the execution of the defined process.

Figure 1-1c
Defined Implementation of Lighting Match and Holding It to the Paper

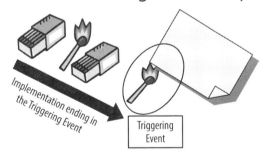

A Defined Implementation = the specific implementation used to obtain the conditions required to support the defined process

Chapter One

The key is that just having a defined process is not enough if that process is never implemented. A defined change is always contingent on having both an accurate defined process and the implementation of that process. So the defined implementation defines the specific factors, "*implementation factors,*" that must be present, including the activities and actions that must take place in order to implement the defined process.

Implementations have two facets. The first facet is that of defining the specific condition that must exist in order for the specified defined process to execute. This condition is called the *triggering event*. The examples from above included the specific condition of the lighted match next to the paper as shown in Figure 1-1c and the specific condition of the pot of water on the lighted burner. It is important to note that a triggering event is the specific condition that exists that triggers the execution of a specific defined procwess and is NOT the process or processes that produces that specific condition.

In other words, having the pot on the lighted burner and having the lighted match next to the paper represent conditions that exist at a specific point in time. It is these specific conditions that actually start the defined process of combustion of the paper and the defined process of thermodynamics for the boiling of the water. Therefore, the triggering event is NOT the process of putting the pot on the lighted burner or the process of lighting a match and placing it next to the paper. Instead, the triggering event is one of the end conditions (results) of the defined implementation. The triggering event is that part of the implementation that describes the "final how" the defined process will be executed (in other words, the defined process starting point). The rest of the defined implementation works backward from the triggering event and represents the second facet of an implementation.

The second facet of a defined implementation describes the rest of the "how and what" needs to happen in order for a specific defined process to execute. The second facet describes, among other things, how the triggering event condition will come to be. In essence, this second facet of the implementation defines what process or processes and other implementation factors need to take place (or have taken place) in order for the execution of a specific defined process to be successful.

In our examples above, it is the placement of pot of water onto the lighted gas burner on the stove and the ignition and placement of the match next to the paper indicated in Figure 1-1c that represents the second facet of the defined implementations.

At this point in time some of you might be saying, "This is crazy. Why not just eliminate the third element of implementation by expanding the defined process to include the placement of the pot on the flame or the lighting of the match and placement to the paper?" To this I would respond "excellent question." However, at this point in time it would be better for you to hold that thought until later in the book when we discuss chain of events and the interdynamics between change elements and the environment to gain a better understanding of the answer to this question. In the meantime, you will just need to accept the concept that there will always be a triggering event/implementation no matter how broadly you define the defined process.

Figure 1-1d represents a summary of our three elements of change using the example of the defined change of burning a piece of paper.

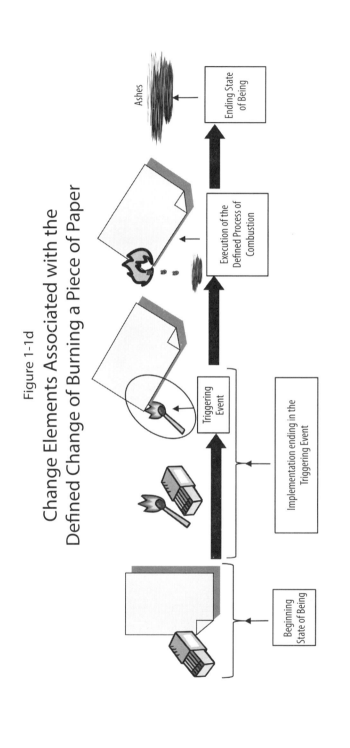

Figure 1-1d
Change Elements Associated with the Defined Change of Burning a Piece of Paper

While it is hard to imagine that all the change occurring around us can be broken down into just three key elements, the ramifications associated with these three elements are significant. We will come to learn that the dynamics and interdependency of these elements will often determine if a change will, in fact, occur. For example, you can have a defined process that will not produce the defined change in any set of circumstances (that is, the defined process is wrong and will never produce the defined change or vice versa, an incorrectly selected defined change will never result from a specific defined process). You can also have a proven process that given a specific set of circumstances can never be implemented.

Some of you might now be wondering why don't I always observe a consistent defined change if I have a defined process and a defined implementation that have been proven to work. In other words, if Mary wants to obtain a certain defined change and successfully implements a defined process to obtain that defined change, then why does Sam not obtain that same defined change even though he uses the exact same defined process and defined implementation? Or, why does Mary obtain the defined change one day and not the next day even though she used the exact same defined implementation and defined process on both days? We can use change science to help answer these questions by next focusing on the implications that exist for change because of the environment associated with that change.

ENVIRONMENTS

While the three elements discussed above are always required to obtain a defined change, it must be recognized that all change is taking place in an environment.

From the perspective of change science, we will define an *environment* as the context, circumstances, and conditions that exist in a specific defined space at a specific point or period of time in which the change elements must operate.

As depicted in Figure 1-2, in theory there can be as few as one environment, which would be represented by the entire known and unknown universe, or there could be countless environments if you treated the space associated with every smallest subatomic particle as being an individual environment.

Figure 1-2
Different Types of Environments

Environments can come in all sizes and shapes and respresent the <u>specific defined space</u> in which the change elements must operate!

However, at this point in time the key concept to understand in change science is that all change occurs in an environment. Therefore, in order to fully understand change you must take into consideration the conditions existing in the given environment under which the observation and/or examination of the defined change is taking place. If the conditions in a given environment cannot support the factors associated with a defined process or defined implementation, then the defined change associated with that process or implementation will not take place. So "different environments and/or different conditions within an environment" are answers to the questions as to why a set of change elements works for one person and not another or why that set of change elements works today but not tomorrow.

Later in the book we will explore the subject of environments in much more detail covering such topics as external versus internal conditions, relevant conditions, environmental dynamics, and risk dynamics. For now, the important change science concepts to understand are:

1. Change is defined as the transformation or alteration from one state of being to another state of being.
2. Three elements for change must exist in order to obtain change.
3. All change takes place in a given environment; and in order for a defined change to take place in a given environment, the conditions that exist in that environment must be able to support all the elements for change.

With these concepts in place, we can move on to the final set of change science definitions to be covered in this chapter. We will now define the types of change that exist.

TYPES OF CHANGE

Have you ever daydreamed what Earth must have been like before there was any life as we know it today? It does not matter whether you consider this from a religious or agnostic perspective, prior to life everything would have been changing in a strictly naturally-occurring context, free from any sort of cognitive influence. Change in a given environment would be subject only to the continuous interaction of the conditions in that environment and the change elements associated with the known and unknown laws of science. This becomes the basis for the definition of the first type of change associated with change science.

1. *Naturally-occurring change* is a defined change that is obtained through the naturally-occurring implementation and execution of a process associated with the interactions between the laws of science and the environment.

    - *Naturally-occurring change* takes place naturally with no cognitive influence or intervention.
    - *Successful naturally-occurring change* is obtained when the interaction of the environment and the laws of science naturally produce a defined change (that is, new state of being) that is expected from such an interaction. In technical terms, the environment supports the defined implementation of the defined process required to obtain the expected defined change that has naturally occurred.
    - *Unsuccessful naturally-occurring change* exists when conditions in the environment are such that the laws of science are unable to naturally produce a given defined change. Again, in technical terms, the defined implementation of the defined process required to obtain a given defined change is restricted by the conditions that exist in the given environment and an expected naturally-occurring change does not take place.

The second type of change assumes that some sort of cognitive influence is associated with a defined change. This cognitive influence can exist from any level of the spectrum of life. In other words, a bird building a nest (cognitive influence) changes the state of being in a given environment just as a human building a house changes the state of being in that given environment. While the magnitude between the bird's nest and the human's house might be different, the fact that neither of those states would have existed in the given environment without cognitive influence is the real underlying principle to understand. In other words, neither the nest nor the house would have existed in that environment left strictly to the laws of science interacting with the environment. Even though the laws of science come into play in the actual construction of the nest and house, they only come into play to the extent they are associated with a change that is influenced by cognitive activity. So the second type of change is defined as cognitively-influenced change.

2. *Cognitively-influenced change* is a defined change that is obtained through the implementation of a process associated with the interaction between the laws of science, the environment, and some cognitive influence that impacts the specific defined change (that is, specific state of being).

    - Cognitively-influenced change still follows the laws of science (both known and unknown).
    - Cognitively-influenced change still is subject to the conditions that exist in a given environment.
    - Cognitively-influenced change has a cognitive influence that impacts the environment or change elements relative to the resulting defined change.
    - Cognitively-influenced change can be used by a person or entity to obtain a *desired defined change.*
    - *Desired defined change* is a defined change the result of which is desired (wanted) by a specific individual or entity. It is important to note that a desired defined change can be naturally-occurring or can represent an end objective of a cognitively-influenced change.
    - A change can be impacted by cognitive influence even if it does not result in a desired defined change (that is, change can be cognitively influenced even if it is not

directly related to the specific intent of the person or entity that is creating the cognitive influence).
- *Successful cognitively-influenced change* occurs when a desired defined change is obtained in a given environment through the successful implementation of a process associated with the required defined change and for which a cognitive influence exists.
- *Unsuccessful cognitively-influenced change* occurs when a desired defined change is not obtained from the cognitive influence of the environment or change elements. Causes can include:
    - The desired defined change is impossible given the laws of science and the conditions that exist in a given environment no matter what given defined process or given defined implementation is selected or no matter what cognitive influence is brought to bear.
    - The cognitive influence fails to properly define a given defined process that is adequate to obtain the desired change.
    - The cognitive influence fails to properly define a given defined implementation that is adequate to obtain the desired change.

Once again, simplicity prevails in change science with just two general types of change. What is interesting about these two types of change is that they represent an either/or scenario (a closed loop structure). In other words, if a defined change is not classified as one type of change, then it has to be classified as the other type of change. So if one wants to argue that once the bird exists, all cognitive influence or actions associated with the bird are, in fact, naturally occurring; the only ramifications are that you have expanded what is considered naturally-occurring change and reduced what would be considered cognitively-influenced change.

In the end, the real ramifications lie in whether or not a defined change is or will be successful and if not, why not.

With these general change science definitions and concepts under our belt, we can now move on to a deeper analysis of what these concepts represent and what other change science definitions, principles, and concepts we can derive. Let the journey into change science continue with an exploration of Change Science Principles.

CHAPTER TWO

Change Science Principles

I do not create complexity; I just try to define it!

Tom Somodi

In the last chapter we learned that change is the transformation or alteration of the current state of being to a different state of being as it relates to a person, place, or thing or as it relates to the interrelationships between persons, places, or things. From this definition it naturally follows that change is constantly occurring around us, universal to all that we know, experience, and observe. If we are not careful, this concept can become overwhelming to comprehend. To think that everything we are or that we come in contact with is constantly changing is difficult to conceptualize. Yet from the grass you are walking on to hair on your head, change is taking place every second of every day. How can anyone even begin to grasp the magnitude of the situation, much less learn how to understand and channel change to improve the world we live in?

The answer is to simplify the complexity by developing a set of definitions, principles, and concepts to help explain and understand change. That is what change science is all about: creating these definitions, principles, and concepts and using them to establish a basis that can be challenged, expanded upon, and refined over time.

We began this process in the last chapter by establishing the elements of change. These are the components of change that are common to all change. They include Element 1, the defined change, which is the requirement to identify and define the specific change that you wish to obtain or examine. From there we define Element 2, the defined process, which is an identification of any process factors that will be required, including the sequence of activities and actions that need to take place in order to obtain the defined change represented in Element 1. Finally we define Element 3, the defined implementation, which represents the specific implementation factors, activities, and actions that must occur in order to implement the defined process represented in Element 2.

To round out our discussion we explain that these change elements need to be placed in the context of a given environment. We discover that all change occurs in an environment, and every given environment has a set of conditions that exist at any point in time within that environment. Therefore, in order to fully understand change, you must take into consideration the conditions existing in the given environment under which the observation and/or examination of the defined change is taking place. We have now reached a point at which we can more deeply explore the interrelationship between the elements of change and the environments they interface with. This allows us to expand upon the definitions and concepts we have in place. The best way to do this within the science of change is to develop some principles.

THE ENVIRONMENTAL OVERRIDE PRINCIPLE

The change science principle of *environmental override* states that if the conditions contained within a given environment will not support the requirements of a specific defined process or specific defined implementation, the defined change associated with the defined process and/or defined implementation will not be obtained.

Therefore, it does not matter if you are using a proven process and/or a proven implementation to obtain a certain defined change. The reality is that the defined change will not be obtained using that defined process and/or defined implementation if the conditions in a given environment are not available to support that specific defined process and/or defined implementation.

For example, let us assume you want to freeze some water into ice cubes. The defined change is taking water (the beginning state of being) and transforming it into frozen ice cubes (the ending state of being). The defined process is to place an ice cube tray containing water into a freezer and keep it in that freezer until the water has transformed to ice. The defined implementation is the actual placement of the ice cube tray containing water into the freezer. From these assumptions, we can see that our defined process and defined implementation are adequate to obtain the defined change. However, if the actual environment of the freezer is not at least 32 degrees Fahrenheit or less, then the defined change will not be obtained even though the defined process and defined implementation were conceptually flawless. In other words, the temperature condition in the freezer (that is, the environment) is not low enough to in fact support the defined process.

Even when experts, authors, and consultants tell you they have a proven method to obtain change (for example, lose weight or implement a new business system), the success of that methodology will still be totally dependent on the environment in which this methodology will be operating. Keep in mind these methodologies from experts are nothing more than a defined process and a defined implementation, so the environmental override principle of change science must be applied.

This is why a so-called "proven diet" will work for Sam but not for Chris. The environments Sam and Chris are operating in can be different at several levels. For example, Chris's body (his body would be considered an environment) is different from Sam's body and therefore, might not have all the necessary conditions required for the diet to work even though it works in Sam's body. Or Sam's house (which would be considered an environment) is different from Chris's house. So conditions such as the food each one has in their house and the existence or nonexistence of a spouse and children in the two households—the list goes on— can easily create an environment that will not support the methodology of that particular diet in Chris's house while supporting the diet in Sam's house.

Note, if there is one concept to take away from this book that will help you cope and better understand the change you deal with daily in your life, I think the environmental override principle is probably the number one principle of change science that you want to remember!

The principle of environmental override can also help explain the lack of commitment dilemma described in the Introduction of this book. Often the principle of environmental override is enough to explain why a proven process and implementation fail, including explaining the lack of commitment phenomenon. This is why I say that if there is one change science principle to learn and take away from this book, it would be the principle of environmental override.

However, many experts and consultants would argue that part of their change methodology recognizes the issues associated with environmental override and that they compensate for this issue within their methodology. Their methodology would, therefore, still support an argument for a lack of commitment. I agree that in some cases this argument may have validity. However, the principle of environmental override is but one principle within change science that needs to be taken into consideration when explaining the lack of commitment phenomenon or why change fails. So while environmental override is an important underlying change science principle, I will be developing other change science principles and concepts that, when taken into consideration in conjunction with the principle of environmental override, will fill out a much more complete picture of why change succeeds and fails.

In addition, it is important to note that just because the principle of environmental override exists does not mean that there are not ways to counter its effects, thereby improving the probability of obtaining successful change. Developing this capability will be one of many objectives as we continue on our journey into change science.

THE CHANGE/TIME CONTINUUM PRINCIPLE

THE KINEOGRAPH.

Many of you have been exposed to the flip book. A flip book contains a series of pictures that vary gradually from one page to the next so that when the pages are turned rapidly, the pictures appear to simulate motion or some other type of change (text and picture from Wikipedia).

Now I want you to think about being frozen in time. If time is frozen, then the environment would also be frozen with everything at a frozen state of being. No movement, no activity—in essence, no change! Then think about moving forward just one second and again freezing time. Once again everything in the environment would also exist in a frozen state of being. However, this new state of being in the environment would be after any and all change that took place during that one second interval of time. Like the flip book, you would have moved from one picture to the next picture with the next picture being slightly different from the first picture. If you continue this process of freezing time after some interval of time has occurred, then you will have established a model of the change science principle of the change/time continuum. Again, a given environment changes from one state of being to another state of being each time an interval of time passes just as the flip book changes from one picture to the next picture.

The change science principle of *change/time continuum* states that in order to have change in a given environment (that is, progress from one state of being to another state of being), the passage of an interval of time (time interval) must occur.

Therefore:

1. Change will not exist in a given environment without the passage of time.
2. Change occurs over a continuum of time or change/time continuum.
3. The greater the length of the *time interval/interval of time* on the change/time continuum (that is, interval of time that passes between one state of being and the next state of being), the greater the potential amount of total change in conditions within that given environment.

Bottom line, change does not exist without time since everything would be frozen in a single state of being. The principle of change/time continuum also reinforces the fact that change is constantly occurring around us on a continuous basis (continuum). There is a saying that many of you are probably familiar with that states, "If you do not like the weather today, just wait and it will change." As much as we complain, the reality is that we unconsciously accept, and actually come to expect, the change in our lives and the change that exists around us. The change science principle of change/time continuum is at the center of it all.

Visually the principle of change/time continuum looks like the graphic in Figure 2-1.

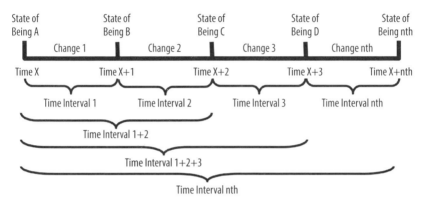

Figure 2-1 indicates how the conditions, which equal the state of being, in a given environment progress based on the actual change that occurs during the time interval selected in the change/time continuum. For example, the condition that exists in the environment at the point in time X+2 equals the State of Being C, which reflects Change 1 that occurred in Time Interval 1 plus Change 2 that occurs in Time Interval 2 on the change/time continuum.

The principle of change/time continuum also interacts directly with the principle of environmental override. Environment override is only associated with the conditions in a given environment as of a particular point in time. It is as if you are looking at just one picture in the flip book. Therefore, if change in a given environment is occurring on a continuum, then the conditions in a given environment are also changing on that change/time continuum. So if a defined process and/or defined implementation do not work at one point in time in a given environment, it does not mean that they will not work at a different point in time on the change/time continuum when the conditions in that given environment have changed.

The converse is also true. Just because the conditions in a given environment will support a defined process and defined implementation at one point in time on the change/time continuum, it does not mean that the conditions in that given environment will support the same defined process and defined implementation at another point on the change/time continuum.

Think of this example. You drive to work every day on the same set of roads, leaving at 7:00 so you can be at work on time at 8:00. The triggering event of leaving at 7:00 and driving this specific set of roads (that is, the defined process) works for 25 days in a row, and you are never late for work (that is, you have successful defined change). Then on the 26th day, there is a car accident on one of the roads on your route, and you are late for work (that is, an unsuccessful defined change) because of being trapped in a traffic jam.

This is clearly a case of the interaction of the change/time continuum principle and the environmental override principle. For days 1 through 25 on the change/time continuum, the conditions in the given environment support the defined process and the defined implementation. Then on the 26th day, changes that occur on the change/time continuum between the 25th day and 26th day are such that the conditions that exist in the given environment at the particular point in time of execution of your defined process no longer support the selected defined process and defined implementation. In other words, the principle of environmental override exists on day 26. Interestingly enough, barring some other unforeseen set of changes in the given environment, there is a strong probability that the conditions in the given environment will once again support the defined process and defined implementation on day 27, and a successful defined change will occur.

CHANGE AS IT RELATES TO TIME

The principle of change/time continuum raises some interesting questions. If change cannot exist without time, then does it hold that time cannot exist without change? Does time in the traditional sense exist or is it really only an integrated measurement of change, in which case change is the true underlying concept that is important? In addition, if change occurs on a continuum, then what are the ramifications associated with the ability to travel in time? While these questions are not technically central to change science, the study of change science might help further the definitions and concepts surrounding the subject of time. In Chapter 1 we explain how this book represents just the beginning in our quest to establish change as a science and how change science can be used to help solve problems or provide explanations that exist in other sciences and disciplines. The change science concepts regarding change and time might just be one of those examples.

THE CHAIN OF EVENTS PRINCIPLE AND PERPETUATING CHANGE

In order to understand this principle we will start by revisiting the three elements of change.

Element 1—Defined Change
Element 2—Defined Process
Element 3—Defined Implementation

Chapter Two

Every defined change has a defined process and defined implementation associated with it. In addition, every defined process has a set of specific factors (that is, requirements) associated with it, and every defined implementation has a set of specific factors associated with it. In order for the defined process and defined implementation to be successful, all the required factors must be present in (that is, supported by) the conditions that exist in a given environment. For example, if a defined process has water and air as required factors, then the conditions in a given environment must include water and air in order for the defined process to execute successfully.

In summary, in order for you to derive a successful defined change, you will need to have a defined process associated with the defined change that will be supported by the conditions in a given environment, and this defined process will require a defined implementation including the triggering event that will be supported by the conditions in that given environment.

However, when we take a second to think about it, the "sequence or order" of the three elements of change actually occurs in reverse order. That is, first a specific implementation with a triggering event occurs in a given environment that creates a new set of conditions in that given environment. These new conditions can then support the factors associated with the defined process that will in turn result in a successful defined change. Therefore, the sequence/order of our three change elements now looks like this:

Element 3—Defined Implementation
Element 2—Defined Process
Element 1—Defined Change

When you consider this new order of the change elements in conjunction with the change/time continuum, the underlying concepts of the change science chain of events principle begin to solidify. The heart of this principle lies in the fact that changes that occur in one interval of time create new conditions in an environment that then provide the basis for the execution of a new set of processes in the subsequent period of time. In essence, the processes that are executed in the first interval of time create the conditions including the triggering events (that is, implementations) for the processes that will be executed in the next interval of time on the change/time continuum.

Put another way, there is a continuous sequence of events whereby a defined implementation produces environmental conditions (that is, states of being) that support an associated defined process which results in a successful associated defined change represented by a new set of conditions in the environment. This new set of conditions will in turn support a new set of defined processes.

In the end, this sequence of triggering events (chain of events) is constantly occurring in a given environment over the change/time continuum creating perpetual change in that environment.

Thus, the formal change science definition of the chain of events principle is as follows:

The *chain of events* principle states that the defined changes that occur because of defined processes that are executed during one time interval on the change/time continuum create the conditions in a given environment, including the triggering event condition (that is, the defined implementations), that implement the next set of defined processes in the subsequent time interval on the change/time continuum in that given environment, and this chain of events continues as time progresses along the change/time continuum creating *perpetuating change.*

Therefore, *perpetual change* is the result of a continuous cycle of triggering events (that is, defined implementations) created by the execution of defined processes in one time interval on the change/time continuum, which in turn creates conditions that become the triggering events/implementations for the next set of defined processes to execute in the subsequent time interval on the change/time continuum, all of which continues as time progresses along the change/time continuum.

Visually, the principles of change/time continuum and chain of events look like the graphic in Figure 2-2.

Figure 2-2
Time/Change Continuum and Chain of Events Principles

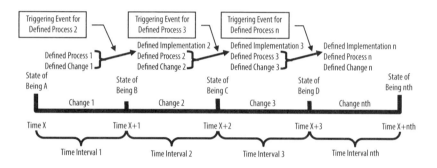

Figure 2-2 depicts how the Defined Change 1 resulting from the execution of the Defined Process 1 during Time Interval 1 results in the triggering event for the execution of the Defined Process 2 in Time Interval 2. In other words, *Defined Process 1 is equal to the Defined Implementation 2.* Therefore, the change that occurs in a current time interval in an environment becomes the starting point in a chain of triggering events in all future time intervals, thereby creating perpetuating change in that environment.

Let's look at an example. Let's say you want to water your garden (let's call this Defined Change 3).

1. Defined Change 3 = water garden

The Defined Process 3 associated with the Defined Change 3 is to use the water from a garden hose that is running from the house to a sprinkler located in the garden.

2. Defined Process 3 = run water through a hose from the house to a sprinkler in the garden

It is 7:00:00 pm, and the conditions in the given environment include a garden hose running from the faucet at the house to the sprinkler located in the garden. However, the faucet at the house is turned off. Therefore, the Defined Implementation 3 associated with the Defined Process 3 is to turn on the faucet.

3. Conditions at 7:00:00 pm = (a) garden hose running from house to sprinkler and (b) faucet at house turned off

4. Defined Implementation 3 = turn on the faucet

However, turning on the faucet represents another Defined Change 2 that requires an associated Defined Process 2 of using your hand to physically turn the faucet.

5. Defined Change 2 = turn on the faucet

6. Defined Process 2 = physically turn the faucet with your hand

Therefore, the Defined Implementation 2 associated with the Defined Process 2 is for you to grab the faucet. But at 7:00:00 pm the conditions in the given environment have you sitting in your chair inside the house.

7. Conditions at 7:00:00 pm = you are sitting in your chair in the house

8. Defined Implementation 2 = grab the faucet

Once again another Defined Change 1 is required (that is, moving from your current state of being sitting in your chair to the ending state of being of grabbing the faucet). Of course, associated with Defined Change 1 is Defined Process 1 of walking from your chair to grabbing the faucet and also an associated Defined Implementation 1 of getting out of your chair.

9. Defined Change 1 = grab the faucet

10. Defined Process 1 = walk from your chair and grab the faucet

11. Defined Implementation 1 = get up out of your chair

So at 7:00:00 you get up out of your chair, (the triggering event for Defined Process 1) and walk to the faucet grabbing the faucet at 7:01:00. Therefore, the conditions in the given environment at 7:01:00 pm still have the garden hose running from the faucet at the house to the sprinkler located in the garden, but the faucet at the house is still turned off. However, the conditions have also been impacted by the execution of Defined Process 1 resulting in the success of Defined Change 1 with your grabbing the faucet. It also represents the execution of Defined Implementation 2 that is the triggering event for Defined Process 2.

Now at 7:01:00 you begin to turn the faucet, which is the execution of Defined Process 2, and you completely open the faucet at 7:01:15. So the conditions in the given environment at 7:01:15 have the garden hose running from the faucet at the house to the sprinkler located in the garden with the faucet at the house now turned on, which, in fact, is the result of the success of Defined Change 2.

Finally at 7:01:15 with the faucet turned on, the Defined Implementation 3 has occurred, which is the Triggering Event for Defined Process 3, and at 7:01:25 water has flowed through the hose from the faucet and is flowing through the sprinkler watering the garden. Defined Change 3 is now successful, and the conditions in the given environment at 7:01:25 include water on the garden.

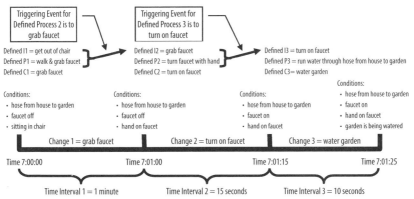

Figure 2-3
Example of Watering Your Garden

Figure 2-3 summarizes our example visually. You can clearly see how the defined process and resulting defined change in one time interval become the defined implementation for the defined process in the next time interval. So the execution of Defined Process 1 and resulting Defined Change 1 between 7:00:00 and 7:01:00 results in the triggering event or implementation for Defined Process 2 that occurs in Time Interval 2.

The chain of events principle with resulting perpetuating change is an extremely powerful concept and goes to the heart of what is occurring in the world around us. It is because of this principle that naturally-occurring change takes place in an environment with the events (that is, changes) that occur in one time period triggering the changes that will take place in subsequent time periods— perpetual, constantly occurring, and theoretically never-ending.

Chapter Two

Cognitively-influenced change, on the other hand, attempts to alter (that is, influence) this naturally-occurring chain of events. The objective of cognitive influence is to obtain a specific desired state of being that, barring such cognitive influence, might not otherwise occur if the naturally-occurring change of events was left to its own. Therefore, in order for cognitive influence to exist, the influence must be focused on the chain of events so as to attempt to obtain a specific ultimate defined change.

On the History Channel on cable television there was a series illustrating what would happen if there were no longer any impact on Earth from humans. In other words, if there were no longer any human cognitive influence on the environment we call Earth, what would happen? It was interesting to see how over time (that is, the future change/time continuum) the chain of events associated with naturally-occurring change would impact Earth's environment to reverse the prior cognitive influence associated with mankind. However, the cable television series also gave a perspective of just how much impact mankind has had over the years in cognitively influencing the naturally-occurring chain of events to reach the existing environmental state of being of Earth. From the buildings we have built to the dams we have erected to the pollution we have created to the crops we have planted, the impact from cognitive influence on the chain of events has been significant.

The chain of events principle helps explain why change is constantly taking place around us. More importantly, it provides a starting point to develop an understanding of just how, through cognitive influence, we can attempt to alter a future chain of events in a given environment so as to obtain a desired change.

CHANGE SCIENCE PRINCIPLE OF SIMULTANEOUS CHANGE

The principle of *simultaneous change* states that change will occur simultaneously during any time interval along the change/time continuum across all environments no matter how the environments are defined.

The basis for the principle of simultaneous change is really quite straightforward. As we have indicated already, there can be as few as one environment, which would be represented by the entire known and unknown universe, or there could be countless environments if you treated the space associated with every smallest subatomic particle as being an individual environment. However, if we focus strictly on having only a single environment (that is, a single all-inclusive defined space), then within any given time interval on the change/time continuum, change will be occurring universally and simultaneously across that entire single environment. Therefore, even if you break the single environment down into many separate environments, change will still occur simultaneously across all the environments no matter how they are defined.

The key is that even though you as an individual may not directly experience a change or observe a change that is occurring in an environment outside of your immediate presence, it does not mean that such change does not exist/take place.

An easy to understand example is the visit my wife and I made to Australia. Even though we were halfway around the world, during any interval of time on the change/time continuum, change continued to take place simultaneously back home in the Midwest of the United States even though we were not there to directly observe it or experience it. Obviously, there were times on our side of the globe where the types of change we might expect were based on its being daytime while simultaneously back home the change

Chapter Two

occurring was what we might expect because it was in the middle of the night. However, change was occurring simultaneously on the change/time continuum no matter what our observable perspective was.

The ramifications of the principle of simultaneous change are in some ways both mind-boggling and practical. They are mind-boggling in that it is often difficult to comprehend that during any given time interval along the change/time continuum change is executing simultaneously somewhere in the most distant corner of the universe at the same time you experience the change in your life here in the small defined space of the universe that you occupy. What's more, the change that occurred out there somewhere in the universe might be so far away that any recognition of such a change sometime in the future here on Earth may never be detected.

On the other hand, the ramifications of simultaneous change can become very practical, useful, and even imperative to us in our daily lives. Let us look at three examples:

1. It is good to know that while we are in the midst of the change that is occurring while we are sleeping, the simultaneous changes associated with the Sun heating the other side of the Earth are imperative to our continued existence.
2. You need to drive from Chicago to Detroit in the wintertime, and you have flexibility to make the drive sometime during the next three days. You want to base when you leave on the expected future weather conditions along your route. These expected weather conditions are, in turn, based upon changes that are in fact occurring elsewhere in the United States simultaneously within the time interval in which you are making your decision. In other words, weather forecasts are made based upon conditions associated with changes taking place

simultaneously elsewhere that are predicted to result, in turn, in future weather conditions in your location.
3. The materials you need to operate a machine at work are at a location XYZ six hours away. You have no materials available at your company. The change associated with the truck leaving location XYZ must take place simultaneously while you are sleeping. If this change does not take place six hours in advance of the start of operations, you will not have the materials necessary to perform your job when you arrive at work in the morning.

In the end, it would be a scary situation if the only change taking place during any given time interval on the change/time continuum was the change occurring in the immediate environment that we could observe or directly experience.

IS CHANGE REALLY OCCURRING SIMULTANEOUSLY EVERYWHERE?

There might be some of you still questioning if there is not in fact somewhere in the vast universe where change is not simultaneously occurring. Without trying to be overly technical or theoretical, we can say that, given the way change has been defined within the science of change, a single change at any location in the universe, by definition, will create change everywhere in the universe. Remember that change is not only the transformation or alteration of the current state of being to a different state of being as it relates to a person, place, or thing but also as it relates to the interrelationships between persons, places, or things. It is this inclusion of the "interrelationship" between everything that dictates that even

> if a single change exists in one location in the universe, then the state of being relative to everything else also changes. This, in essence, then represents change everywhere in the universe that is generated from that single change. So even if you can find an environment (that we will define as "V") that has absolutely nothing in it (that is, it is completely void of anything), the fact that a change occurs in an environment next to the void environment (that we will call "C") still represents a change that is also associated with the void environment. This is due to the change in the relationship between V and C at the point in time on the change/time continuum prior to the change in C (that is, the beginning state of being relationship) and the relationship between V and C at the subsequent point in time on the change/time continuum after the change in C (that is, the ending state of being relationship). However, if you are still skeptical, then move forward under a pragmatic context in that, outside the theoretical, the concepts associated with the change science principle of simultaneous change we will be discussing in this book will be useful to you from a pragmatic perspective.

SIGNIFICANCE OF CHANGE SCIENCE PRINCIPLES

The four principles of change science outlined in this chapter form the basis of an understanding of the change that is constantly occurring around us. You should recognize not only the significance each change science principle represents by itself but also the significance that exists in the interrelationship among the principles. At the center, the principle of environmental override states that just having a valid defined process and valid defined implementation is not enough. The proper conditions in a given environment at any point in time to support all the required process and implementation factors must also be available. If the conditions do not match the required process and implementation factors, you will not obtain a successful defined change.

However, if a defined change does not occur at a particular point in time, all is not necessarily lost because the principles of change/time continuum and chain of events are also at play. These two principles describe how change is perpetually occurring over a change/time continuum. Therefore, the conditions/state of being are also constantly changing. This then provides the possibility that the conditions in the environment will match a set of required process and implementation factors at some future point in time.

Of course, these first three change science principles take place simultaneously along the change/time continuum across all environments no matter how the environments are defined.

Finally, with no cognitive influence, these principles of change science would indicate that the naturally-occurring change that exists in a given environment over a change/time continuum will be strictly dictated by the dynamics associated with the laws of science both known and unknown. In other words, the chain of events and resulting perpetuating change in the given environment over a change/time continuum are subject exclusively to the laws of science.

Therefore, cognitively-influenced change attempts to impact this naturally-occurring chain of events so as to try to obtain a specific desired defined change. However, once again, these attempts to influence are still subject to the change science principles, especially the principle of environmental override. That is why the principle of environmental override can be a major reason why much of the desired defined change we strive for ultimately fails no matter how much commitment we have.

Now it is time to move on and examine in the following chapters how we can continue to build off of these concepts that we

Chapter Two   59

have established up to this point in the book. We will dive more deeply into such areas as the structural nature associated with the elements of change, the study of environmental dynamics, and the study of risk dynamics. We will start by taking a closer look at the subject of change dynamics.

CHAPTER THREE

Change Dynamics

The power of a concept increases through the relationships it has with other concepts!

Tom Somodi

We now have established a solid starting point for the understanding of change science through the definitions and principles presented in Chapters 1 and 2. However, as you might have expected, these change science definitions and principles do not act in a context of singularity. Instead, the elements of change, environments, and change science principles all interact and can influence each other in specific ways.

The term *dynamics* can have various meanings, including specific meanings relative to physics. However, in change science, you will see the term *dynamics* used in the context of something that has continuous activity and interactions.

Therefore, *change dynamics* is defined in change science as the continuous activities, interactions, and interrelationships that exist between the elements of change, environments, and change science principles.

So in this chapter we are going to take a closer look at how the principles of change, processes, implementations, and environments all interrelate with each other.

DEFINED PROCESSES AND CHANGE DYNAMICS

The second element of change, a defined process, represents the specific activities, dynamics, actions, variables, elements, and any other factors (that is, everything we have defined as process factors) that move us from one state of being to another state of being (that is, a defined change) in a given environment. To obtain a defined change in a given environment, you must have a defined process take place in that environment, and that defined process must specifically explain how we move from one state of being to another state of being in that environment.

Defined processes have a direct relationship with all of the change science principles described in Chapter 2. As already indicated, a defined process will not take place in a given environment unless the conditions in that environment support the required process factors 100 percent (change science principle of environmental override). So just conceptually having a proven defined process is not enough. You must also have an environment that contains all the conditions necessary to support all of the process factors required by the defined process you have selected.

A defined process also has a direct interrelationship with the change science principle of change/time continuum. Since we are moving from one state of being to another state of being, any defined change that occurs in the environment will always represent an interval of time on the change/time continuum. Therefore, the defined process associated with any given defined change will also require an interval of time on the change/time continuum. In other words, a defined process cannot take place without having an interval of time (that is, movement along the change/time continuum). By default *the process factors associated with a defined process will always have an interval of time as one of their elements.*

Finally, a defined process is directly incorporated into the chain of events principle of change science. The defined change that occurs through the execution of defined processes in one interval of time on the change/time continuum creates new conditions in a given environment. In turn, these new conditions in that environment become the triggering events and process factors used by the subsequent set of defined processes executed during the next interval of time on the change/time continuum. That is correct: it is the change that occurs because of the execution of processes in a given environment that becomes the conditions that exist in that environment in subsequent intervals of time on the change/time continuum.

Figure 3-1
Execution of a Process in the Chain of Events

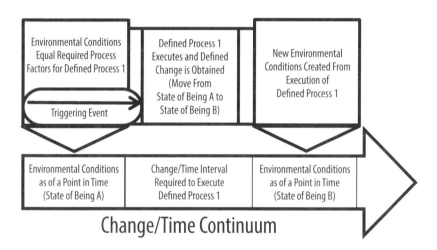

Figure 3-1 depicts how a process moves the conditions in a given environment from a state of being A to a state of being B on the change/time continuum as part of the chain of events. In other words, a *defined change* from state A to state B is depicted in Figure 3-2.

Figure 3-2
Defined Change = Change in Environmental Conditions Resulting From Execution of a Process

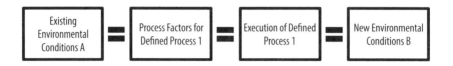

In future chapters we will explore the structural nature of processes in more detail, including the selection of processes, the interrelationship between processes, the laws of science (both known and unknown), and cognitive influence. For now, let's move on to implementations and change dynamics.

DEFINED IMPLEMENTATIONS AND CHANGE DYNAMICS

The defined implementations change element can be more difficult to comprehend than the defined process change element. Therefore, do not be discouraged if you need to spend a little more time thinking about these concepts.

A defined implementation represents the conditions that must exist in a given environment in order for the actual execution/implementation of the defined process to take place and how those conditions are obtained. So the defined implementation details the specific implementation factors that must be present, including the activities and actions that must take place, in order to implement a specific defined process.

Here is a good way to understand implementations. View an implementation as the specific activities, dynamics, actions, variables, elements, and any other factors (that is, everything we have defined as implementation factors) "required to match" the conditions in a given environment to the process factors needed to successfully execute a defined process thereby obtaining the associated defined change. This lengthy explanation sounds more complicated than it is. If you break it down logically, it would look like this:

1. The principle of environmental override says that a defined process will not take place if the conditions in a given environment will not support the necessary process factors associated with that defined process.
2. However, the chain of events principle dictates that change will occur in that given environment over the change/time continuum.
3. Therefore, just because the conditions in the given environment will not support the required process factors of a defined process at a specific point on the change/time continuum, it does not mean that the conditions in the given environment will not support the required process factors "at a future point" on the change/time continuum.
4. It is the defined implementation that describes how a given environment needs to change over the change/time continuum using the chain of events from a set of conditions that do not support a defined process to a set of conditions that do support a defined process. In other words:

    a. In the case of a defined process that has already been executed in the given environment: the implementation describes the specific activities, dynamics, actions, variables, elements, and any other factors *that have occurred* in that given environment between a prior point on the change/time continuum and the point on the change/time continuum where the defined process was actually executed.

  b. In the case of a defined process that we want to execute in the given environment: the implementation describes the specific activities, dynamics, actions, variables, elements, and any other factors *that are required to occur* between one point on the change/time continuum and a subsequent point on the change/time continuum in order to create the conditions necessary in that given environment to support the actual execution of the defined process.
  c. In both cases the defined implementation describes the "how" of changing a given environment from a condition of not supporting a defined process to a condition of supporting the defined process.

When you look closely at the above breakdown, you can recognize how the various change science principles are intertwined with the change element of defined implementations. We can also derive additional insight into how defined implementations are integrated into change dynamics by examining and expanding off of the discussion regarding defined implementations from Chapter 1.

In Chapter 1 I explained how defined implementations have two facets. The first facet is that of defining the specific condition that must exist in order for the specified defined process to execute. In change science, this condition is called the triggering event. It was emphasized that a triggering event is the specific condition that exists that triggers the execution of a specific defined process and is NOT the process or processes that produces that specific condition. Instead, the triggering event is one of the end conditions (results) of the defined implementation. The rest of the defined implementation works backward from the triggering event and represents the second facet of an implementation.

Once again, the triggering event is that part of the defined implementation that describes the "final how" the defined process will be executed (in other words, the defined process starting point). Therefore, the triggering event represents an **ending condition** in the environment produced from the implementation that is the **starting condition** of the defined process. *In other words, it is the formal handoff between the defined implementation and associated defined process!*

In Chapter 1, I also explained how the second facet of a defined implementation describes the rest of the "how" of what must happen in order for a specific defined process to execute. The second facet describes both how to derive the triggering event condition and how to obtain any other required conditions necessary to support the process factors associated with the defined process.

Given that the only way to change the conditions in a given environment is through a defined process, *in essence, this second facet of the implementation defines what defined process or defined processes and other implementation factors need to take place (or have taken place) in order to create all the conditions necessary in the environment for the successful execution of a specific defined process.*

At this point it is important to recognize that the second facet of a defined implementation is composed of a defined process or multiple defined processes. Therefore, all of the discussion above, regarding defined processes and change dynamics, also apply within this context of the defined implementation.

As depicted in Figure 3-3, the second facet of implementations is nothing more than the execution of a defined process or multiple defined processes along the change/time continuum as part of the chain of events. As such, the "objective" is to create a set of conditions (defined below as relevant conditions) in a given environment that will support the execution of a predetermined defined process, thereby yielding the ultimate defined change that is desired/required.

Figure 3-3

Change in Environmental Conditions Resulting from the Execution of a Defined Implementation with the Objective = Execution of Process 1

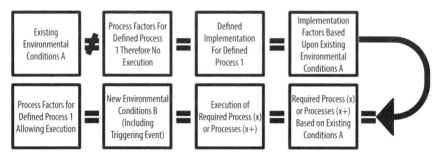

Another way to look at it is that an implementation describes the chain of events that has occurred, or needs to occur, in a given environment in order for a specific defined process to successfully execute somewhere along the change/time continuum. Successful implementations look like this:

1. In the case of a process we want to execute in a given environment:

    a. Define/determine all of the process factors (including the triggering event) required to have a successfully executed specific defined process.
    b. Compare these process factors to the conditions existing in a given environment at a specific point on the change/time continuum.
    c. Based upon the existing conditions in the environment, determine how the environment should be changed through the chain of events in that environment (that is, what the implementation factors are) in order to obtain a successful execution of the defined process.

d. Execute the defined implementation based upon this set of existing conditions in the environment.
2. In the case of a defined change that has already occurred in a given environment:
   a. Determine what process factors existed as part of the chain of events within the given environment that were executed as the defined process that in turn resulted in the defined change.
   b. Determine what the implementation factors were that:
      - changed the conditions within the environment from an inability to support the above specific defined process at a specific point in time on the change/time continuum to
      - a set of conditions within the environment that ultimately successfully supported the execution of this specific defined process in a subsequent time on the change/time continuum.
   c. Identify these implementation factors as representing the defined implementation that was executed in the environment.

Figure 3-4
Implementation of a Process in a Chain of Events

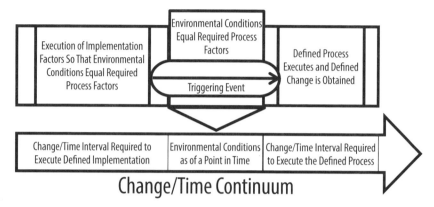

Figure 3-4 is a depiction of what we have just discussed regarding the defined implementation of a defined process. You can see how as part of the chain of events an implementation during an interval of time on the change/time continuum leads to a state of being at a point in time on the change/time continuum where the "environmental conditions and required process factors match up." This allows the defined process to execute so that the defined change is successfully obtained. Figure 3-4 also depicts how one of the conditions derived from the implementation represents the triggering event that starts the execution of the defined process (that is, it is at the end of the implementation and at the start of the process).

Finally, in Chapter 1, I also presented the following question and asked you to wait for the explanation: Why not just expand the defined process to include the placement of the pot on the flame or the lighting of the match and placement to the paper, thereby reducing implementation factors associated with the defined implementation? The answer is that a defined process is generally a closed loop in nature in that it can often be executed in multiple environments. In addition, a defined process can often have multiple types of triggering events as possibilities to initiate its execution.

For example, when the defined change is to burn a piece of paper and the defined process selected is combustion, then the burning of the paper has a specific starting point (the state of being is a piece of paper exposed to heat) and a specific ending point (the state of being is the burning of the entire piece of paper). While combustion cannot occur in every environment we select (for example, it would not work in outer space where there is a lack of oxygen), the process of combustion relative to the paper can definitely occur in multiple environments. It could occur in our house, outdoors, in the United States, or somewhere else in the world.

More importantly, the combustion of the paper could have multiple triggering events depending on the environment. As in our example, the triggering event could be a lighted match held next to the paper. However, the triggering event for the defined process of combustion of the paper could just as easily be a condition in which the paper is exposed to a bonfire; to an electric hot plate that is turned on; or, more unlikely, to a lighting strike.

Likewise, in the example of boiling a pot of water, the process of placing the pot on the burner would not have triggered anything if in our example the burner had been turned off when the pot was placed on it (that is, the triggering condition would not have existed). We would have had to execute another process to turn on the burner before the process of boiling a pot of water would have executed. This is a good example of how there can be multiple possibilities (depending on the sequence of the chain of events) of processes that could create the triggering event condition of the pot being on a lighted burner. This also shows that the process is not the triggering event for the next defined process but the resulting condition from the process.

The key is that if we look at the defined process from a perspective of being a closed loop, we recognize that there can often be multiple potential environments and triggering events (or combination thereof). Therefore, it is generally easier and/or more efficient to construct defined implementations to address the specifics associated with the specific environment and specific triggering event selected than to continue to expand the defined process backward. We will further address these concepts later in the book when we take an even closer look at defined processes and defined implementations.

ENVIRONMENTS AND CHANGE DYNAMICS

Remember that any defined change and, therefore, any defined process and defined implementation take place within a given environment. We defined such an environment as the context, circumstances, and conditions that exist in a specific defined space at a specific point or period of time in which the change elements must operate. It is difficult to have a meaningful discussion of defined changes, defined processes, and defined implementations without having a clear understanding of the interrelationship and interaction they have with the given environment in which they must operate.

To start with, we must realize that there can be as few as one environment, which would be represented by the entire known universe and possibly beyond, or there could be countless environments if we treat the space associated with every smallest subatomic particle as an individual environment. Therefore, there is a certain amount of arbitrariness associated with defining what a given environment is. Later on in the book we will develop a further understanding of how, by utilizing the change science principle of environmental override along with some other basic rules, we can begin to establish a better context under which to define what a given environment should look like.

For now, we will focus on a higher level of understanding as it relates to the interrelationship between environments, processes, and implementations. We will start with an introduction to the concept of relevance.

Relevant Environment and Conditions

A *relevant environment* is defined as an environment that has a defined space, time period, and conditions (or the potential to have conditions) associated with it so as to be relevant to a specific defined change and, therefore, to any defined processes and defined implementations that might be associated with the specific defined change.

Relevant conditions are defined as the subset out of the universe of all conditions that exist in a given relevant environment that are relevant to the process factors and implementation factors associated with a defined process and defined implementation under examination.

Obviously, selecting an environment that is totally irrelevant to the desired defined change and associated defined process and defined implementation makes no sense. Given that a defined process and defined implementation can only be successful if the conditions in the given environment have the potential to support the process and implementation factors under consideration, it also makes no sense to select processes and implementations that we know will not work in a selected environment. For example, as mentioned earlier, we know we cannot have combustion without oxygen, so selecting combustion as our process when we know our environment lacks oxygen (for example, outer space or a vacuum chamber) is a nonstarter.

However, this is not to say that a process and/or implementation will not work in multiple environments. To the contrary, processes and implementations often can and do have the capability of working in alternative environments. The important concepts at this point are that there needs to be an evaluation to determine a) whether a given environment is relevant to the desired defined change under consideration and b) whether the process and/or implementation being contemplated can be executed in the environment selected.

Later on (Chapters 4 and 5) we will address additional concepts regarding environments. For now you should note that a defined change can have multiple environments associated with it, especially if there is an extended time period associated with the defined change. For example, if the defined change is to lose X amount of weight, then chances are multiple environments will be associated with this defined change. Any defined process and defined implementation associated with this defined change will need to take these multiple environments into consideration. The multiple environments might include the physical body, which will be a consistent environment during the entire change/time continuum. However, the work environment, home environment, and various environments associated with traveling are also environments that will need to be considered when evaluating the defined process and defined implementation selected.

Finally, as depicted in Figure 3-5, we should recognize that at any point in time, there is a universe of possible processes available for execution in a given environment, all based upon the laws of science (both known and unknown). In addition, any given environment has a universe of conditions that are available for possible use in the execution of a defined process.

Figure 3-5 also shows that as we move along the change/time continuum for a given environment and the conditions within that given environment change because of the chain of events, processes will execute within that given environment whenever there is a triggering event and the conditions within the given environment continue to support all the process factors associated with a defined process.

Therefore, within any given environment there will be a universe of processes that are executing and a significant universe of processes that are not executing as we move along the change/time continuum for that given environment. There will also be a universe of conditions that exist in a given environment some of which are relevant to a specific defined process that is currently executing and some of which are not.

Figure 3-5
The Chain of Events for a Given Environment XYZ

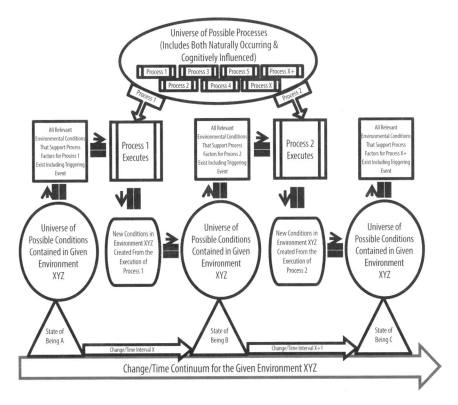

Defined implementations, on the other hand, are directly related to both the defined process and the environment in which we are attempting to execute the defined process. So while a defined implementation is directly associated with a given defined process, it is also dependent on the environment in which that defined process will be executed. Therefore, the ability to have a single implementation associated with a given defined process that is universal across all possible environments is more difficult to obtain.

It should also be recognized that while in some environments there might only be a single defined implementation associated with a given defined process that will work in that specific given environment, in other environments there could be a multitude of possible defined implementations that would work for the same given defined process. This will all be explained in more detail in later chapters, but for now these are the important concepts about environments and change dynamics to begin to understand:

1. Environments can cover a broad range of sizes and shapes from very large environments (for example, our galaxy or the universe) to very small environments (for example, subatomic).
2. In some cases the selection of the environment under examination can be somewhat arbitrary, but a good starting point is selecting an environment that is relevant to the defined change you are examining.
3. An environment typically has a vast array of conditions that exist at any point in time or over any interval of time on the change/time continuum. Therefore, we should focus only on the relevant conditions within the environment that can impact the defined process and/or defined implementation associated with a defined change.
4. While it is highly unlikely that a defined process and/or defined implementation will work in every environment, it is

not unusual for a defined process and/or defined implementation to be able to be executed in multiple environments.
5. It is also possible to obtain a defined change in multiple environments although the defined processes and defined implementations associated with obtaining that defined change may vary from one environment to another environment.
6. The universe of potential defined processes that exists is probably almost endless. A given defined process from this universe of potential defined processes will execute in any environment that has the relevant conditions that will support the process factors associated with that defined process. Therefore:

   a. Within any given environment there will be a subset of this universe of defined processes executing during any interval of time on the change/time continuum.
   b. The chain of events within the given environment continues to create new conditions within the given environment as we proceed along the change/time continuum.
   c. Therefore, the subset of defined processes will continually vary within this given environment as we proceed along the change/time continuum. This is due to the creation of new triggering events and the ability of the given environment to support the process factors related to an ever-changing array of defined processes.

7. On the other hand, defined implementations are related not just to a defined process but also directly to the given environment that a defined process will execute in.

a. This means that an implementation will be subject to the conditions existing within a given environment at any point in time on the change/time continuum.
b. And, as already noted, the chain of events within the given environment continues to create new conditions within the given environment as we proceed along the change/time continuum.
c. Therefore, it is more difficult, if not impossible, to obtain a single implementation that is universal across all of the possible environments that a given process can potentially be executed in.
d. However, this does not mean that we cannot have multiple defined implementations for a given defined process that will work in a given environment.

CHANGE DYNAMICS PROFILES AND ANALYSIS

We now have a good understanding of how the principles of change and the elements of change interact with each other to help solidify the concept of change dynamics. In future chapters we are going to develop deeper understandings of how environments work; the ins and outs of defined change, defined processes, and defined implementations; and the risks involved in obtaining the change in life that you desire. But before we move on, we still need to tidy up a few topics relative to the concepts surrounding change dynamics.

The open-ended question is: "How can we package all this information regarding change dynamics into a structure that is easier to manage, communicate, and facilitate for initial decision making?" To accomplish this, there are tools that can be used that are derivatives of the change dynamics concepts we have just presented. These tools are Change Dynamics Profiles and Change Dynamics Analysis.

The starting point for our discussion of these tools is the introduction of the concept of definitional parameters. We will see that definitional parameters become the cornerstone for a change dynamics profile and change dynamics analysis.

In change science *definitional parameters* are defined as those parameters that define the assumptions and specific characteristics used in determining a defined change and its associated defined process and defined implementation. Definitional parameters include:

1. A clear description of the defined change we are examining
2. The environment(s) involved and the conditions associated with those environments
3. The length of the time interval on the change/time continuum (assuming there are restrictions) associated with the defined change under consideration
4. Defined processes under consideration to obtain the desired defined change
5. Defined implementation strategies under consideration
6. Any other critical considerations associated with the defined change under examination

Definitional parameters are used to start defining some of the more important relevant characteristics associated with obtaining a specific defined change or how a defined change under examination came to be. When they are linked together under a single analysis, the definitional parameters can be a useful starting point for either trying to determine how to obtain the defined change we desire or examining a defined change that has already taken place.

The definitional parameters are packaged together and become the foundation for use in a change dynamics profile and/or change dynamics analysis.

Change Dynamics Profile

A *change dynamics profile* outlines all the specific criteria necessary to try to obtain a specific desired defined change. It includes:

1. A description of the defined change we are examining
2. Environment(s) under consideration
3. The starting state of being in the environment(s) under consideration and its specific position on the change/time continuum; in other words, conditions that exist in the environment(s) we are considering
4. The length of the time interval on the change/time continuum (assuming there are restrictions) associated with progressing from the starting state of being to the ending state of being
5. Possible defined processes under consideration to obtain the desired defined change and the match up of the associated process factors to the relevant conditions that exist in the environment(s) under consideration
6. Possible defined implementation strategies based upon the answers to the above questions

It is important to note that a change dynamics profile is not the same as an implementation plan. In future chapters you will learn that an implementation plan focuses on specific execution strategies. In contrast, a change dynamics profile is a much broader analytical analysis of all of the dynamics surrounding a given defined change. It captures not only some of the aspects of specific execution strategies but also the analytical thought process that went into deriving those execution strategies.

More importantly, a change dynamics profile provides a tool for performing an initial go/no go analysis. By doing a high-level review and analysis of exactly what will be involved in order to obtain a specific change under consideration, we often can derive enough of an understanding about the dynamics involved to make an initial decision as to whether or not we should proceed with the efforts. In this regard we should note the following:

- We as individuals, organizations, and society are performing change dynamics profiles and reaching go/no go decisions based upon these profiles as a regular part of our daily lives. In some cases they might be formal, but in most cases in our daily lives they are ad hoc and on the fly. Our subconscious is constantly creating and reacting to change dynamics profiles all the time.

    For example, let's say you live in the city, and you want to go to the store that is three blocks away (that is, change your location from home to the store). You open the door and see that it is raining (that is, you assess the conditions that exist in the environment in which you must execute). You immediately think of various possible processes you could use and the implementations required to execute those processes (that is, you can run dressed as you are, you can get a raincoat out of the closet, you can go upstairs to your bedroom and get an umbrella, or you might even just wait until it stops raining and then walk to the store). This analysis is performed taking into consideration how critical the need is to go to the store (that is, what are the change/time continuum considerations) and also other expected chain of events considerations (that is, how long is the rain expected to last). This change dynamics profile occurs in a matter of seconds, and you make a go/no go decision on the spot and begin to execute to that decision.

- Using change dynamics profiles can also help when we are trying to analyze the merits of someone's claims. Early on in the book we raised the issue of the claims made by experts (self-proclaimed or otherwise). Many of these experts will claim to have the proven solution to accomplish the change we want to make. We have now reached a point of understanding in this book that we can start to improve our ability to analyze these claims using the fundamentals of change science as our tools. By utilizing a change dynamics profile to examine someone's claims of having an ideal solution, we can develop a direct link between the claims and the actual reality that is specific to us.

  For example, someone claims to have the ideal solution to weight loss (the defined change). If you approach their claims using a change dynamics profile, there is a good chance you can assess with some degree of certainty the likelihood as to whether or not the solution will work for you. Their solution should provide an explanation of the process they are claiming will work. From this process you need to assess what the specific process factors are. Remembering the principle of environmental override, you would next compare these process factor requirements to the conditions that exist in the environment(s) in which you will be executing. If there is an immediate match, then you have an immediate go for a decision. If there is not a match, then you must try to determine if there are any implementation strategies that can change the conditions in your environment(s) in order to match the process factors. Keep in mind that some claims will recognize this dilemma and provide potential implementation strategies as a part of their overall solutions. In either case, if the answer is yes and the implementation can be executed in an acceptable interval of time on the change/time continuum, then a go for an answer is still obtained. However, if after you have conducted this high-level review and analysis the answer is no or the time interval and/or implementation efforts are not acceptable, then you should not spend any more time exploring this solution.

- A change dynamics profile is a structured approach and, as such, increases the chances of making improvements in decisions and in time management. Obviously, the amount of effort we want to apply preparing a change dynamics profile depends upon how critical the change under consideration is. However, even for more routine change decisions, the quick use of a high-level change dynamics profile can help us make a more informed and, therefore, improved decision.
- A change dynamics profile can also help reduce the overall amount of time and effort you put into making decisions about change in your personal and/or professional life. Most people can give immediate examples of contemplated change in their personal lives or at work that they struggled with and stressed over. By defining these change issues using a change dynamics profile, it is not uncommon to quickly obtain a clearer understanding of whether or not a particular change makes sense. If it does make sense, you also have a better understanding of the requirements necessary to make it happen.

In future chapters, you will increase your knowledge about processes, implementations, and environments. However, I hope you see that just having a basic understanding of the change dynamics associated with the three elements of change and the principles of change gives you enough knowledge to start having an immediate impact on the change decisions you are making at a personal, business, or societal level. Leveraging off of the structural nature of a change dynamics profile will help in these efforts.

Change Dynamics Analysis

While a change dynamics profile is a tool to use when considering change decisions that are in the future, a change dynamics analysis is used for examination of a change that has already taken place. We can often learn about how to proceed in the future if we understand the dynamics of what has taken place in the past. Past success or failure is almost always the best starting point for decisions you need to make in the future.

A *change dynamics analysis* attempts to define all the specific change dynamics *that have occurred* in order to derive a specific defined change that is under consideration. A change dynamics analysis can also be used to try to determine why a specific defined change *did not occur* in a given environment. It includes such items as:

1. A description of the defined change being examined
2. The environment in which the defined change took place
3. The starting state of being in the environment and its specific position on the change/time continuum; in other words, the conditions that existed in the environment in which the defined change took place
4. The length of the time interval on the change/time continuum associated with progressing from the starting state of being to the ending state of being

5. The defined process used to obtain the desired defined change and how the associated process factors matched up to the relevant conditions that existed in the environment at various points in time on the change/time continuum
6. Implementation strategies used based upon the answers to the above questions

Again, the use of a change dynamics analysis is a tool that provides a structured approach to these types of efforts. By breaking down a given defined change that has occurred, or has not occurred, in a given environment into its individual definitional parameters, the user can save time and effort in trying to figure out why the particular change under examination was successful or unsuccessful. The information derived can then often be leveraged off of when we need to predict what might or might not happen in the future or what decisions to make relative to specific changes we face in the future.

The more you use change dynamics profiles and perform change dynamics analysis, the better your skills will become, leading to increased incorporation of the change science concepts into your daily life. Hopefully, this will ultimately lead to an improved understanding of the change you are constantly dealing with.

Now it is time to move on to the subject of the structural nature of environments and environmental dynamics.

CHAPTER FOUR

Environments Part I: Structural Nature of Environments

*Change is directly subject to the conditions
under which it must take place!*

Tom Somodi

By now you should be recognizing that our exploration of change as a science is different from much of the discussion you find in general regarding the subject of change. There is an enormous amount of information and discussion out there regarding change. However, as indicated earlier in this book, there is a propensity to focus on, or promote, specific process methodologies and implementation methodologies. In contrast to all that discussion, I hope that you are beginning to see our argument that there is really a science to the subject of change.

The objective should be to realize a much deeper understanding of change that goes beyond what a good process or implementation methodology is. When we view change as a science, a whole new world of understanding opens up to us.

For example, other discussions regarding change also often focus on certain aspects of environments. However, rarely, if ever, do these discussions explore environments to the level of examination that you will find in this book, much less tie the concepts surrounding environments back to such an integrated set of concepts regarding change. This should ultimately help you to not only better master all the change that exists in your life but also to better evaluate all the other discussions regarding change that you encounter.

As you will come to see as you read on, there is a lot to be taken into consideration when exploring the subject of environments and environmental dynamics. In some respects, I consider this lost subject matter when people discuss change. So hang on to your hats because there are some exciting things to learn about environments.

WHAT IS AN ENVIRONMENT?

To start, we need to remember exactly what an environment is. If you recall from Chapter 1, a given environment is defined as the context, circumstances, and conditions that exist in a specific defined space at a specific point or period of time in which the change elements must operate. The key element to this definition is that there are a countless number of conditions that exist in the known and unknown universe. Therefore, if we are ever going to be able to understand the change dynamics associated with a specific change, we must focus on a specific defined set of conditions in a specific space or area relative to all of these possible conditions.

In addition, we must note that our focus is on the execution of a specific set of change elements over an interval of time. Therefore, we are interested not only in the conditions that exist in a specific space/area but also in what is happening to those conditions relative to the specified change elements under consideration at particular points and/or intervals of time along the change/time continuum.

So in the simplest of terms, we can think of an environment as nothing more than a circle or box of specific conditions that are carved out of this vast universe of all the conditions that exist around us. And the main reason we are interested in this circle or box of conditions is because they have some sort of significance to the given defined change that we are examining.

In addition, we know that the change dynamics associated with the chain of events principle in change science tells us that the conditions within our circle/box will be constantly changing over the change/time continuum. In the next chapter we will discover that environmental dynamics represent the study of all of the dynamics that are taking place within a specific given environment because of the change dynamics taking place both internally and externally to this specific given environment.

By understanding the interrelationship between the environmental dynamics that exist and the change elements that we are examining, we can significantly increase both our understanding about the change we are interested in and the probability of obtaining the change we desire.

But before we get into the subject of environmental dynamics, we first need to expand our understanding of the structural nature of environments by exploring such topics as the selection of an environment, types of environments, and the conditions that exist within environments.

SELECTION OF AN ENVIRONMENT

We have already noted that there can be a certain amount of arbitrariness associated with the selection of a given environment. This is due to the fact that there are literally countless options ranging from as few as one environment, which would be represented by the entire known universe and possibly beyond, to countless environments if you treat the space associated with every smallest subatomic particle as being an individual environment.

The following are some examples of a selected environment:

1. Your house or apartment can be viewed as a specific given environment in that there is a defined set of conditions that exists in it, and there are change elements (and the associated change) executing within in your house or apartment along the change/time continuum.
2. A computer, mobile phone, or piece of equipment at work can all be considered a specific defined environment since, once again, there are defined sets of conditions that exist along a change/time continuum and related change elements executing within these defined environments.
3. The conditions associated with the planet Earth can be a defined environment relative to the rest of the solar system or the universe.
4. Finally, if the change elements under examination are associated with the stars and galaxies, then even the universe itself might be the defined environment since these represent conditions that exist in the universe.

The above examples highlight the concept that environments must have an association or possible association with a specified set of change elements. Remember, an environment is only relevant if it is associated with the examination or execution of a specific set or sets of change elements.

In other words, while there can be a countless number of possible defined environments, the science of change states that it is only those environments that you are considering directly associated with the change elements under examination that should carry the distinction of being defined environments. As we will explain below, it is this relationship or relevance between a given environment and a given set of change elements that is the perfect starting point to begin to establish some rules that can assist us when selecting environments.

Rules for Selecting an Environment

In this book on change science, we will be promoting a focus that is based upon a more pragmatic philosophy when dealing with selecting and studying environments. As you will see when we get into environmental dynamics, even with a pragmatic practical philosophy the concepts can start to become somewhat complex, so increasing the complexity by opening the discussion to include broader philosophical discussions will not be a focus of this book.

The other advantage of using a practical approach to defining environments is that we can use some basic rules to assist in our understanding. In Chapter 3 we touched upon how relevance plays a role in the selection of an environment. So let's continue to build off of that discussion and create our first rule for the selection of an appropriate environment.

In Chapter 3 we introduced the definition of relevance as follows:

> A relevant environment has a defined space, a time period, and conditions (or the potential to have conditions) associated with it so as to be relevant to a specific defined change and, therefore, to any defined processes and defined implementations that might be associated with the specific defined change.

Therefore, Rule 1 for defining a given environment is *to define a given environment that is a relevant environment to the defined change under consideration.*

In other words, first look at the defined change under examination. Then determine what given environment or environments make the most sense to use relative to that defined change based upon the defined space (that is, location), time period, and the type of conditions that are required to support that defined change. Note that the use of a change dynamics profile or change dynamics analysis described in Chapter 3 might be perfect in assisting in these efforts.

Here are some examples to help you better understand Rule 1:

1. Let's say that the defined change is to eliminate a headache that you have. Then defining "your physical body" as the environment makes the most sense given that any defined process (for example, the use of aspirin) and defined implementation must take place relative to this given environment.
2. If the defined change is producing a specific product on a production line at work, then it only makes sense to define the given environment as the areas at work associated with that production line.
3. If the defined change you are examining is the relationship of the location of the planets to one another, then the solar system would probably be the best definition of the environment associated with this defined change.

Note that selecting an environment that is totally irrelevant to the defined change, associated defined process, and defined implementation makes no sense. For example, giving aspirin to your spouse when you have a headache (that is, using a body other than your own as the environment) is not logical since the conditions in the other body are totally irrelevant to the desired defined change.

It is also very important to recognize that the number of possible relevant environments to select from can vary significantly based upon the defined change you are examining. For example, in the case of your having a headache, an environment associated with your body is the only relevant environment that exists. It is an example of a very limited specific environmental selection. On the other hand, if you own or work for a company that has manufacturing facilities located all around the world and the defined change is to add manufacturing capacity, you could easily have multiple relevant environments to select from.

Rule 2 builds off the logic of Rule 1 but focuses on environmental override. The environmental override principle states that if the conditions contained within a given environment will not support the requirements of a specific defined process or specific defined implementation, then the desired change associated with the defined process and/or defined implementation will not be obtained. Therefore, it does not matter if you are using a proven process and/or a proven implementation to obtain a certain defined change, because that defined change will not be obtained using that defined process and/or defined implementation if the conditions in that given environment are not available to support that specific defined process and/or defined implementation.

Therefore, Rule 2 for selecting a given environment is *to select a given environment that has the potential to contain conditions that will match the process factors and implementation factors associated with possible solutions.*

Put another way: do NOT select an environment that is unlikely to contain the conditions necessary now or in the future to support the process factors and/or implementation factors associated with the anticipated defined processes or defined implementations. Examples of Rule 2 include:

1. If the defined process includes the use of a windmill to create electricity, you would not want to select an environment that has limited access to wind (for example, between tall buildings or among a forest of trees).
2. If your defined change is to change your location using a boat (for example, go on a vacation on a boat), you would not pick an environment in which a body of water did not exist since one of the conditions will be a body of water.

Chapter Four

Rule 3 recognizes the need for some level of stability in the environment you are selecting. You remember from Chapter 3 that the defined process you select in order to obtain a specific defined change will always require an interval of time on the change/time continuum as one of its process factors in order to achieve execution.

Therefore, Rule 3 for selecting a given environment is *to select a given environment in which the conditions required to support the execution of the possible defined processes under consideration have enough stability over the expected time intervals associated with the change/time continuum.*

Rule 3 is different from Rule 2 in that the environmental override principle underlying Rule 2 assumes the conditions required to support a defined change do not exist and are unlikely to exist during the time horizon required to obtain the desired defined change.

Rule 3, on the other hand, recognizes that there can be situations in which an environment can have the conditions necessary to support a specific defined change. However, the stability of those conditions is such that there is a strong likelihood that the conditions will not exist long enough in that given environment to support the required interval of time on the change/time continuum. For example, you would not build a factory to produce a product (producing a product is the defined change) in an environment in which the stability of available raw materials is inadequate to support the desired production capacity/interval of time. Likewise, if your desired defined change is to control your diabetes by using insulin, you would not select to live in an environment where the access to an adequate supply of insulin is not stable enough to ensure availability when required during the change/time continuum.

As a side note, Rule 3 can become very significant when the desired change requires an extensive time interval in order to execute. This is due to the fact that as the time interval increases, the likelihood of the required conditions in a given environment remaining stable decreases with time. In addition, the number of environments associated with a given change will also often increase.

A great example of this is someone who wants to lose weight on a diet. This change usually takes an extended period of time. Therefore, the number of environments that needs to be taken into consideration is usually large (for example, home, work, play, etc.). In addition, the conditions in these sorts of environments are also usually subject to a fair amount of change over an extended period of time. In my opinion, it is these dynamics that make something like losing weight so difficult, no matter what methodology you are using or how much commitment you have.

In the next section of this chapter we will be introducing the concepts of primary and secondary environments. So while Rule 4 might not make total sense now, it should be clearer after we finish our discussion later on. For now, just understand that a primary environment is the environment directly associated with the execution of the defined change. Secondary environments are environments surrounding the primary environment, and, therefore, activities that occur in a secondary environment can potentially impact the conditions that exist in the primary environment. An easy to understand example: if you are ill, the primary environment is your body while the secondary environment would be your immediate surroundings (that is, you might be at home, at work, or in a hospital).

So Rule 4 states that *when selecting an environment, take into consideration not only the environmental dynamics of the primary environment but also the environmental dynamics of the secondary environments.* For example:

1. If your defined change is to control your allergies when you are in your home (the home being your primary environment), execution of your defined change would probably be easier if your home were located in an area of the country (the secondary environment in which your house is located) where allergy conditions are low to begin with. This is, of course, as opposed to an area of the country known to have conditions that aggravate individuals who have allergies.
2. If your defined change is to produce a product on a machine that requires highly skilled labor (the machine is the primary environment and the area surrounding the location of the machine is the secondary environment), you would want to take into consideration the availability of skilled labor relative to the location of your machine.

Note that while these two examples appear to represent the same dynamics, they do not. In Example 1 the defined change is to control allergies within your house. No defined process on how to obtain the defined change has yet been selected, and the primary environment is, therefore, the house. In Example 2, the defined change (that is, produce a product) and the defined process (that is, use a specific machine that requires skilled labor) have already been selected. Therefore, the primary environment is the machine itself since the conditions within the machine will dictate if a product is produced or not. However, in both cases, the selection of the primary environment is impacted by the different potential secondary environments surrounding the primary environments.

Therefore, Rule 4 would suggest that we attempt to select a primary environment that maximizes the potential of positive influences from surrounding secondary environments.

In summary, while we could spend time developing even more rules for selecting an appropriate environment, we recognize that, in the end, selecting an appropriate environment relies heavily on logic and common sense. If we use these rules along with some high-level change dynamic profiles or analysis and add in some common sense, the selection of an appropriate environment should be clear in the majority of situations.

Once an environment or set of possible environments has been selected, the next step is to further refine this selection through the use of primary and secondary environments.

Primary and Secondary Environments

A *primary environment* is the given defined environment selected for the execution of the defined process associated with the specific defined change under examination.

Secondary environments are environments that are external to the primary environment with a first-degree secondary environment representing the secondary environment that directly borders the primary environment.

Up to this point in time we have focused only on the given defined environment in which the change was expected to be executed. In order to better understand environmental dynamics outlined in the next chapter, it is important to differentiate between the given defined environment in which the change is expected to execute and those environments surrounding that given defined environment. Therefore, from now on, we will identify the given defined environment selected for the execution of the change elements associated with the specific defined change under examination as the primary environment.

Environments surrounding a selected primary environment will be identified as secondary environments. In addition, there will be times when we want to establish a level or degree of relationship between a primary environment and its surrounding secondary environments. To this end, *a defined environment that is directly surrounding a primary environment will be referred to as the first-degree secondary environment.* If we decide to define multiple layers of secondary environments surrounding the primary environment, *these layers of secondary environments will increase in degree relative to their position (that is, first-degree, second-degree, third-degree and so on).*

CHANGE SCIENCE AND OTHER DISCIPLINES

While I do not want to confuse our discussion, it is probably a good idea to address how the definitions here of primary and secondary environments relate to some of the other scientific disciplines. Other scientific disciplines also often try to limit the focus of their analysis or discussion to relevant areas of interest. For example, in physics the word "system" has a technical meaning, namely, it is the portion of the physical universe chosen for analysis. Everything outside the system is known as the environment, which in the analysis is ignored except for its effects on the system.

So you can see that in change science, the definition of a primary environment is really the equivalent to this definition of a system in physics. However, what is important to note is that change science is attempting to further define what is occurring in the universe in the context of the change that exists in the universe. This focus on change requires a set of definitions and concepts that build off of and are interrelated to each other in a cohesive context. Therefore, specific definitions used within change science are intended to be in a context that relates specifically to change and the theory of change.

Bottom line, it is the intent of this book to increase your understanding of the world we live in from a context of the change that is occurring all around us. As clearly pointed out, change science is directly related to and dependent on

> laws and concepts that exist in other disciplines. However, it is an objective of this book to create a set of definitions and concepts specifically related to the science of change. So throughout this book, you will be exposed to definitions and concepts that have similarity to terms and concepts found in other disciplines. If you are so inclined, it will be your objective to examine these points of intersection from the context of change.

TYPES OF ENVIRONMENTS

Earlier in this chapter we used the example of your human body as the primary environment when discussing the desired defined change of eliminating a headache. When discussing different types or classifications of environments, the human body becomes a great example since it represents a broad range of environmental types. Let's take a moment to think about our body in the context of a primary environment.

1. As mentioned earlier, if the defined change under examination is to cure your headache, then your body represented the only ONE RELEVANT primary environment you can consider. So your body was an exclusive primary environment relative to all other possible primary environments.
2. Another characteristic of your body as a primary environment is that it has a fixed boundary to it. Your skin and body features represent a permanent boundary to all secondary environments and do not tend to vary in size and shape during the change/time continuum under consideration. There are some primary environments that can change in shape and context. For example, you might define a cloud or storm as a

primary environment which, of course, has boundaries that can vary in size and shape during the change/time continuum under consideration.

Therefore, your body is self-contained, much like a box or other container that has a specific set of boundaries as defined by their size and shape.
3. Another characteristic of your body as a primary environment is that there are subsystems within your body that can also be considered primary environments which are fixed in location relative to your body in general. For example, depending on the defined change under examination, your brain or your heart could easily represent primary environments in and by themselves. However, their location in your body is fixed relative to your body in general. Your brain will always be in your head and, therefore, fixed relative to the other parts of your body. More importantly, movement of your brain is directly dependent on the movement of your body. It cannot move to a different location in a room unless it moves in conjunction with your entire body.
4. Finally, Number 3 above highlights another characteristic of your body as a primary environment in that it is mobile. It has the potential to move across, through, and into other environments creating a new set of secondary environments as it moves. It is mobile relative to the other environments that surround it providing an opportunity to both influence and be influenced by a changing set of secondary environments.

The above thought process should make it much easier to understand the following definitions of the various types of environments found in the world of change science:

An *exclusive primary environment* is a primary environment that has the distinction of being the ONLY possible environment that is relevant to a specific defined change under examination (for example, your body relative to the defined change of eliminating your headache is an exclusive primary environment).

A *self-contained environment* is any primary or secondary environment that has a fixed set of boundaries during a specified time interval on the change/time continuum (for example, the self-contained boundary that your skin and other body features create or the case of your cell phone relative to surrounding secondary environments represents a self-contained environment).

A *fixed environment* is any primary or secondary environment that is fixed in location relative to all or certain surrounding environments during a specified time interval on the change/time continuum (for example, your brain can be a primary environment that is fixed in location relative to your body, or a house on a street can also represent a fixed environment).

A *mobile environment* is any primary or secondary environment that can have movement in its location relative to surrounding environments, thereby having the ability to create a set of new surrounding environments as it moves (for example, the mobility of your body or a cloud in the sky is a primary environment relative to surrounding secondary environments).

Upon close examination of the above discussion, one word should have begun to pop out at you. That word was "relative." Of course the theory of relativity is a major concept in physics, but while it is somewhat pertinent to what we are discussing here, I will leave it to trained physicists to explain those concepts to you. However, as it pertains to change science, it is important to understand that our ability to obtain or understand a specific defined change is highly dependent on the environmental dynamics associated with these various types of environments. This will be discussed in more detail in the next chapter on environmental dynamics.

Relative to this chapter on the structural nature of environments, our discussion continues with a deeper examination of the conditions that exist within an environment.

CONDITIONS

Classifications of Conditions

Conditions represent actual states of being such as the temperature of the air in a room, a building that exists on a city street, a specific molecular structure, or the existence of a specific star. Conditions can usually be measured and/or defined in some sort of substantive or structural context.

Conditions also represent the end result of a defined change and are directly related to the change dynamics that are occurring along the change/time continuum.

By definition, a defined change is represented by the change in the state of being between two points in time on the change/time continuum. *It is extremely important that you understand that since conditions represent specific states of being, then a defined change can also be defined as a change in a condition or conditions between two points in time on the change/time continuum.*

Just as there is a benefit to defining different types of environments, there is also benefit to classifying conditions based upon their characteristics. Differentiating conditions will further help us better understand certain dynamics that take place in and among environments and will help us later in the book when we further explore processes and implementations.

Relevant Conditions

As you might expect, any given environment will normally have a significant number of conditions associated with it at any point in time on the change/time continuum. In the prior chapter we briefly introduced relevant conditions as the subset of the universe of all conditions in a given relevant environment that are relevant to the process factors and implementation factors associated with a defined process and defined implementation under examination.

Therefore, any condition in the universe of conditions within the relevant environment that is <u>not</u> relevant to the process factors and implementation factors associated with the defined process and defined implementation under examination has to be considered an *irrelevant condition.*

Relevant conditions can be further broken down by the following characteristics:

- *Complementary relevant* conditions are relevant conditions that support the defined change and/or are directly equal to the required process and/or implementation factors.
- *Conflicting relevant conditions* are relevant conditions that are relevant because they in some way do not support the defined change and will obstruct the execution of processes and/or implementations required to obtain the defined change.
- *Variable relevant conditions* are relevant conditions that at one point in time, or for an interval of time on the change/time continuum, have no direct impact on the change dynamics that are executing but that can become either a complementary and/or conflicting relevant condition at a future point or interval of time on the change/time continuum based upon the results of future change dynamics that execute within the environment.

To solidify our understanding of these different characteristics, let us think about an example where the desired defined change is to change our location from outside of our house to the inside of our house. The defined process will be to walk from the outside to the inside of the house.

However, there is a doorway with a door that can be locked that represents one of the conditions that exists within the environment in which the process will execute. The door represents a relevant condition in that your defined process must include turning the door handle to let yourself into the house.

If we assume that the future condition of the door being locked or unlocked at any point in time is unknown, the door would be considered a variable relevant condition in that, even though it has no current impact, it can have an impact at such time as we wish to execute the process and walk into the house. In other words, it can become either a complementary (unlocked) and/or a conflicting (locked) relevant condition at a future point of time on the change/time continuum. This would be based upon the results of the change dynamics that execute within the environment between now and the point in time we wish to enter the house.

However, if we always carry a key to open the door, then that key represents a new complementary relevant condition, As such, the condition of having a key would negate the conflicting characteristic of the door being locked provided your defined process included testing the door and opening the lock if required. In this case, the fact that the door can be either locked or unlocked now becomes an irrelevant condition.

The usefulness of these definitions should be clear. Just knowing if a condition is relevant has limited value unless we determine the context in which it is relevant. Taking an inventory of the conditions that are complementary will help us assess what conditions are missing relative to the process and implementations factors that are required. This, in turn, helps us develop a strategy to obtain those missing required conditions.

Likewise, if we determine that conflicting relevant conditions exist, then we must develop a strategy to compensate for or mitigate these conflicting conditions. In our example above, carrying a key to the door eliminates a possible conflicting condition that the door might be locked when we want to enter the house.

Finally, sometimes conditions exist in an environment that are or can be variable; depending on the change dynamics that exist in the environment, these variable conditions can become either complementary or conflicting. Therefore, they are relevant in that if they are not taken into consideration as part of our analysis or strategy, they could represent either a missed opportunity or a problem moving forward.

Classification of Conditions Based Upon Underlying Origin

Conditions can also be further broken down into four classifications based upon aspects of the change dynamics associated with their underlying origin:

- *Naturally-occurring conditions* represent those conditions derived exclusively from the change dynamics associated with the laws of science (both known and unknown) in the given environment during a given time interval.
- *Cognitively-influenced conditions* represent those conditions derived from change dynamics that would not have occurred in the given environment during a given time interval without cognitive influence.
- *Naturally-occurring triggering event conditions* represent triggering event conditions derived exclusively from change dynamics associated with laws of science in the given environment during a given time interval.
- *Cognitively-influenced triggering event conditions* represent triggering event conditions derived from change dynamics that would not have occurred in the given environment during a given time interval without cognitive influence.

We know that change will occur in an environment with or without cognitive influence. Understanding the change dynamics associated with naturally-occurring change is central to an understanding of our discussion in the next chapter on environmental dynamics. If naturally-occurring change is ignored, then the relevant naturally-occurring conditions that exist as a result of this change will represent complete unknowns relative to any analysis we are performing or strategy we are attempting to execute.

Likewise, if cognitively-influenced change exists because of the activities of individuals other than ourselves, ignoring any of these relevant cognitively-influenced conditions will again represent complete unknowns relative to any strategy we are attempting to execute.

Finally, we have two choices when attempting to obtain a specific desired defined change. We can do nothing and leave it 100 percent contingent upon the environmental and change dynamics associated with naturally-occurring change and the cognitively-influenced change of others. Or we can attempt to influence this naturally-occurring and external cognitively-influenced change through the use of our own cognitively-influenced change. In either case, having a good comprehension of the types of naturally-occurring and cognitively-influenced change and the resulting associated relevant conditions will be instrumental in understanding the likelihood that our desired defined change will be obtained.

Constant Conditions

Constant conditions are defined as conditions within an environment that do not tend to change over extended time intervals on the change/time continuum. While a constant condition can also be a relevant condition and incorporated into a defined change as a process or implementation factor, it tends to be fixed/constant (that is, stable) in its characteristics over an extended period of time on the change/time continuum. For example, if the primary environment we select is a city, the buildings within that city would most likely be considered constant conditions within the primary environment.

The fact that a significant number of conditions in a given environment are constant conditions helps us as we develop our strategy or perform our analysis. For example, the fact that oxygen is a constant condition in the air that surrounds us helps eliminate it as a consideration if oxygen is also a required process factor and a defined process is executing in the open air.

Dominant Conditions

Dominant conditions are defined as conditions within an environment that tend to dominate the change dynamics that are executing over a specific time interval on the change/time continuum. These conditions are characterized by the dominance they have on all the change activity that is occurring over a specified period of time on the change/time continuum. For example, if a hurricane is located within the primary environment we select, then the conditions associated with the hurricane will most likely dominate all other conditions and change activity within the primary environment for whatever period of time the hurricane remains active.

Therefore, determining if any dominant conditions exist or might exist over the associated change/time continuum becomes an important consideration when developing a strategy. It is important to note that dominant conditions are not always obvious or can be subtle in nature. A car accident can create a dominant condition of a traffic jam on your route to work. Or a special showing at a museum may create a dominant condition of a crowded museum. Both of these are subtle but can significantly impact the desired change of going to work or visiting the museum.

Dominant conditions can also take place because of cognitively-influenced conditions. For example, a defined change might require a condition of the approval of someone in your organization before the process associated with the defined change can proceed. The lack of such approval (that is, a cognitively-influenced condition) represents a dominant condition relative to the defined change.

Defining these characteristics for the various environmental conditions will become very meaningful in future chapters as we attempt to make decisions regarding process and implementation strategies or as we attempt to analyze the "whys" or "ifs" of a particular defined change. For example, before we select a specific defined process to use, we will want to know if there are any conflicting relevant conditions that exist in the primary environment for that process. In addition, we will want to know whether those conflicting relevant conditions can be eliminated or mitigated as part of the implementation process.

We will also want to know what sort of naturally-occurring and/or cognitively-influenced conditions we can expect to exist in our primary environment. This is important in order to determine whether these conditions will be relevant and, if so, if they will be complementary or conflicting relevant conditions.

ENVIRONMENTS VERSUS CONDITIONS

Given the similarity in many of the definitions and concepts discussed above regarding environments and conditions, many of you might be somewhat confused. It is not unusual to sometimes struggle with the difference between an environment and a condition. Since an understanding of these concepts will be critical as we move forward in our discussion of environmental dynamics, processes, implementations, and risk, let's take some time here to make sure we solidify our understanding.

In the simplest terms, environments *do not exist except in the context of a frame of reference* to enable us to narrow our focus when we are examining a specific defined change. Because an environment does not exist in a factual context except for how we define it, there can be a certain amount of arbitrariness when an environment is defined. The more broadly we define the primary environment, the more irrelevant conditions or information we must deal with. However, if we define a primary environment too narrowly, then we increase the probability of more external influence or a lack of the available relevant conditions required to obtain a successful defined change.

The use of environments in change science greatly enhances our ability to focus and conceptualize what is critical relative to the defined change we are dealing with. Remember, in order to obtain a change, you must execute a process, and that process has certain requirements (process factors) that must exist in order to be executed. Relativity tells us that for that change to be significant to us, it must be in a context (that is, an environment) we can observe and/or examine and/or conceptualize.

The use of environments also makes it easier to understand the various types of influences that are occurring that can impact the defined change under examination. A good example of this is a NASA spacecraft launch. Such a launch can be impacted by the weather conditions that exist along its launch path. Therefore, it is easier to focus on those conditions if we define the launch path as a primary environment. However, we also know that the weather along the primary environment will be externally influenced by weather that is occurring in the surrounding secondary environments. It is interesting to note that the size of the secondary environment can shrink as we progress along the change/time continuum. This is because the ability for weather patterns all around the world to impact the primary launch path environment will decrease as we approach the actual time of launch.

In other words, while weather patterns that are hundreds of miles away from the launch path might externally influence the primary environment 10 days out from launch, those same weather patterns will no longer have the ability to externally influence the primary launch path environment when we are hours away from launch. This means that the secondary environment surrounding the primary launch path environment decreases in size as we progress along the change/time continuum as it relates to weather.

It can also be useful in our example to use additional primary environments consisting of specific weather patterns. If we believe that a specific weather pattern in our secondary environment might ultimately influence our primary launch path environment, we might want to define that specific weather pattern as its own primary environment. By doing this, we can more easily focus on the conditions and change dynamics associated with that specific weather pattern. This then can help determine more accurately if and when that specific weather pattern might influence our primary launch path environment.

You should now have a better understanding of why the concepts and definitions associated with environments are important in the world of change science. So the next question is how do environments compare to conditions?

As noted above, unlike environments, *conditions represent actual states of being* such as the temperature of the air in a room, a building that exists on a city street, a specific molecular structure, or the existence of a specific star. Conditions can usually be measured and/or defined in some sort of substantive or structural context.

Conditions also represent the end result of a defined change and are directly related to the change dynamics that are occurring along the change/time continuum. By definition, a defined change is represented by the change in the state of being between two points in time on the change/time continuum. Since conditions represent specific states of being, then a defined change can also be defined as a change in a condition or conditions between two points in time on the change/time continuum.

Depending on the context, a condition can represent both a specific state of being and/or a specific defined environment. For example, a specific building can represent a condition if the defined change we are examining represents moving an item from one location to another location in a city and the building is located such that it must be taken into consideration when executing the defined change. On the other hand, that same building could be defined as a primary environment if the defined change under consideration is moving an item from one floor in the building to another floor in the building. In the end, it is the same building but is differentiated by the context under consideration.

Likewise, a storm can be a condition that exists relative to a specific defined change under examination (for example, the change associated with walking from your house to a store down the block). However, it could also be considered a primary environment if the change dynamics under examination are the change dynamics directly associated with that specific storm. Again, same storm with a differing context.

So in summary, *while an environment represents a specific defined frame of reference, conditions represent specific states of being.* Hopefully, this has further clarified your level of understanding surrounding environments and conditions so we can move onto the next topic: environmental dynamics.

TRANSITION INTO ENVIRONMENTAL DYNAMICS

During this chapter we have expanded upon our understanding of environments by exploring the structural nature of environments. The concepts we have established become important as we now transition into the next chapter on environmental dynamics.

In the next chapter we will explore further the activity that exists within a single given environment and the interactivity between various given environments. The chain of events principle and the change/time continuum principle tell us that change will be constantly occurring. Therefore, the conditions within any selected environment will be impacted not only by the change activity occurring within the selected environment but, most likely, also by the change activity occurring in other environments surrounding the environment that has been selected.

The change activity in these various environments might be complementary, variable, or conflicting with the change dynamics we are seeking. Therefore, the concepts associated with environmental dynamics will help you to recognize, plan for, and possibly even control this activity in order to increase your chances of obtaining the defined change that you desire.

CHAPTER FIVE

Environments Part II: Environmental Dynamics

Nothing happens until something moves.

ALBERT EINSTEIN

In Chapter 3 we had an extensive discussion about the role the interrelationship between environments, processes, and implementations plays in the world of change dynamics. While we will revisit many of those concepts again here, it would be a good idea for you to reread the section on environments in Chapter 3 just to reinforce your understanding of the concepts of those interrelationships. In this chapter we are going to continue to build off of those concepts with particular focus on expanding our discussion with a deep dive into environmental dynamics.

In Chapter 3 on change dynamics we also indicated that in change science you will see the term "dynamics" used in the context of something that has continuous activity and interactions. As with our definition of change dynamics, *environmental dynamics* also uses "dynamics" in this context and is defined in change science as the continuous activities, interactions and interrelationships that exist within and between environments. Environmental dynamics focuses not only on the how, why, and what is happening to the conditions within a given environment but also on the interrelationships between environments.

ENVIRONMENTAL ADJUSTMENTS

In order to examine environmental dynamics, we need a method of differentiating between the change dynamics occurring internally to a specific environment versus the change dynamics taking place outside of the specific environment. To this end we start by defining the concept of environmental adjustments.

Environmental adjustments are defined as all of the changes (that is, the universe of changes) that occur in a given environment during a given time interval on the change/time continuum. Environmental adjustments can be further broken down into:

- *Internal environmental adjustments*, which are environmental adjustments that are 100 percent derived from conditions and change dynamics that are internal to a selected primary environment during a given time interval on the change/time continuum
- *External environmental adjustments*, which are environmental adjustments in a primary environment that are partially or completely influenced by the change dynamics that have occurred externally to the selected primary environment (that is, from a secondary environment)

In the last chapter we differentiated between primary and secondary environments. Now we are also differentiating between:

- The change that is occurring within the primary environment because of the change dynamics that is exclusively self-contained within the primary environment (that is, internal environmental adjustments).

- The change in the primary environment that has been influenced by change dynamics that is external to the primary environment (that is, influenced by external environmental adjustments taking place in secondary environments). In other words, in many cases there is a direct interrelationship between the change dynamics taking place in a primary environment and the change dynamics taking place in the secondary environments surrounding the primary environment.

As you might expect, this interrelationship is bidirectional with the change occurring in the primary environment radiating outward into surrounding secondary environments and the change occurring in secondary environments radiating inward into the primary environment.

Let's use Figure 5-1 as an example set for some of the definitions that have just been outlined:

1. If environment A is the selected primary environment, then:

    a. Environments B and C through Xx are secondary environments to primary environment A.
    b. Environment B is the first-degree secondary environment since it directly boarders primary environment A. Environment C would be the second-degree secondary environment since it represents the second layer of secondary environments surrounding primary environment A.
    c. Environments B and C through Xx can be externally influenced by external environmental adjustments radiating outward from primary environment A.
    d. Primary environment A can be externally influenced by external environmental adjustments radiating inward from environments B and C through Xx.

Figure 5-1
Structural Dynamics of Internal and External Environmental Conditions

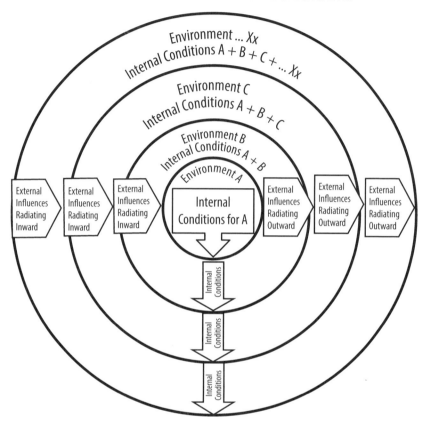

2. Internal conditions for a given environment will always equal all the internal conditions within the boundaries of that given environment; therefore:

   a. The internal conditions for environment B include all the environmental conditions defined by environment A plus the incremental conditions of environment B.
   b. The internal conditions for environment C include all the environmental conditions defined by environment

A plus the incremental conditions of environment B plus the incremental conditions of environment C.
c. The internal conditions for environment Xx include all the environmental conditions defined by environment A plus the incremental conditions of environment B plus the incremental conditions of environment C through environment Xx.

The bottom line is that we are now introducing the fact that when we are dealing with change in a given environment (that is, a primary environment), we are dealing not only with the change dynamics occurring in that primary environment but also with the possibility that the conditions in the primary environment can be influenced by the change dynamics taking place in surrounding environments (that is, secondary environments). In addition, we should also recognize that the change dynamics taking place in the primary environment can also possibly radiate outward and impact the conditions in the secondary environments surrounding the primary environment.

Therefore, within any primary environment, the conditions will be influenced/affected by both the change dynamics existing within the primary environment and the change dynamics taking place outside of the environment (that is, within the secondary environments). As we will discover in more detail later in the chapter, change emanates outward from its origin. So depending on the amount of energy associated with a given change, the effects of that given change can transcend multiple environments. For example:

- If the change executes in the primary environment, it can potentially radiate outward into the surrounding secondary environments. A good example of this would be the explosion of a bomb. The execution of the explosion in the primary

environment radiates outward into the secondary environments that surround it, thereby significantly influencing the conditions in both the primary and secondary environments.
- If the change executes in a secondary environment, it can potentially emanate into the primary environment. An example of this can be something as simple as leaving a window open in your house (the house being the primary environment) and rain blowing in from the outside (the wind and rain are executing in the outdoors that is a secondary environment).

This, of course, further complicates our ability to understand and control all the change around us, much less obtain the desired change we are looking for. Therefore, to ignore these environmental dynamics when dealing with change would be a mistake. However, as we shall see in Chapter 6, we have developed ways personally, organizationally, and societally for dealing with these environmental dynamics in our daily lives. At this point in time, we need to recognize that a fuller recognition and understanding of environmental dynamics will improve our ability to analyze and obtain the change we are interested in.

For example, we have already begun this process when we introduced Rule 4 for selecting an environment earlier in Chapter 4. Rule 4 states that when selecting a primary environment, we must consider the potential impacts from the secondary environments that surround it.

Relevancy

In the last chapter we introduce the concept of relevant and irrelevant conditions. While the relevancy of the conditions are in relation to the process factors and implementation factors under examination, there is also a relevancy to environmental adjustments that are associated with the universe of environmental adjustments found in a given environment.

Relevant environmental adjustments are defined as the subset out of the universe of all environmental adjustments taking place in a given environment that are relevant to the change dynamics required to obtain a given defined change under examination.

Irrelevant environmental adjustments, in turn, are any environmental adjustments out of the universe of all environmental adjustments taking place in a given environment that are not relevant to the change dynamics required to obtain a given defined change under examination.

While there may be cases in which the number of environmental adjustments and conditions in a primary environment might be limited, in general, any given environment will have countless conditions and changes to those conditions (that is, environmental adjustments) taking place. It is also safe to say that generally the larger the primary environment selected, the greater the likelihood that more conditions and environmental adjustments will exist in it as opposed to the selection of a smaller primary environment.

In addition, the larger the size of the primary environment, the greater the amount of internal conditions that are likely to exist and, therefore, the greater the likelihood that influence on all of the internal conditions will be more significantly derived from the change dynamics contained within that primary environment. It only stands to reason that the larger the size of the primary environment, the smaller the number of secondary environments and, therefore, the more internal environmental adjustments versus external environmental adjustments that will likely exist. This has already been pointed out in Figure 5-1. The number of internal conditions of B is the sum of the conditions in A and the incremental conditions in B. Therefore, the total number of internal conditions in B would be greater than the internal conditions in A alone.

Luckily for us, the number of conditions and environmental adjustments occurring in the primary environment we select may not always be an issue. We have already introduced rules for selecting an environment along with the concepts of relevant and irrelevant conditions. Based upon these rules and concepts, what really is important is whether the relevant conditions exist or can exist within a selected primary environment and whether those relevant conditions will remain stable enough over the time interval required on the change/time continuum.

So, most of the conditions and environmental adjustments executing in a primary environment will probably be irrelevant to the defined change under examination. *Therefore, (and this is very important to remember) we should focus only on the relevant conditions within a primary environment and those relevant environmental adjustments (both internal and external to the primary environment) that can impact or influence the conditions as they relate to the defined change under examination.* All other conditions and environmental adjustments that exist (again both internal and external to the primary environment) can be ignored.

RELATIVITY

It is the interaction of environments relative to one another and to us as individuals, organizations, and society that is at the heart of environmental dynamics. There is a day-to-day example that is familiar to many of us that helps us to understand this point. People around the world are constantly monitoring the weather. On any given day, the weather often influences the defined change we are exposed to and the defined change that we attempt to execute. Impending rain storms, snow storms, sunny days, heat waves, and so forth all can influence what defined change we decide to execute and the defined change we are exposed to on any given day.

Yet these various weather conditions are actually conditions that exist in defined environments in our atmosphere. And since these weather environments are mobile environments, they move into and out of the primary environment in which we are directly located, influencing the defined change that is occurring around us. The location of any given weather environment relative to our environment becomes significant. In other words, the defined change we observe, execute, and are exposed to is relative to the environmental dynamics that we are exposed to at any point in time on the change/time continuum.

For example, being out in a desert without any shelter is significantly different from being out in the desert in an air-conditioned house (that is, a self-contained fixed environment). However, persons living 1,000 miles away would not be observing or exposed to any of those conditions since those environmental dynamics are not relative to the environment in which they are located.

Therefore, in change science, we will be defining *relative environmental dynamics or relativity* as those environmental dynamics that exist relative to the environment under observation and examination at a specific point or during a specific time interval on the change/time continuum.

As a final note, it is important to understand that relativity is sensitive to the point or the time interval on the change/time continuum we are observing. For example, the environmental dynamics of a solar eclipse that is occurring 100 hundred miles away at one point in time on the change/time continuum does not have relativity to us since we are not exposed to it or observing it. However, if because of the movement of the Earth we are now exposed to the solar eclipse and can observe it and be affected by it, there would be relativity to the solar eclipse at that point in time on the change/time continuum.

Keep in mind that per the change science principle of simultaneous change, at any point in time on the change/time continuum, defined change is simultaneously occurring throughout the known and unknown universe. However, in change science, only a certain amount of that change has relativity to us: the change that we can actually observe and to which we are exposed to at any specific point or interval of time on the change/time continuum.

This is not to say that a change that has occurred elsewhere in the universe at one point in time on the change/time continuum and that has no relativity to us at that point in time will not *affect* (that is, be an external influence) what we observe or are exposed to at a later point in time on the change/time continuum. In change science we refer to this as a change effect.

A *change effect* is any condition that currently exists in an environment (either a primary or secondary environment) that is the result of a defined change that executed in a different environment at an earlier time interval on the change/time continuum.

A dramatic example of this is the observation today of change that has occurred billions of years ago. We are now able to observe certain types of energy that were created by changes that occurred billions of years ago elsewhere in the universe. However, it is important to note that what we are observing is *not* the change itself since that change actually took place billions of years ago on the change/time continuum. What we are observing today is the result from that change (that is, the change effect) that has finally reached our current environment as a condition that we are exposed to.

We will explore this phenomenon in more detail in our next discussion on inter-environmental influence.

INTER-ENVIRONMENTAL INFLUENCE

Imagine that we are standing on your porch watching a lightning storm that is taking place a few miles away. We see a lightning bolt hit the ground and a few seconds later hear the loud crash of thunder associated with that lighting strike. We know that both the lightning and thunder are created almost simultaneously by the defined change of the lightning strike. We also know that the delay between viewing the lightning and the point in time that we hear the thunder is due to the fact that the energy associated with the lightning travels at the speed of light while the energy associated with the thunder travels at the slower speed of sound waves through our atmosphere. What does this simple example have to do with environmental dynamics?

First, we should recognize that the effect of the lightning strike is not limited to the immediate area (that is, the path of the lightning and point of contact on Earth) in which the change takes place (that is, the primary environment). Obviously, there are changes in the state of being (that is, new conditions) at that place on the Earth. But there are also changes in the conditions of surrounding environments (that is, secondary environments) as the light and sound energy emanate outward from the direct path of the lightning. *This change in conditions in surrounding secondary environments created by the change that executes in the primary environment was defined earlier as a* change effect *in the secondary environments.*

In other words, this change effect represents the influence (that is, new conditions of light and sound energy in the secondary environments) that is created in the secondary environments because of the specific change that takes place in the primary environment.

A second observation to note is that the change effect in the surrounding secondary environments is not limited to a single point of time on the change/time continuum. In fact, as depicted in Figure 5-2, there is the change effect of the light (that is, a condition we observe in the environment of our porch) at one point in time on the change/time continuum and a second change effect as represented by the sound observed by us at a subsequent point of time on the change/time continuum.

For example, Figure 5-2 indicates that individuals in an environment five miles out from the occurrence of the lightning strike observe the light from the lightning strike in only .00003 seconds while it takes 24 seconds before they hear the sound of the thunder. The same event had a significant difference in time between the two change effect conditions of light and sound in the secondary environments.

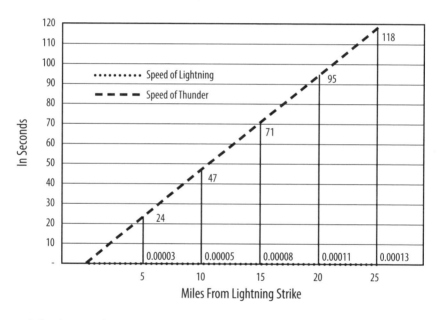

Figure 5-2
Speed of Light Versus Sound Across Multiple Environments

The key is that the effects of change are not always limited to a single point in time on the change/time continuum. Instead, the change effects can transcend across an extended time interval on the change/time continuum as they emanate outward across multiple environments from their originating source.

In addition, the distance and length of the time interval associated with a specific defined change is directly related to two sets of dynamics. First is the amount and type of energy associated with the originating specific defined change. The second is the change dynamics that are occurring in the secondary environments relative to the new conditions created in the secondary environments because of the change effect from the original specific defined change.

In physics we are told that energy cannot be created or destroyed, and only its form can be changed (that is, energy can take the form of kinetic energy, chemical energy, magnetic energy, and the like). Therefore, in the physical world (that is, naturally occurring), all change has energy associated with it, and the conditions that we observe are nothing more than energy in its various states of being. So when a change occurs, the energy associated with the change can take new forms, some of which can be released into surrounding environments.

What happens to the released energy is directly related to two major factors: first, the amount and type of energy that is released and, second, the conditions this energy creates in its primary and surrounding secondary environments relative to the conditions that are required to support the change dynamics that are executing at that point in time on the change/time continuum. In other words:

1. For any given type of energy, the greater the amount of energy that is released, the larger the potential change effect in the primary environment and the larger the number of surrounding secondary environments it can potentially affect/influence. In our example of lightning strikes, lightning has even been observed from orbiting NASA spacecraft showing the significant amount of energy associated with this change. Another example would be the change occurring when a star releases an enormous amount of energy that, in turn, can transcend almost a countless number of surrounding envi-

ronments over an extended time interval on the change/time continuum.
2. This emanating energy creates new conditions in its primary and surrounding secondary environments. Therefore, some if not all of that energy can be changed within these environments as part of the change dynamics that are executing in those environments at that point in time on the change/time continuum. For example, some of the light emanating from our Sun is absorbed within the change dynamics that are taking place on our planet Earth and, therefore, will no longer continue to emanate as light into other secondary environments. Likewise, the sound waves of thunder associated with our lightning strike are absorbed by the conditions that exist in surrounding environments, limiting the distance and time interval in which they exist on the change/time continuum.

In change science we refer to these dynamics as the dispersion of change or change dispersion.

Change Dispersion

Change dispersion is the type, intensity, and direction of energy associated with a defined change emanating outward into its primary and surrounding secondary environments from its epicenter in the primary environment in which it was executed.

The faster the change dispersion of the energy from the epicenter of the change in the primary environment, the faster it will reach surrounding secondary environments. While not mathematically proven relative to this book, we can conceive how Einstein's theory that the speed of light is the maximum speed energy can travel is applicable to the concept of change dispersion. To travel any faster, the release of energy in the primary environment would have to be simultaneous with the change effect in the closest secondary environment, which would be impossible. In other words, if you have two side by side environments (that is, a primary and its first-degree secondary), then there has to be an interval of time on the change/time continuum for energy to move between the two environments. Consistent with Einstein's theory, this shortest interval of time for energy to move between these two environments would be represented by the speed of light. To move any faster, the two environments would, in fact, have to be one and the same environment, and the change (that is, energy) would have to occur simultaneously at a single location in space and at a single point in time on the change/time continuum.

NOT A TRAINED PHYSICIST

This is a good place to insert a very important qualifier. It is important to note that I am not a trained physicist. The focus of this book is on developing a basis for the science of change. Therefore, as already pointed out:

1. In order to develop a basis for change science, we must establish a set of definitions and concepts strictly associated with a focus on change science.
2. Certain definitions and concepts might overlap terms and concepts common in other scientific and behavior disciplines but are intended to be interpreted in this book relative to developing the discipline of change as a science.
3. It is my hope that students of other scientific disciplines will explore change science in more detail as it relates to their other scientific disciplines in an effort to advance both their underlying discipline and change science as a discipline.

> 4. Finally, I am trying to find a balance between definitions and concepts that is substantial enough to justify change as an independent science while still being relevant enough for general understanding and usefulness to the public at large. In other words, definitions and concepts that are both substantive from a scientific perspective but pragmatic enough for the casual user.
>
> It is in this context that we will use the term "energy." It is understood that terms such as "energy," "mass," "matter," "relativity," "systems," and the like all have very specific, significant, and sometimes complex definitions and theories associated with them in other disciplines, which are beyond the scope of this book. Therefore, for pragmatic purposes, we will use the term "energy" in a very broad and general context. We will assume that change requires energy in order to take place and that conditions can be viewed as energy in very specific states of being at any point in time on the change/time continuum.

As discussed above, the change effect/influence associated with a change dispersion on a specific environment is directly related to the "interaction" it has with the other conditions that exist in that environment at that specific point in time on the change/time continuum. In other words, the change effect from a change dispersion becomes a new condition within that specific environment at the point in time that it exists in an environment. Depending on the other conditions that exist within that environment at that point in time, the change effect condition can be either relevant or irrelevant to the change dynamics that are taking place in that environment.

It can be helpful if we think about what happens when our Sun has a change in its environment that releases light energy outward into space (that is, a change dispersion of the condition of energy in the form of light):

1. Some of that light reaches the Earth where it interacts with the conditions on Earth that exist at that point in time on the change/time continuum. For example:

    a. Some of it might become a condition associated with the change dynamics within an environment where it is absorbed as heat.
    b. Some of it might become a condition associated with the change dynamics where it is reflected off an object that we, in turn, can see as part of the change dynamics associated with our vision.
    c. And some of it becomes irrelevant to any of the change dynamics in these secondary environments other than to be reflected back out into space.

2. Some of the change dispersion light energy associated with the initial change that took place on the Sun just continues outward as an irrelevant condition to every environment it passes through, never changing from its existing state of being.
3. Our observation of the light that is associated with this change dispersion is not our observation of the change itself but the observation of the change effect of the original change that took place on the Sun. This can be a difficult concept to grasp.

    a. In order to directly observe the change that took place on the Sun, we would have had to have been personally a condition that existed as part of the change dynamics in the primary environment at that specific point or interval of time on the change/time continuum.

b. This is because of the fact that during any given period of time on the change/time continuum the principle of simultaneous change is at play and *change is occurring SIMULTANEOUSLY in every environment that exists.*

c. Therefore, we can only directly participate in the change that is occurring during any period of time on the change/time continuum in the primary environment in which we exist. Everything else that we observe or experience represents the change effects associated with change that occurred during a previous period of time on the change/time continuum. Therefore, what we observe is, in essence, the result of continuously looking backward in time at events that took place on the change/time continuum for which change effect conditions are still available.

d. It is important to remember that in addition to the principle of simultaneous change, this is also consistent with the change science principles of chain of events and the change/time continuum.

Observation and Change Dispersion

At the time of writing this book there has been much excitement in the scientific community relative to our ability to observe energy associated with change dating back toward the beginning of the known universe. Some would argue that we are traveling back in time. However, technically we are not traveling back in time, but instead what is really happening is that we are observing a change that occurred billions of years ago on the change/time continuum. The change effect condition of the energy remaining from those changes occurring billions of years ago is becoming a condition that has been incorporated as a process factor within a process that changes this energy into images that we are able to observe in the present.

So there are two types of possible observations that we can make relative to a given defined change. First, within the primary environment in which we exist, we experience/observe the defined change that is executing during that specific time interval on the change/time continuum. The second type of observation is when we are in a secondary environment and we observe the change effect of a defined change that executed in a primary environment at an earlier point in time on the change/time continuum.

I must note here that some might argue that technically we are never directly observing a specific defined change. This is because of the delay between energy release from a change and the time interval it takes for the energy to reach us and for us to process that energy into a cognitive observation. For example, there is technically a slight delay (that is, an infinitesimal amount of time) for light to reflect off an object that is right next to us and reach our eye where it is turned into perceptions of the images in our minds. Therefore, we are always observing something backward in time.

However, while this might be technically correct, from a pragmatic perspective it is generally irrelevant to the objective at hand when dealing with change in our lives.

Therefore, for our purposes, we are going to consider *direct observation* as taking place when someone is located in such a way relative to the defined change that he or she is able to directly experience and/or observe the defined change as it executes during the time interval on the change/time continuum.

This would most likely mean that the person would be in the primary environment. However, depending on how the primary and secondary environments are defined, there is the potential that he or she could be located in a secondary environment.

A *secondary observation* will be considered to take place when we are located in such a way relative to a defined change that there is a sufficient time delay on the change/time continuum so that our experience and/or observation is related to a change effect condition in our environment resulting from the defined change that took place (that is, from the change dispersion of that defined change).

For example, observing two cars collide in front of you would be a direct observation. Hearing the change effects of screeching tires and the sound of the crash from around the corner of the building would be a secondary observation.

While I have tended to avoid philosophical discussions, it might be helpful to explore a philosophical question here in order to help us expand our understanding about the concepts we have been discussing.

The question takes various forms but, in essence, asks the question that if a tree falls in a deserted forest, does it make a sound?

Technically, sound requires observation (either direct or secondary) by something that can sense the energy of the sound waves of the falling tree. Since the change dispersion associated with the falling of the tree does not have adequate energy to reach anything with the ability to observe it either directly or in a secondary context, the sound is never observed. However, that does not mean that the tree falling does not exist. As pointed out earlier, there are big differences between the existence of a change, the impact of the change effects from a change, and the observation of a change versus the observation of the change effects of the change.

Remember that change is occurring simultaneously throughout the known and unknown universe. Therefore, the change associated with the tree falling exists even though it does not have direct or secondary observation. In addition, there is also the possibility that change dispersion associated with the falling tree could have an influence on the secondary environment surrounding the falling tree. For example, if the tree falls in the autumn, the energy released (that is, change dispersion) when the tree hits the ground can create change effect conditions in surrounding trees in that some leaves in those trees are shaken loose and fall to the ground.

In addition, the falling of the tree creates a new set of conditions in the chain of events for that primary environment (the environment in which the fallen tree lies). For example:

1. Over a given time interval on the change/time continuum, the tree may have rotted (a defined change in the primary environment).
2. This supported the growth of a fungus (a second defined change on the change/time continuum in the primary environment).
3. This created the possibility of a release of spores (a third defined change on the change/time continuum in the primary environment).
4. The spores were carried via the wind (a change dispersion on the change/time continuum emanating from the primary environment into surrounding secondary environments).
5. That ultimately infected someone walking down the road in a secondary environment one mile away from the fallen tree (in essence, a change effect condition that was a relevant condition associated with the defined change of infecting the individual).

Change Dispersion Dynamics

To review, change dispersion is defined in the context of the type of energy, the intensity or strength of that energy, and the direction of that energy as it emanates outward from its source (the defined change that created it). As already discussed, change dispersion is the transfer of energy from the epicenter of an executed defined change into its primary environment and surrounding secondary environments.

Once this energy is released into these environments, it represents new conditions (change effect conditions) in those environments. Those change effect conditions will be either relevant or irrelevant to the change dynamics occurring within that environment. If they are relevant conditions, they will be incorporated in a defined, or set of defined, changes that are executing in that environment. If the change effect conditions are irrelevant, the energy associated with the change dispersion will continue to emanate outward into a new secondary environment. This will continue until such time as the change effect conditions associated with the change dispersion are no longer irrelevant, and, therefore, all the energy is fully consumed in the change dynamics of its primary environment and all the secondary environments that it emanates into.

Let's look at these concepts through a series of very basic visuals. In Figure 5-3 we see an example of a single environment that we will label Environment A. For this example, we will assume that only one defined change takes place during any time interval on the change/time continuum, and, therefore, there is only one epicenter in environment A. It should be noted that in reality, depending on how the environment has been defined, there will almost always be more than just one defined change taking place within an environment during any given interval of time on the change/time continuum. However, for our purposes it is best to keep everything simple and make an assumption of a single defined change within a given environment.

In Figure 5-4 we depict different types of change dispersion. If the energy released from a defined change is very fast, it will emanate outward very quickly and, therefore, will have a very flat angle relative to the epicenter. The lighting and thunder example described earlier depicts this sort of differentiation with the lighting moving away very quickly like Line 1 in Figure 5-4.

The length of the line represents that amount of energy emanating from the epicenter before it is consumed by the change dynamics that exist in the primary and surrounding secondary environments. Keep in mind that the amount of energy emanating outward from the epicenter can be impacted by three sets of dynamics:

1. The first is the total amount of energy released from the defined change to begin with. For example, a firecracker will release less energy than a stick of dynamite.
2. However, the amount of energy that actually emanates outward into the primary and secondary environments can also be impacted by the other conditions and change dynamics that exist in those environments when the defined change takes place. For example, the amount of energy emanating outward into secondary environments from a stick of dynamite exploding in an open field will be more than that of the same stick of dynamite exploding inside a primary environment that is a reinforced bunker.
3. Finally, the type of energy will impact how much energy emanates outward. For example, X-rays can pass through certain materials while being absorbed by others. So depending on the makeup of the materials surrounding the epicenter of the release of a beam of X-ray, the length of the line associated with that X-ray might be long or could be short.

Thus, as indicated in Figure 5-4, if all of the energy is consumed within the primary environment (that is, Line 2), then the length of the line is totally contained within the boundaries of the primary environment. However, if the length of the line extends beyond the boundaries of the primary environment (that is, Lines 1 and 3), then all or some of the energy emanates into surrounding secondary environments where it represents a change effect in those secondary environments.

Finally, it is important to note that these visuals represent a two-dimensional depiction of the change dispersion. In reality, change dispersion operates in a world of multiple dimensions and, therefore, can and will emanate out in multiple directions. If we once again think about the explosion of a stick of dynamite, we can better understand this concept. Imagine a stick of dynamite that is placed on the ground and exploded in the middle of an open field (that is, the defined change). The energy from this explosion will emanate in all directions around the epicenter of the explosion. Some energy will emanate downward into the ground while other energy will emanate outward in all directions into the open space surrounding the epicenter of the blast. So while it is easier to depict change dispersion in a two-dimensional context, please remember that in reality we are living in a multidimensional world.

In Figure 5-5 we take our analysis of change dispersion to the next level by taking into consideration the principles of the chain of events and the change/time continuum. Each set of lines represents a simple example of individual defined changes along a single epicenter in a single primary environment. We can see that each defined change has its own set of change dispersion taking place that is unique to the change dynamics associated with each defined change. In essence, each set of lines represents new conditions that will exist at future points in time on the change/time continuum in the primary and secondary environments.

Finally, in Figure 5-6 we depict multiple primary environments each with a single epicenter and single set of defined changes along the change/time continuum. This figure is an example of how all the change dispersion taking place along the change/time continuum in multiple environments interacts with each other. Any line emanating from one environment into another environment represents a change effect in that environment. In other words, the energy at a prior point in time on the change/time continuum in one environment emanates into a surrounding secondary environment at a later point in time on the change/time continuum where it becomes a condition in that secondary environment at that point in time (that is, a change effect in that secondary environment).

This is not intended to overwhelm you. However, this simple two-dimensional example using only three environments with a single epicenter in each environment is intended to give you a flavor of just how significant and complex the change is that is occurring all around us. It also depicts one more reason of justifying change as a science in that only through the use of a scientific discipline can we hope to truly understand and harness the change in our daily lives to our benefit.

Figure 5-3
Example of an Evironment with a Single Epicenter

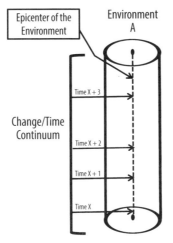

Figure 5-4
Examples of Different Types of Change Dispersion

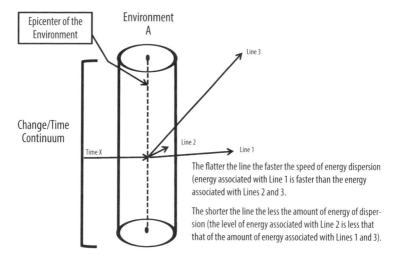

The flatter the line the faster the speed of energy dispersion (energy associated with Line 1 is faster than the energy associated with Lines 2 and 3).

The shorter the line the less the amount of energy of dispersion (the level of energy associated with Line 2 is less that that of the amount of energy associated with Lines 1 and 3).

Figure 5-5
Different Types of Change Dispersion Along Multiple Points on the Change/Time Continuum

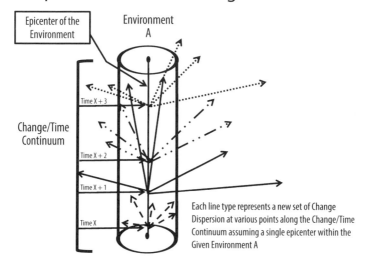

Each line type represents a new set of Change Dispersion at various points along the Change/Time Continuum assuming a single epicenter within the Given Environment A

Figure 5-6
Different Types of Change Dispersion Along Multiple Points on the Change/Time Continuum Across Multiple Environments

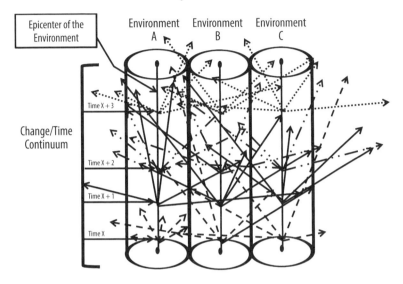

Butterfly Effect

It might once again be helpful in our understanding of environmental influences to explore another philosophical question called the butterfly effect that many of you have probably heard of and that is discussed in chaos theory.

The question has been stated in various contexts but fundamentally asks whether the flapping of a butterfly's wings can lead to a major impact on weather conditions in a larger context (for example, be a part of conditions that ultimately lead to a major storm or hurricane).

The trick in examining this question is to look beyond both the magnitude of the energy associated with the change (that is, the small amount of energy emanated from a single flap of a butterfly's wings) and the apparent insignificance of the event. By using the principles of change science and the concept of change dispersion, we should understand that the change associated with the flapping of a butterfly's wings becomes a new condition in the primary environment in which it executes. Like any other condition, it is either relevant or irrelevant based upon the environmental dynamics and change dynamics taking place from that point forward on the change/time continuum.

Therefore, in theory, even though there is very little energy released and the change event might be considered insignificant, it may represent a triggering condition or be a small part of a larger system of changes occurring over an extended period of time on the change/time continuum. This in turn can create a situation in which such an event does play a role in a much larger change. Let's look at an example that might help us better understand this.

As depicted in Figure 5-7, let's assume we have an extremely accurate scale (Figure 5-7a). On one side of the scale we place a one-half pound weight (Figure 5-7b). In Figure 5-7c, we start placing sand one grain at a time on the other side of the scale. The amount of change and associated energy is very small given that these are single grains of sand. However, as we proceed along the change/time continuum, we eventually reach a point where the amount of sand has the exact same weight as the one-half pound weight (Figure 5-7d). However, when the additional single grain of sand is added in Figure 5-7d, we end up with the scale actually tipping ever so slightly to the left as shown in Figure 5-7e. In essence, that last single grain of sand was a sufficient enough change (creating a triggering event condition) to make the new conditions in the environment of the scale move ever so slightly to favor the sand.

Figure 5-7

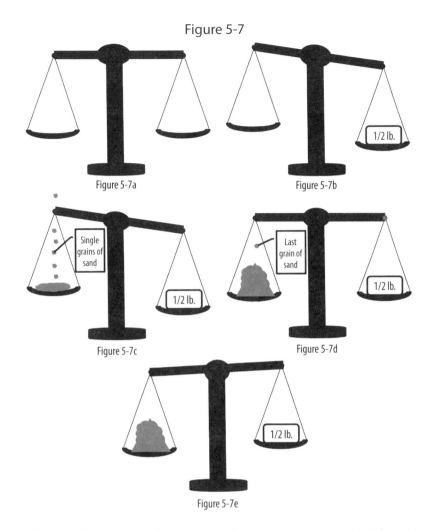

Bottom line, while the change dispersion associated with each new grain of sand is very small, each still has an effect on the balance of the scale until over a certain length of time on the change/time continuum, a single grain of sand triggers a change in the scale in favor of the sand.

Another example of small changes creating major changes has been associated with avalanches. There are indications that minor levels of sound (for example, a distant snowmobile or gunshot) and/or movement of small animals in the snow have represented sufficient amounts of energy to trigger a major avalanche.

So while it is probably highly unlikely that the flapping of a butterfly's wings will lead to a major set of weather conditions elsewhere in the world, we should not necessarily conclude that small changes in an environment cannot lead to or ultimately trigger a much larger change in a primary or secondary environment. It is not always the amount of energy but the condition created with each change relative to the other conditions that exist in an environment that can be the true influencing factor.

BEYOND ENVIRONMENTS

In the end, as indicated in Figure 5-6, the subject of environments and environmental dynamics can be extremely complex. So as we have discussed, it is very important to use the science of change to help cut through this complexity, utilizing such concepts as relevant environments and relevant conditions when analyzing or attempting to obtain a given defined change. However, obtaining a defined change goes beyond the discussions we have had so far regarding environments, environmental dynamics, and change dynamics.

We need to expand our understanding of the underlying elements of change including a deeper understanding of defined change itself and concepts associated with the actual selection of defined processes and defined implementations. In addition, all this knowledge about change is incomplete unless we also take risk considerations into account.

These subjects, starting with a deeper examination of defined change, will be the focus of the remainder of the book.

CHAPTER SIX

Defined Change

The human mind is an incredible thing!

Tom Somodi

You may still be struggling to get your arms around what change is and around contradictions that may exist with some of the traditional perspectives you and the world may have about change. For example:

1. There is often discussion about how complex change is and how difficult it is to manage change and obtain successful change. Yet I am pointing out that, in fact, change is all around us and constantly occurring. How do we reconcile this?
2. If change is constantly occurring around us, how do we so readily manage to survive in our day-to-day lives?
3. Given that we have often experienced a great deal of anxiety or frustration at work and in our personal lives when dealing with change, why is some change acceptable or routine and why does other change create issues for us?
4. What can we do to better cope with all the change that exists in the world around us?

Up to this point we have focused on establishing some basic concepts for the science of change to use as a foundation to explore these and other questions. We have indicated that the best way to deal with a complex subject is to break it down into specific definitions and principles. Now it is time to look deeper into some of the structural aspects of change. We will now use the definitions and principles associated with change science to further explore the three elements of change:

1. defined change
2. defined processes
3. defined implementation/triggering events

In this chapter we will focus on the change element of defined change. We will investigate in more detail naturally-occurring and cognitively-influenced change and successful and unsuccessful change. We are also going to discuss how we deal with change in our daily lives and develop an understanding of (a) just how incredibly powerful our mind is at dealing with all that change around us and (b) how human beings have a history of progress in their ability to deal with and manage the change that exists in society. Finally, we will continue to introduce concepts that build on our discussion of how to improve our chances of obtaining successful change.

DEFINITIONS AND CONCEPTS REVISITED

Let's start by quickly reviewing some of the pertinent definitions and expanding on some of the discussions regarding defined change found in Chapter 1.

Definition of Change and Defined Change

Change is the transformation or alteration of the current state of being to a different state of being as it relates to a person, place, or thing or as it relates to the interrelationships between persons, places, or things.

Defined change is the first element of change and represents an identification/definition of the exact change you want to obtain or examine.

As explained in Chapter 1, change is constantly occurring around us. Examples are endless, and it is exactly this magnitude in the amount of change occurring around us that makes it critical to clearly define the change that we are interested in obtaining or examining.

Types of Change

Chapter 1 also describes two overriding types of change:

- *Naturally-occurring change* is a defined change that is obtained through the naturally-occurring implementation and execution of a process associated with the interactions between the laws of science (both known and unknown) and the environment.
- *Cognitively-influenced change* is a defined change that is obtained through the implementation of a process associated with the interaction between the laws of science, the environment, and some cognitive influence that impacts the specific defined change (that is, specific state of being).

The simplicity of having just two types of change is consistent with many scientific concepts found today (for example, look at the complexity and yet simplicity associated with $e = mc^2$). The concept of two types of change also provides a basis for some very fundamental principles:

1. Change will occur no matter what.
2. It is a completely closed loop structure in that it is either naturally-occurring or cognitively-influenced. In other words, if a defined change is not classified as one type of change, then it has to be classified as the other type of change.
3. Because it is a closed loop structure, it is universal in its ramifications.

    - You can have two opposing positions as to whether or not a particular defined change is naturally-occurring or cognitively-influenced, but in the end change exists no matter which type it is (closed loop). The example about the bird from Chapter 1 applies. If you want to argue that once the bird exists, all cognitive influence or actions associated with the bird are, in fact, naturally-occurring, the only ramifications are that you have expanded what is considered naturally-occurring change and reduced what would be considered cognitively-influenced change.
    - Change is universal across all belief systems. For example, if someone believes the universe is associated with a higher being, then he or she might view the amount of cognitively-influenced change as more significant than someone who does not share the same belief system.

So why do we bother differentiating between naturally-occurring and cognitively-influenced change? Because from a pragmatic perspective, in our daily lives, it is important to realize that naturally-occurring change exists all around us, but we and others have the ability to try to cognitively influence the change that is, or will, occur in our lives.

In fact, our cognitive actions are constantly influencing the change that is taking place in the environment we are in whether or not we are consciously aware of it. Every time you jump into your car and drive to some other location, for example, you are cognitively influencing the change occurring in your environment.

Conscious Versus Unconscious Cognitive Influence

This brings us to the next important concept of conscious versus unconscious cognitive influence. The human mind is incredible!

We need to realize that we are constantly cognitively influencing the change that is occurring in our environment through our conscious and unconscious selection of defined processes and defined implementations. Even in the simple example of changing from one location in a room to another location in the room, there are multiple defined processes that can be selected. We can go in a straight line or go around the perimeter of the room; we can walk, crawl, run, and so on.

Your selection is, of course, influenced by the environmental conditions that exist at the time you choose your defined process. The defined implementation and defined process might be affected by such variables as location of furniture, opened or closed doorways, or even the possibility that other people might be moving at the same time you are moving.

Again, what appears to be simple suddenly can become complex. It makes you really realize the true power of the human mind: we are dealing naturally and unconsciously with so many variables, alternative processes, and alternative implementations while managing the continuous change around us. Our minds are constantly choosing and implementing processes to manage the change we desire and the change that is naturally occurring in our environment.

However, the selection of the defined process to get to the desired defined change is only the beginning. Without the proper defined implementation of the defined process, execution will not take place, and the desired defined change will fail. For example, you cannot drive across town in your automobile if you have not acquired an automobile to begin with (a defined implementation).

Finally, the selection of defined implementations and defined processes can flip back and forth between our conscious and unconscious based upon the environmental conditions that exist at any point in time. For example, exiting your house might generally be an unconscious selection of defined implementations and defined processes but a very conscious selection if the house is on fire.

Therefore, an understanding of naturally-occurring and cognitively-influenced change helps us recognize the magnitude of the challenges associated with the development and implementation of processes to accomplish certain desired defined change. This provides us with a deeper understanding as to why a desired defined change either succeeds or fails.

We now have a good starting point in the development of an understanding of how to increase our chances of obtaining our desired defined change. It allows us to analyze what went right if we obtain our desired defined change or what went wrong if we fail to obtain our desired defined change. Through this analysis we can better determine how we might adjust our selection of defined implementations and defined processes to improve our odds of obtaining the desired defined change we are seeking or to determine if we should just walk away from our desired defined change given the efforts or likelihood associated with a successful outcome.

The take-away is that naturally-occurring change will exist in our environment no matter what we do. However, we do have an opportunity to cognitively influence—either consciously or unconsciously—the change in our environment in an attempt to obtain the desired defined change we want. Therefore, our awareness of the relationship and dynamics that exist between naturally-occurring and cognitively-influenced change provides an opportunity to understand and analyze why a particular change succeeds or fails. With this information and understanding we can increase the likelihood of obtaining the desired defined change in the future.

Most importantly, we now recognize that much of change constantly occurring around us is acceptable and even manageable, because our human minds have the capability to develop and implement processes in both a conscious and unconscious routine manner. The mind is continuously selecting defined process and defined implementation strategies, taking into consideration the environmental conditions that exist at a particular point in time and/or the environmental conditions we anticipate will exist as the change/time continuum unfolds in front of us.

The fact that the human mind is incredible helps answer many of the questions raised at the beginning of this chapter! We can understand how we deal with change that is constantly occurring around us. We now recognize that, as humans, we have learned to marginalize the vast majority of change that is in our immediate environment. We either deal with this change in a routine manner through unconsciously developed implemented processes or consciously control the change through cognitive influence in order to derive the change we desire.

Cognitive Influence and Organizations and Society

It is also significant to note that cognitive influence reaches well beyond the individual and can also be applied conceptually to organizations and society.

An *organization* or *society* can be defined in the science of change as two or more individuals combining together to cognitively influence the environment to obtain certain desired defined change that would be difficult, if not impossible, to obtain at an individual level.

Just as individuals use their minds to influence the change around them, they have combined their intellect through the use of organizations and societies in an attempt to influence the change that exists in the environment. This is done with an objective to manage, control, and ultimately obtain certain desired defined change that is relevant to a broader group of individuals. This is illustrated by a society changing the environment to provide an infrastructure of roads and highways, to collect garbage, or to fight fires as well a business organization that changes the environment by providing a specific product or service to a broad range of consumers.

In every case, individuals have come to recognize that the ability to influence change can be enhanced when we combine our intellect and resources through the use of organizations and societies. More importantly, think of all the change that is occurring around us that has been relegated to these structures and the impact they have on our daily lives to address all that change. You no longer have to worry about the change in your environment associated with the change in the amount of garbage that accumulates around you or how you are going to get your next gallon of gasoline to keep your car running. You have societal and business organizations to handle all this change for you.

I don't know about you, but, as you might expect, I personally find this all quite amazing and, more importantly, powerful in our quest for determining answers about how we handle all the change that is constantly taking place. To think that the human mind has such an enormous capability to manage, control, and adapt to all this change is incredible.

Even more incredible is that, as individuals, we have somehow come to recognize that through organizations and as a society our combined intellect and resources can even further magnify our ability to influence change. There are many that will argue that this capability has had mixed results (for example, the existence of wars or pollution). For our purposes, we will leave that philosophical discussion for others to explore. Instead, we will be satisfied that we have begun to build a solid foundation of understanding how and why we are capable of surviving in a world that is full of constant change.

THE EVOLUTION OF SOCIETY AND REPEATABLE CHANGE

We now recognize just how powerful the mind is at routinely dealing with and executing processes to obtain desired defined change. But what is really exciting is viewing change in the context of the broader society. Remember that originally we began as primarily a gatherer/hunter and then agrarian society. Our primary focus was on survival, and to do so we had to eat. So, most of our attention at the individual level was on "changing" the resources around us into food. More importantly, the defined processes developed and executed tended to be at the level of the individual or small group.

Then an interesting phenomenon began to take place. Certain individuals and groups developed and implemented processes that converted resources into food more efficiently than others. As people began to develop these processes into repeatable change, it allowed certain individuals and groups to consistently produce more food than they required to survive and to reliably provide this excess to others. This in turn allowed other people to focus on the development and execution of defined processes focused on desired change other than food to survive.

In change science, *repeatable change* is defined as change that we would expect to exist on some type of reoccurring basis because of the consistent and repeated implementation and execution of defined processes. Repeatable change can be derived from:

- Individuals or groups (such as organizations or society) that consistently and repeatedly implement and execute defined processes to provide benefit and fulfill the requirements for such change to others.
- Individuals through their use of consistently and repeatedly implemented and executed defined processes.
- Naturally-occurring sources because of the consistent and repeated implementation and execution of processes based upon the laws of science.

Now society could expand its standard of living because people could focus on changing metal into tools, stone into roads, and the list goes on. The Industrial Revolution was no more than an acceleration of society's ability to focus on developing and implementing processes that created desired changes. More importantly, society came to rely on the fact that desired change could be obtained from individuals or groups who could consistently implement and execute efficient processes to provide repeatable change. Not everyone needed to change resources into food because there were individuals and organizations who could provide that change through repeatable change.

As advanced as we like to consider ourselves, the expansion and improvement of repeatable change continues to be a main driver in increasing our standard of living. As an additional example, think of transportation. As the change of resources into food became centralized under fewer and fewer individuals, the need to change the location of these products became more important.

Originally, farmers packed up their wagons and headed for the markets in town. This eventually led to coops where product was delivered to a central location for further distribution. Today the basic requirement to change a product from one location to another location is still the same. However, there is no need for us to individually execute a process whereby we load a product into our car or personally board a plane to change/deliver the product to a new location. Instead, companies (organizations) like FedEx and UPS have developed superior processes that can provide us the service/change as a repeatable change.

The significance of the availability of repeatable change cannot be overemphasized. Repeatable change allows us as individuals, organizations, and a society to support even more change faster and to push for continuous improvements in the development and execution of the processes required to favorably support the change we desire.

Entire industries and management theories have grown up around repeatable change. There are countless examples of how organizations attempt to control all the desired change in their environment through the use of repeatable change. From the repeatable production lines in their manufacturing facilities to the implemented processes they have established to process the payrolls, organizations use repeatable change to manage and control change in order to consistently obtain the results they desire.

In addition, repeatable change is not restricted to just external sources. As individuals, we rely heavily on repeatable change to control, manage, and—most of all—cope with all the change in our lives. Once you determine what you feel is the best way to travel to work, for example, you probably continue to implement this process daily thereafter in the form of repeatable change. If you have children and you have determined a standard routine for putting your children to bed at night, you probably try to maintain that routine over time by, in essence, attempting to create repeatable change. The use of repeatable change is a major reason why as individuals we are ultimately able to cope with all the change that exists around us in our daily lives.

Finally, it is important to note repeatable change can be naturally occurring and is not just due to cognitive influence. Nature is full of repeatable change that under the laws of science will naturally occur if conditions in the environment support them. From the tides that occur every day on Earth, to a multitude of chemical reactions we see in the environment we live in, to the combustion that takes place in the engines of our automobiles, we have come to rely on all sorts of these naturally-occurring repeatable changes.

ANXIETY AND FRUSTRATION ASSOCIATED WITH CHANGE

By now you should be starting to become much more comfortable with the reality of all the change that is constantly occurring, knowing that as individuals, organizations, and society, we have built-in capabilities and methods for managing and accepting all this change. From the capabilities of the human mind to the use of repeatable change, individuals, organizations, and society have methods of dealing and coping with constant change. In fact, not only have we historically been dealing with change, but we have also developed capabilities that allow us to do it at an ever increasing pace.

However, if I were you, I probably would be asking the big BUT question.

BUT if I have capability to deal with all this change, both the change around me that I am unaware of and the change that I desire to obtain, then:

A. Why do I become anxious and frustrated with change?

B. Why am I not more successful obtaining the change that I desire?

Regarding Question A on anxiety and frustration, a good starting point is developing an understanding of some critical factors that play into one's reaction and response to certain change. Let me ask you a few simple questions:

1. What do you think has the potential of creating more anxiety and frustration: the change associated with taking a bus to work in the morning or the change associated with having an operation to repair your knee?
2. What do you think has the potential of creating more anxiety and frustration: the change associated with rearranging a room of furniture in your house or the change associated with moving all of your furniture to a new house in a different state?
3. What do you think has the potential of creating more anxiety and frustration: the change associated with driving your car across town or the change associated with flying on an airplane across the country?

While the answers seem absurdly obvious and probably the associations between the questions appear to be similar in characteristics, there are definitely differences between the examples that are relevant.

In the first question, the major reason anxiety and frustration associated with the operation on your knee are more likely to occur is due to how much more significant having an operation is relative to taking a bus to work. So the level of **significance** associated with a specific change will tend to influence the potential stress, anxiety, and frustration you experience.

In the second question, it is the level of **difficulty** that is a driver in determining the potential for anxiety and frustration. It is far more difficult to move an entire household of furniture to a house in another state than it is to simply rearrange a few pieces of furniture. We need to recognize that no matter how you want to personally define difficulty, the more difficulty you have associated with a change the more likely you are to experience potential anxiety and frustration.

Finally, the third question raises the issue of **control**. When you are driving the car you are completely in control. So generally speaking, you are more likely to experience less anxiety, stress, and frustration when you are in control than when you are not in control—as in the case of relying on an airline and its pilot to fly you where you want to go. It is an interesting dynamic that having control of a situation can often greatly reduce the level of stress associated with a defined change, even when that defined change fails to occur.

A lack of control can also be associated with the unknown. Even though a change might be fairly simple, if an individual, organization, or society faces a defined change that contains a lot of unknowns, the unknowns create a feeling of a lack of control. This then increases the potential for anxiety and frustration.

For example, taking a train from one city to another city can be a relatively straightforward way of obtaining the defined change of moving your location from one place to another place. However, if you have never taken a train before and/or you are in a new city, there can be a great deal of anxiety and frustration associated with this defined change because the unknown creates a perception of a lack of control. This perception of a lack of control in turn increases the potential for anxiety and frustration. If you continue to take this same train in the future between the cities, chances are your anxiety and frustration will probably decrease, given that you become more familiar with the defined change, resulting in a feeling of being more in control.

It is also important to realize that significance, difficulty, and control are not just individual characteristics but are, in fact, dynamics that can be interacting with each other relative to the same defined change. For example, a defined change can be very significant, but if you believe that you have a great deal of control over the change, then the anxiety and frustration that might otherwise exist can be tempered or even completely negated.

So from a science of change perspective, significance, difficulty, and control play a considerable role in the amount of anxiety and frustration that can be associated with any given defined change. The following rules apply:

- The greater the significance associated with a defined change, the greater the potential for anxiety and frustration.
- The greater the difficulty associated with a defined change, the greater the potential for anxiety and frustration.
- The greater the control you have associated with a defined change, the lower the potential for anxiety and frustration.
- Significance, difficulty, and control can be interacting simultaneously relative to a given defined change, thereby creating a set of mixed dynamics relative to the anxiety and frustration that exists with that defined change.

It is important to note that these rules apply to us not only as individuals but also as organizations and societies. In fact, much of history has been influenced by the anxiety and frustration associated with an organization or a society's inability to deal with the change it was facing. For example, there is a good chance that you have been employed by, or maybe even managed, a business organization that completely reorganized itself because of its frustration about its inability to remain competitive in the changing marketplace in which it was operating. Or how about a society that goes to war because of its anxiety over an actual or perceived loss of control in its access to food, water, or other resources?

Before we leave this discussion of significance, difficulty, and control, let's take a quick look at Question B above. Could the fact that you realize that you are not always successful in obtaining your desired defined change perhaps be an underlying reason in many cases why anxiety and frustration exist? If you know that the change you desire will always take place, then there would be no reason to have any anxiety or frustration. However, through experience, you have come to recognize that desired defined change cannot be guaranteed.

You also have learned to realize that this inability to obtain guaranteed change is often affected by the significance, difficulty, and control associated with the defined change. So questions A and B are, in fact, interrelated. Significance, difficulty, and control impact anxiety and frustration levels because you have come to understand that significance, difficulty, and control can also impact the likelihood of obtaining defined change. From babyhood on you have accumulated a vast conscious and unconscious knowledge base relative to defined change. This knowledge base has inherently provided you with the ability to realize that change is not guaranteed and has created a recognition that significance, difficulty, and control can play a major role in obtaining successful defined change.

It has also inherently created defense mechanisms in the form of anxiety and frustration that help bring certain defined change from the unconscious to the conscious where you are more likely to focus on it relative to everything else going on in your daily life. Even though in the end there might not be anything you can do about increasing the potential for success, this knowledge base provides you with an opportunity to focus on the defined change with the hope of increasing the chances for a successful defined change.

Is this set of dynamics good or bad? I believe that the answer is generally positive. While anxiety and frustration caused by the underlying drivers of significance, difficulty, and control can sometime paralyze us or create negative consequences, these emotions are in fact the natural response associated with bringing issues/change into the forefront of our conscious attention. This in turn helps us focus on changes that require immediate and/or our full mental attention.

The key is to learn to try to reduce negative frustration and anxiety by recognizing that much of it is caused by a lack of experience or knowledge while continuing to benefit from the positive aspects of bringing awareness to change that requires additional attention. In either case, additional research and examination will probably be required to address the frustration and/or anxiety.

ANSWERING THE PERTINENT QUESTIONS

We are now in a position to take one last look at the list of questions that were posed at the beginning of the chapter. Through an understanding of the concepts outlined in this chapter, you should be able to begin to make significant progress in constructing answers to these questions.

1. There is often discussion about how complex change is and how difficult it is to manage change and obtain successful change. Yet I am now pointing out that, in fact, change is all around us and constantly occurring. So how do we reconcile this?

    Question 1 points to the conflict between the perceived world and the real world. In Chapter 1 we discussed how change is often perceived as something we have to obtain as opposed the fact that it is something we are experiencing constantly around us. In this chapter we determined that naturally-occurring change will exist in our environment no matter what we do. However, we do have an opportunity to either consciously or unconsciously cognitively influence the change in our environment in an attempt to obtain the desired defined change we want.

Therefore, understanding the relationship and dynamics that exist between naturally-occurring and cognitively-influenced change provides an opportunity to understand and analyze why a particular change succeeds or fails. With this information and understanding we can create a basis to increase the likelihood of obtaining the desired defined change we are striving for in the future.

2. If change is constantly occurring around us, how do we so readily manage to survive in our day-to-day lives?

This chapter introduced us to the power of the human mind and explained how as humans we have learned to marginalize the vast amount of change that is in our immediate environment. We either subconsciously deal with this change in a routine manner through unconsciously developed implemented processes or we consciously control the change through cognitive influence in order to attempt to derive the outcome we desire (that is, desired defined change).

However, over the generations of human existence, our capability to manage the change around us has developed beyond that of individual capacity. Organizations and societies emerged combining the ability to cognitively influence change across multiple individuals, thus permitting changes that would be difficult if not impossible to obtain at an individual level.

This led to the development of repeatable change that was ever increasing in sophistication and reliability. This repeatable change allowed us as individuals to further remove ourselves from having to directly deal with much of the day-to-day change existing in our lives.

So, it is the human mind that provides us the enormous capability to manage, control, and adapt to all of this change together with our willingness to create organizations and societies that combine our intellect and resources so as to magnify even further our ability to influence the change that exists in our daily lives.

3. Given that we have often experienced a great deal of anxiety or frustration at work and in our personal lives when dealing with change, why is some change acceptable or routine to us and why does other change create issues for us?

In this chapter, the science of change introduces the concept of how significance, difficulty, and control play a considerable role in the amount of anxiety and frustration that can be associated with any given defined change. Based upon our personal life experiences and the relationship of these concepts of significance, difficulty, and control to the change we are encountering, anxiety and frustration can and will exist. However, this anxiety and frustration can, in fact, also play a vital role by bringing critical issues/change to the forefront of our immediate attention.

While such an understanding will probably not eliminate the anxiety and frustration, it has the potential to stimulate us to increase our knowledge and understanding about what is causing the anxiety and frustration. This in turn can help us to better manage this anxiety and frustration and to reach courses of actions that are more positive in their overall long-term ramifications.

4. What can we do to better cope with all the change that exists in the world around us?

The reality is that through a history of firsthand experiences, individuals, organizations, and societies have come to learn, either consciously or subconsciously, that a desired defined change cannot be guaranteed. This is why there is an appeal in the claims made by many experts that to obtain a certain desired change, all you have to do is follow a specific course of action or methodology and it will happen.

However, this chapter once again points back to the fact a desired defined change cannot be guaranteed, no matter how much commitment we have or what methodology we follow. This fact is an underlying reason why anxiety and frustration exist relative to significance, difficulty, and control. If we know that the change we desire will always take place, then there would be no reason to have any anxiety or frustration.

Recognition of the fact that a desired defined change cannot be 100 percent guaranteed is our starting point in answering the question of "What can we do to better cope with all the change that exists in the world around us?" Once we accept this conclusion, we are in a position to open ourselves up to learning what the underlying study of the science of change has to offer.

One of my objectives in this book is to help you better learn to cope with all the change that exists around you by exposing you to the principles, concepts, rules, and dynamics associated with the science of change. It is very difficult to personally repair your automobile if you do not know how it works. Likewise, it is difficult to know how to manage the change that exists in your life if you do not know how change works. So it is now time to continue to build off of what we have learned up to this point about the science of change by taking a deeper look at defined processes and defined implementations.

CHAPTER SEVEN

Defined Processes Part I: Structural Nature of Defined Processes

If you want truly to understand something, try to change it.

KURT LEWIN

In Chapter 6 we began our expanded discussion of the elements of change by focusing on the first element of change: defined change. In Chapter 3 we explored change dynamics to develop a better understanding of the interrelationships, interactions, and dynamics that exist between processes, implementations, environments, and principles of change. In fact, it might be prudent if you took some time to review Chapter 3 since a clear understanding of concepts discussed there regarding processes and implementations will definitely be helpful as we now move into a deeper discussion into these two change elements.

In Chapters 7, 8, and 9 we will continue our discussion of the three elements of change by looking further at the second and third elements of change. Chapters 7 and 8 will examine defined processes, and in Chapter 9 we will focus on defined implementations. As previously indicated, a clear understanding of processes and implementations is critical. This is due to the fact that we can have the best defined change ever conceived, but if we are not able to determine a defined process and defined implementation that will work within the environment we are dealing with, then that defined change will just never take place.

Of course, our discussions on defined processes and defined implementations will leverage off of what we learned about change dynamics and environments in Chapters 3, 4, and 5. Knowing that a defined process and defined implementation must take place in the context of these change dynamics and environmental considerations should help us in our understanding of the defined process and defined implementation associated with a specific defined change under examination. For in the end, the change dynamics and environmental considerations will ultimately determine if a defined process and defined implementation will, in fact, work.

So let us get started with a deeper look at defined processes. We will do this in two parts. Chapter 7 on Defined Process Part I will focus on the structural nature of defined processes, and Chapter 8 on Defined Process Part II will focus on the selection of defined processes.

Part I of our discussion on the structural nature of defined processes begins by revisiting and exploring deeper the definition of a defined process.

DEFINITION OF A DEFINED PROCESS

As explained earlier, a *defined process* represents the specific activities, dynamics, actions, variables, elements, and any other factors (all of which have been defined as process factors) that move us from one state of being to another state of being (that is, a defined change). To obtain a defined change we must have a process take place that specifically explains how we move from one state of being to another state of being.

On the surface this definition can seem pretty straightforward. However, some of us might ask, what does this really mean? So let's break it down in detail:

1. At the center of any change there must be at least one underlying "activity" that occurs. In change science we equate this to the action of some underlying law of science or set of laws of science (both known and unknown). In this context, a particular law of science represents an expression of what we expect to occur scientifically, provided a specific set of conditions exists. These laws of science represent the foundation for the various scientific disciplines from physics to chemistry to quantum mechanics and so on.
2. However, in order to obtain a particular defined change, it is common to have more than just one underlying activity. *Therefore, since you can have multiple activities, you can have multiple processes incorporated into a single defined process.* In addition, it is often the specific interaction of these various underlying activities (that is, the "dynamics" that are occurring between these activities and/or various processes) that is critical in obtaining a given defined change. For example, certain activities might need to execute in a specific sequence in order to obtain a specific defined change.
3. It is also not unusual to have some sort of "action" embedded in a process in order to obtain a specific defined change. For example, let's assume our defined change represents the activity of turning pancake batter into a pancake by using a frying pan. This will probably require the "action" of flipping the partially fried pancake (a process in and by itself) at some point in time during the defined process of making a pancake if we want to in fact obtain the desired result.
4. Finally, there are other "variables" and "elements" required in order for a defined process to execute and provide us with the

defined change we desire. These can include the time interval required to fully execute the process, ambient temperature requirements, ratio of components, or the existence of specific required equipment or tools.

To further reinforce the definition of a defined process, let us look at another example. Let us say we want to have a bonfire in our backyard that will last two hours. So the defined change is to go from a state of being of no bonfire to that of having a bonfire that lasts for a time interval of two hours. To obtain this defined change, we decide to rely on a defined process of the combustion of firewood in our backyard fire pit (the primary environment). So a breakdown of our defined process looks like this:

- Activities = 1) the use of the laws of science associated with combustion, and 2) the use of the laws of science associated with our ability to stoke an ongoing fire in the fire pit.
- Dynamics = the interaction of the combustion of the firewood in the fire pit and the incremental stoking of the fire at specific times over the two-hour time interval.
- Actions = the actions associated with the stoking of the fire at certain times during the time interval of two hours including 1) the stirring up of the fire, and 2) the feeding of the fire with additional firewood.
- Variables and elements = 1) enough firewood to support a two-hour fire (that is, an appropriate ratio of firewood to the rate of combustion to maintain a bonfire for two hours); 2) oxygen (which we will consider a constant condition); 3) heat (which we will initially derive from a lighted match and continue to derive from the combustion of the firewood); 4) a tool to help safely stoke the fire; and 5) a time interval of two hours.

These four items describe the "process factors" associated with the defined process we have selected, which, upon implementation, will ultimately result in the desired defined change of a two-hour bonfire in the primary environment of our backyard fire pit.

So now is a good time to continue our examination of defined processes with a closer look at process factors.

PROCESS FACTORS

Obviously, as we have seen above, process factors are the reality of what a given defined process is all about. As defined in Chapter 1 and described above, process factors are the specific activities, dynamics, actions, variables, elements, and any other factors necessary for a specific defined process to occur. As indicated, these factors are not limited to strictly physical conditions. Process factors can also include:

- The length of the time interval required on the change/time continuum for the defined process to execute.
- The sequence of activities and actions that need to take place in the chain of events in order to move from the beginning state of being to the ending state of being associated with the defined change under examination.
- The cost associated with the execution of a defined process that can require an environmental condition that there is a monetary, or some other type of intrinsic cost, that needs to be covered in order for the defined process to execute.

What tools exist to assist us in our attempts to determine the specific process factors that are incorporated in the defined process we are interested in? The answer is process maps.

Process Maps

A *process map* is an outline that attempts to map out at a high level the critical characteristics and aspects associated with a specific defined process that is under examination. Process maps can be used to help analyze and describe a process. The format of these process maps can vary significantly depending on the user and their application, but for our purposes we would suggest the following structure:

1. As previously discussed, ultimately all change relies on the laws of science (both known and unknown). Therefore, a good starting point is to try to define what scientific principles are involved in the process under examination.
2. Once we have defined what scientific principles will be involved, we can define what "physical conditions" need to exist to support those scientific principles.
3. We also need to determine any other process factors that might be required that are outside the specific physical conditions necessary to support the specified scientific principles (for example, cost).
4. Then we need to define any sequence associated with the execution of the scientific principles and/or other process factors that have been determined to be required.
5. Finally, we should attempt to define what time interval is associated with this process so as to provide an adequate amount time necessary to complete the required sequence associated with the process factors.

Let's take a closer look at each of these steps.

Step 1: Define what scientific principles are involved in the process under examination.

We have already learned in Chapter 5 that at some level a defined change is energy changing from one form to another. Therefore, the laws of science (both known and unknown) will always apply to the defined process associated with a defined change. So from a purely technical perspective, all the laws of science and their associated required process factors should be defined within the defined process.

However, there are both technical and pragmatic aspects to this exercise. From a purely technical perspective of change science, we should be very specific about what laws of science are at play and, therefore, what exact process factors need to be taken under consideration. As a promoter of change as a science, I would argue that when absolutely necessary such a comprehensive technical approach should be applied.

On the other hand, I also recognize that many individuals wanting to benefit from the science of change will not necessarily have access to this level of expertise. Only a limited number of people are physicists, chemists, or individuals trained in other scientific disciplines. Therefore, a more pragmatic approach will probably need to be applied.

Such a pragmatic approach would dictate that we should not be afraid here if our thought process is not 100 percent scientifically accurate. In some cases users may need to be highly scientific and detailed. However, for the majority of cases, we can probably get by with general concepts. Therefore, we can use standard or generically known scientific concepts and principles where possible.

For example, in the backyard bonfire described above, if we want to burn something, we might just say combustion with process factors of a combustible material, fire, and oxygen as opposed to a scientific breakdown of what happens when combustion takes place. If the defined change is to move from one doorway across a room through another doorway on the other side of the room, the use of concepts such as walking, running, or crawling will probably be adequate versus trying to define all the detailed scientific components associated with movement in human beings.

The risk of being too general is that our underlying assumptions might not be accurate from a technical perspective, and we might inadequately define to the plus or minus the required process factors. *The level of significance should be a guide here.* Unless the defined change is extremely significant or technical in nature, we are probably safe using generalities when defining what scientific principles and associated required process factors are at play. However, if the defined change represents something highly significant (for example, something directly associated with your health or well-being) or technical in nature, then we should increase our research or solicit the input of experts when defining what scientific principles and associated process factors are at play.

Step 2: Define the process factors associated with the scientific principles selected.

Once we determine what scientific principle(s) are or will be at play, it should not be difficult to define at some level the process factors associated with those scientific principles. As discussed in Step 1, again the level of detail need only be consistent with the level of significance, relevance, and technicality associated with the scientific principle(s).

For example, a high-level determination that the ability to walk may be sufficient without having to go into all the detailed process factors associated with the scientific principles of why or how an individual has the ability to walk. Thus, in most cases, the important process factors associated with walking are:

- The underlying ability to walk.
- Enough energy and stamina at the time to walk.

- An available path between the two points on which to walk (for example, if there is a river, there is a bridge over the river).
- No obstructions or restrictions relative to the path (for example, a locked gate in which case a key is an additional process factor).

While these process factors are, in fact, critical to the process of walking, they are still high-level in nature and do not require in-depth scientific knowledge. On the other hand, if the defined change is to determine a defined process that would help an individual who is not currently capable of walking to walk again, then a deeper scientific definition of the process factors associated with what is required to walk could easily be necessary.

So once again, *the level of definition of process factors will be greatly influenced by both the defined change under examination and by pragmatic underlying requirements and relevancy.*

Therefore, just as we have a definition for relevant conditions, we will also define *relevant process factors* as those process factors out of a universe of possible process factors that are relevant to the defined change under examination, taking into consideration such dynamics and characteristics as significance and underlying pragmatic requirements.

Step 3: Determine if there are any other required process factors other than those process factors associated with the scientific principles selected.

Keep in mind that our ultimate goal is to select a defined process that either provides a way to obtain a desired defined change or that explains why a specific defined change took place. Since it will be important for us to also determine if the environment we choose can support the defined process we select, then we need to make sure we have considered "all" the relevant process factors associated with the defined process we select.

To this end we need to examine if there are any other process factors in addition to those associated with the scientific principles that need to be considered. For example, the process of walking can be executed anytime of the day, but the defined process of walking from home to the store in order to buy groceries is only relevant if the walking occurs relative to the hours that the store is open. Therefore, the hours of operation of the store become a process factor in addition to the process factors associated with your ability to walk to the store.

Step 4: Determine any sequence of activity associated with the execution of the process factors.
Since there is a time interval associated with the defined process, we need to determine if there is any sequence associated with the execution of the process factors. For example, when we define the process factors associated with digestion, there is a specific sequence associated with those process factors. The process factors associated with the mouth occur in sequence before the process factors associated with the stomach.

Therefore, if there is a sequence in which the process factors interact, that sequence also becomes another process factor in and by itself and needs to be taken into consideration. Keep in mind that we can have a situation in which all the process factors exist in an environment as conditions, but if there are other conditions (for example, a conflicting relevant condition) that obstruct the sequence of the execution of the process factors, that defined process will fail in that environment.

Step 5: Determine the required time interval.
We will begin by noting that as discussed in Chapter 5, the fastest a given defined process can execute (that is, the shortest time

interval) is the speed of light. For a defined change, and therefore a defined process, to take place any faster than that would require the beginning and ending states of being to be located at the same point in space at the same point in time on the change/time continuum: this would be impossible. So in change science, the shortest interval of time for energy to change from one state of being to another state of being is the speed of light.

Given that there a great deal of energy in the universe that is in motion at the speed of light, there is, therefore, also a great deal of change occurring around us executing at the speed of light. However, there is also a large amount of change that requires a longer time interval on the change/time continuum to fully execute. Determining the length of this time interval for any given defined process can become critical and needs to be defined as a process factor.

One of the main reasons the process factor of the time interval is important is the environmental override principle. Since the conditions that exist in an environment are continually changing because of the change dynamics and environmental dynamics discussed in Chapters 3 and 5, there is the possibility that the conditions in that environment will no longer support the defined process as we proceed along the change/time continuum. Obviously, the risk associated with this possibility increases as the length of the required time interval process factor increases.

As we will see later in this chapter when we discuss effectiveness and efficiency, understanding the process factor of the required time interval will also be helpful when we compare one potential defined process against an alternative potential defined process. As we might expect, the length of the time interval can have a significant impact when comparing the option of one defined process against a second defined process option.

In order to obtain a reasonable estimate of the time interval process factor, we need to look at the time requirements associated with the underlying scientific principles we have already defined in Step 1. For example, in the case of neutralization of an acid with a base, assuming we know the proportion of acid and base we have and the rate at which neutralization occurs, we can calculate the time interval relative to the defined change and associated defined process of neutralization.

Once we determine any underlying required time intervals associated with the scientific principles, our next step would be to evaluate if there are any adjustments required to these time intervals because of any of the additional process factors identified in Step 3 or resulting from the sequence of activities noted in Step 4. In some cases we might have multiple time intervals associated with various scientific principles and additional process factors that are at play within our defined process. In these cases, we want to use the longest time interval that we have determined for our final time interval process factor.

Importance of Determining Appropriate Process Factors

Determining the appropriate process factors associated with a given defined process is important on several levels:

1. Comparison of various alternative defined processes.

    As we will soon be discussing, it is not unusual to have alternative defined processes to select from when explaining or attempting to obtain a specific defined change. Therefore, comparing the process factors associated with each alternative (such as the time interval process factor associated with the various alternative defined processes) can play a significant role in the determination of which alternative to select.

2. Selection and/or analysis of alternative environments.

   Just as there is the potential to have alternative defined processes available to select from to obtain a specific defined change, there can also be multiple primary environments to select from for the execution of the defined change. Given that each potential environment can have its own set of conditions and environmental dynamics associated with it, certain defined processes (that is, process factors) may work better than others based upon the primary environment selected. Therefore, a thorough understanding of the process factors associated with each alternative defined process becomes instrumental in making the proper selection of which primary environment to utilize.

3. Analysis of environmental conditions and the associated development of alternative defined implementations.

   Keep in mind that there will also ultimately be a defined implementation associated "with each combination" of defined processes and primary environments selected. The associated defined implementations are based upon the relationship of the actual environmental conditions that exist at any point in time on the change/time continuum relative to the process factors that are required. Therefore, a clear understanding of all the required process factors for each defined process under examination is a must.

   In other words, evaluation of one potential defined process/primary environment combination against an alternative defined process/primary environment combination can be significantly influenced by the required defined implementation associated with each of the alternative combinations under consideration. One defined process/primary environment combination might look superior to another alternative combination until the required defined implementation associated with each alternative is taken into account. The better the understanding of all the process factors associated with each defined process alternative, the less the analysis will represent guesswork and the more reliable the analysis will be.

4. Analysis of claims and methodologies by authors and experts.

As stated, one of the objectives of our study of change science is to provide you, the reader, with an ability to analyze the claims made by the various authors and experts you are exposed to. This analysis should start (and sometimes can end) with a clear understanding of the process factors associated with the claims and methodologies being promoted. Now that you understand that in order for a defined process to work it must be supported by the conditions that exist in the primary environment in which it will be executed, you can see why a clear understanding of the process factors associated with the claims is critical.

It is this type of analysis that can counter an author's or expert's argument that their assertions or methodology can only fail because of a lack of commitment. You should now understand that, given the process factors associated with their assertions and methodologies (that is, defined processes), the ability to succeed can also be greatly influenced by the conditions that exist in the selected primary environment at any point in time on the change/time continuum and/or the ability to execute an associated defined implementation.

I want to stress this point because it provides a new freedom for you relative to the claims of others whether for work, society, or at a personal level. It is not unusual for an author or expert to display an assertion or methodology (defined process) that has been shown to be successful. However, those assertions and methodologies are executed in specific environments utilizing specific defined implementations. Therefore, while a "lack of commitment" might be a reason for failing to obtain a desired defined change using their assertions and methodologies, there is also a strong probability that failure will occur because you will be operating in a new/different primary environment. The analysis required to determine these potential underlying issues starts with a clear understanding of the process factors that are associated with their assertions and methodologies!

THREE ADDITIONAL UNDERLYING ASPECTS OF DEFINED PROCESSES

Before we move on to the discussion of the selection of a defined process, there are three aspects to defined processes/process factors that people often struggle with that I would like to cover first. They include:

1. The interrelationship of defined processes to other defined processes and defined implementations
2. Multidimensional aspects of defined processes and the hierarchy of change
3. Beginning and ending points of a defined process

Let us take a look at each of these individually, keeping in mind that these discussions can apply to both defined processes and the discussion of defined implementations we will be having in Chapter 9.

Chapter Seven

Interrelationship of Defined Processes to Other Defined Processes and Defined Implementations

Probably one of the most difficult aspects related to defined processes for people to comprehend is how defined processes are interrelated and intertwined with each other.

Processes are central to all change. Because of this, it is easy to become confused by all the terminology because of the overlap of the use of defined processes within our explanation of change. For example, as explained under the description of defined processes above, the defined process you select to explain a defined change in a given environment, in and by itself, might be made up of individual activities represented by individual defined processes. So a defined process can be made up of additional defined processes incorporated within it as process factors.

In addition, defined implementations require the ability to create specific conditions in a given environment that, in turn, require the execution of a defined process. Therefore, the implementation factors associated with a defined implementation must include at least one defined process that produces a defined change/condition that is now included into those environmental conditions. In other words, the defined change derived from a specific defined process implementation factor becomes a condition in the primary environment that is necessary to support the ultimate defined process and associated ultimate defined change.

So let us advance our discussion of defined processes by making sure we understand the terminology and the integration of defined processes within the context of change science.

First and foremost, all change requires the three elements of defined change, defined process, and defined implementation. The key here is that the use of the terminology of "defined" is at a micro level. We use the word "defined" to link (that is, specifically associate) a specific defined implementation to a specific defined process that, when executed, will result in a specific defined change.

We have already determined that a specific defined change represents the difference between a state of being at one point of time on the change/time continuum and the state of being at another point in time on the change/time continuum. Therefore, it is also extremely important to remember that a defined change must take place within a given environment (that is, the primary environment) that incorporates this state of being. Consequently, the defined process linked/associated with that defined change must also execute specifically in that same given/primary environment.

Given that the defined process that results in the ultimate defined change must execute in the same primary environment, then it only stands to reason that any defined processes incorporated within that defined process as process factors must also execute specifically in that same primary environment. In other words, all process factors (*including defined processes that represent a process factor*) must execute within the same primary environment as that of the defined process in which they are incorporated.

This is unlike defined implementations that can have defined processes incorporated within them as implementation factors that can execute in multiple environments. While we will look more deeply into defined implementations in Chapter 9, it might still be beneficial here to have a quick review of the differences between defined implementations and defined processes.

Defined Processes Versus Defined Implementations

The discussions in Chapter 3 on processes and implementations should have already provided us with a solid understanding of what processes and implementations are and the role they play in change dynamics. Therefore, we will not spend a lot of time here other than to provide a quick review. A good way to provide such a review of the difference between defined processes and defined implementations is in the context of the questions of how, why, when, and where.

A defined process addresses the questions of how, why, when, and where as they relate to the specific defined change under examination. More specifically, a defined process explains:

1. "How" a specific defined change has taken or will take place. It clearly quantifies all the process factors required in order to move from one state of being to another state of being (that is, obtain the defined change).
2. "Why" a specific defined change will be obtained if the defined process is executed. In other words, it clearly quantifies why a specific defined process and associated process factors have worked or will work in obtaining the defined change under examination.
3. "When" the defined change and, therefore, the associated defined process has taken or will take place. By quantifying the required process factors associated with a defined process, we know that the "when a defined change will take place" will not occur on the change/time continuum until the conditions in a primary environment support these defined process factors.
4. "Where" a defined change will be obtained will always be the primary environment in which the defined process executes. The defined process and defined change must exist in the same primary environment.

So a defined process focuses on answering the questions of how, why, when, and where as they relate to the defined change under examination.

A defined implementation, on the other hand, answers the how, why, when and, where questions as they relate to the *conditions* within the primary environment required to support the specific process factors associated with the selected defined process.

More specifically, a defined implementation explains:

1. "How" the conditions in the environment have equaled or will equal the required process factors associated with a defined process. It clearly quantifies all the implementation factors required in order to obtain the required conditions in the primary environment that match the required process factors.
2. "Why" the conditions in the primary environment have equaled or will equal the required process factors associated with a defined process. It clearly quantifies why a specific defined implementation and associated implementation factors have worked or will work in creating the conditions in the primary environment that support the required process factors.
3. "When" the defined process has executed or will execute in the primary environment. Since the defined implementation includes the quantification of the condition defined as the triggering event, we know that the defined process will execute at the point in time on the change/time continuum that the triggering event condition exists (this of course assumes all of the other conditions required to support the process factors also exist).
4. "Where" (that is, what environment or environments) the required conditions associated with a defined implementation have or will come from. Unlike a defined process that must execute in a single environment (the primary environment), defined implementations can execute in multiple environments. Keep in mind that a defined change and associated defined process executed in a secondary environment can represent a change effect (that is, external impact) on the

conditions in the primary environment. Therefore, the defined changes incorporated as implementation factors within a defined implementation can, but do not have to, execute in multiple environments both sequentially or simultaneously.

In summary:

1. Defined processes explain either:

    a. How a specific defined change was obtained in a given environment (that is, what defined process and process factors "were executed") or

    b. How we can obtain a specific defined change in a given environment (that is, what defined process and process factors "need to be executed").

2. Defined implementations explain either:

    a. How the conditions "were created" in a primary environment so as to support a specific defined process (that is, a specific set of process factors) or

    b. How "we can create" conditions in a primary environment so that they will support a specific defined process (that is, a specific set of process factors).

This review should help solidify our understanding of how defined processes are intertwined, integrated, and incorporated into other defined processes and defined implementations. However, a second area of confusion regarding processes often centers on how they are interconnected at multiple levels within any given environmental framework.

Multidimensional Aspects of Defined Processes and the Hierarchy of Change

Remember that at any point in time, even though we cannot directly observe the vast majority of it, change is "occurring at multiple levels" within the known universe. As depicted in Figure 7-1, the change science principle of simultaneous change states that there is "simultaneous" change occurring within the universe all the way from the subatomic level to the intergalactic level. In change science we refer to this as the *hierarchy of change* or *change hierarchy*.

Figure 7-1
Heirarchy of Change
Levels of Change Occurring Simultaneously in the Known Universe

Subatomic	Atomic	Molecular	Planetary	Interplanetary	Galactic	Intergalactic

More importantly, the *hierarchy of change* also states that change is not only occurring simultaneously at these levels but also interactively between these levels. You cannot have change occurring at the molecular level without change also occurring at the atomic and subatomic level. In other words, change at the molecular level is dependent on change at the atomic level which is, in turn, dependent on the change that is occurring at the subatomic level. This interdependency exists all the way up to and including the change taking place even at the intergalactic level; even the change that exists at the intergalactic level is dependent on the laws of science simultaneously operating all the way down to the subatomic level.

So we might ask: why is this all even germane to our discussion of defined processes? It is significant to us when we are establishing and ascertaining the defined process we want to focus on. *In order to avoid unnecessary analysis and possible confusion when establishing and defining a given defined process and associated process factors, it is best to limit the selection of the defined process/process factors to a level of relevancy along the various levels of change on the change hierarchy that is taking place.*

If we do not do this, the defined processes we are examining can be at levels on the change hierarchy that create unnecessary analysis that is irrelevant to the objective at hand. *In other words, we can create paralysis by analysis if the selection of the defined process is at a lower level on the change hierarchy than is necessary relative to the defined change under examination.*

However, as we would expect, change science provides tools to try to help avoid this dilemma.

Constant Conditions and Relevancy

Constant conditions and relevancy are a set of concepts we have already been exposed to that can help simplify our analysis and thought process as we progress in our study of processes and implementations.

In Chapter 4 we introduced *constant conditions* as follows:

> A condition within an environment that does not tend to change over extended time intervals on the change/time continuum. While a constant condition can also be a relevant condition and incorporated into a defined change as a process or implementation factor, these conditions tend to be fixed/constant (that is, stable) in their characteristics over an extended period of time on the change/time continuum.

Therefore, "relevant constant conditions" that are commonplace conditions do not always need to be traced back to their originating event on the change/time continuum but can be just defined as a given constant condition. By doing so, the analytical procedure associated with the selection and analysis of a defined process can often be greatly simplified. Let us look at some examples to make sure we understand this dynamic:

1. One example would be oxygen and combustion. Oxygen is a required condition for combustion, but there are only rare occasions where tracing the existence of oxygen all the way back to its origins within a given environment is of any value when examining the defined process/change of combustion. Oxygen would normally be considered a constant condition when considering combustion that occurs within the Earth's atmosphere.
2. Another example would be the defined process of walking. The reality is that there are multiple defined processes all the way down to the subatomic level that are executing in order for you to walk. However, the relevancy of all the defined processes associated with your ability to walk at these lower levels on the change hierarchy is in most cases immaterial when selecting a given defined process. Therefore, we only need to include the "ability to walk" as a process factor and treat all the other defined processes that are at work that support the capability of walking at the lower levels of the change hierarchy as constant conditions.

    In other words, if the defined process we choose to execute to move from one location in a room to another location in a room is walking, then the only process factor required is the ability to walk. This is due to the fact that it is assumed that if we have the ability to walk, then all the other defined changes/processes/implementations associated with this ability are constant conditions and will automatically be executed at the time that we begin walking.

    However, note that if the defined change under examination is to help someone who cannot currently walk to walk in the future, then selecting defined processes/process factors at the molecular or even lower levels on the change hierarchy might be absolutely necessary.

3. Finally, this same sort of defined process selection dynamics can be applied for examples of defined changes that incorporate water. If our defined change is to water our lawn, then treating water as a relevant constant condition process factor in the selection of your defined process will be adequate. In other words, the availability of water will be considered adequate as a process factor without the inclusion of how the water itself has been created.

However, if the defined change is the distillation of water, then selecting a defined process and process factors at the molecular level or possibly below will be a requirement.

Beginning and Ending Points of a Defined Process

As discussed in both Chapter 1 and Chapter 3, probably one of the most difficult challenges for many people is determining the starting and ending points of a defined process. The determination of when a defined process begins is often the more difficult to establish because people often struggle with determining when a defined implementation ends (that is, a triggering event takes place) and when a defined process begins. Some might argue with some merit that change is just one continuous process and therefore has no beginning or end. Of course, this is consistent with the change science principle of the chain of events.

However, becoming fixated on such a global concept diminishes our ability to analyze and control all the change around us. By expressing the continuous cycle of change "in the context of incremental defined processes," change science provides us a framework in which we can better obtain a grasp and control over all the change that is continuously taking place. There is no question that there will be times when determining the starting and ending point of a given process will be easy, and/or there will be times when it will be very difficult and debatable. *Nonetheless, examining the chain of events through the use of incremental defined processes is crucial in order to leverage the science of change in our daily lives.*

By using such concepts as defined processes and defined implementations, change science provides us with tools that will help us conceptualize, understand, and improve our ability to control this vast universe of change we are exposed to and are dealing with. In addition, change science does provide some guidelines we can use when tackling the issues associated with determining the starting and ending points for a given defined process:

1. A defined process often has some sort of closed (that is, easily definable) cycle to it. For example:

    a. The process of walking from one side of the room to the other side of the room is an easily definable cycle with the current location in a room as the starting state of being and the new location in the room as the ending state of being. In this case, the defined process would be walking, and the triggering event would be the mind telling the body to take the first step.

    b. The process of a base neutralizing an acid is another easily definable cycle that begins when the acid and base come in contact with one another. A possible triggering event is the pouring of a quantity of acid into a vessel containing a quantity of base.

    c. The process of using a specific machine to stamp a hole into a piece of metal is yet another example. The initial state of being is represented by the metal without a hole, and the ending state of being is represented by the same piece of metal with a hole in it. The triggering event would be pushing a button on the machine to trigger the production cycle of the machine.

2. Just because a specific defined process linked to its associated defined change must execute in a single primary environment does not mean that the same defined process cannot execute in multiple potential primary environments. It is important that we understand this concept because it can be very helpful in defining the beginning and ending point of a defined process. It is also easier to understand the tendency of a defined process to have a closed cycle associated with it (that is, a starting and an ending point) if we can recognize the ability of the defined process to execute in multiple environments.

In other words, the fact that a defined process can be executed in multiple environments tells us that the defined process has a well-defined cycle to it. For example, it is not difficult to imagine how the processes of walking or the neutralization of acids and bases or the ability to punch a hole into a piece of metal using a specific machine can be executed in multiple environments. Thus, the cycle and, therefore, the starting point and ending point associated with these defined processes are easily confirmed.

3. Consistent with the ability for the same defined process to execute in multiple environments is the capability for a given defined process with a defined cycle to have multiple implementations and triggering events. It only stands to reason that if a defined process has a defined cycle associated with it, then there is often also the potential to have multiple implementations/triggering events associated with it. So if we recognize that the defined process we have established has the potential to have multiple triggering events, then the starting and ending points of the execution cycle associated with that defined process should be easier to establish.

a. When we discussed burning a piece of paper, we noted that the triggering event could be the placing of a match to the paper, exposing the paper to an electric hot plate that is turned on, or even throwing the paper into a bonfire (that is, the potential for multiple triggering events). Therefore, in all cases, the defined process of combustion begins at the point where there is enough heat to begin the combustion and ends when there is no longer enough heat, combustible material, or oxygen for it to continue.

b. Even something as simple as walking from one location to another location can have multiple triggering events that help define the starting point of the defined process of walking. For example, we might consciously decide to take the first step. Someone might unexpectedly push us, and we take the first step. Finally, we could even be caught up in a crowd and forced to take the first step. In any case, the defined process of walking begins when we take our first step and ends when we take the last step at our end location.

4. Finally, given that ultimately all change is impacted by the known and unknown laws of science, we can often determine the starting and ending points of a defined process by the characteristics and dynamics associated with the laws of science that are incorporated in the defined process. The neutralization of acids and bases is a prime example. This neutralization is reflective of the laws of science, and, therefore, the defined process of neutralization will begin when an acid and base come into contact with one another and will end when the ratio of the quantity of required acid to required base no longer supports the defined process of neutralization.

However, even with these guidelines, we will generally find a broad range of flexibility in establishing the starting and ending points of a defined process. *The trade-off is generally in the size of the defined process selected along with the length of the time interval it has versus the size of the defined implementation and its associated time interval.* Remember the following generalities:

1. A large defined process (a defined process with a lot of process factors) generally requires a longer time interval to execute.
2. Because a defined process must execute in a single primary environment, the size of the primary environment generally increases as the size of the defined process (that is, the number of process factors) increases.
3. The desired time interval on the change/time continuum to move from a current state of being in the primary environment to a desired state of being is often fixed. Therefore, the ratio of the defined process time interval to the defined implementation time interval will increase or decrease in direct proportion to the increase and decrease in the size of the defined process. For example, if the total time interval available to move from state of being A to state of being B is one hour and if the defined process time interval is 45 minutes, then the defined implementation time interval must be 15 minutes or less. On the other hand, if the defined process time interval is only 20 minutes, then the defined implementation time interval can be increased to 40 minutes or less.
4. A larger number of process factors (that is, an increase in the number of conditions that must be established in the primary environment) and/or a longer time interval associated with a defined process (that is, the amount of time in which the change dynamics and environmental dynamics can negatively impact the conditions in the primary environment)

tend to increase the risks associated with the ability to obtain the defined change.

5. As noted, defined implementations can incorporate multiple defined processes as implementation factors that can in turn execute both sequentially and/or simultaneously in multiple environments. Therefore, it is often possible to obtain more flexibility by shifting away from a defined process that contains a large number of process factors and/or has a long time interval associated with it toward an expanded defined implementation.

6. Therefore, when all things are taken into consideration, *the use of smaller defined processes that leverage off of larger associated defined implementations generally provides an overall structure that decreases the risk and increases the flexibility associated with obtaining a desired defined change.* This is due to the fact that a skewing toward a larger associated defined implementation provides the ability and flexibility to have multiple incremental defined process implementation factors executing sequentially and/or simultaneously in multiple environments.

Given the significance these concepts have relative to both defined processes and defined implementations, we need to explore an example to further reinforce our understanding. Therefore, we will once again use the example of a backyard bonfire to expand on these concepts.

In this example, we want to have a bonfire in our backyard that will last one hour. Thus, the defined change is to go from a state of being of no bonfire to having a bonfire that lasts for a time interval of one hour. To obtain this defined change, we decide to rely again on a defined process of the combustion of firewood in our backyard fire pit. With this as a starting point, let us look at some scenarios relative to the selection of a defined process and defined implementation.

Single Defined Process and Single Defined Implementation

Figure 7-2 depicts a straightforward example where the defined process has a single activity (a single defined process) and also has a single defined process implementation factor incorporated within the selected defined implementation. Enough firewood to last an hour is already in the fire pit with paper inserted to help produce enough initial heat to start the combustion of the firewood, and a box of matches is available right by the fire pit. Oxygen is assumed to be a constant condition and is, therefore, ignored. Most importantly, everything is executing in the single primary environment of the fire pit.

Therefore, the lighting of a match and holding it next to the paper in the fire pit is the defined process implementation factor that is incorporated in the defined implementation that in turn creates the triggering event condition in the primary environment of a lighted match next to the paper. The defined implementation time interval is only 30 seconds.

Likewise, the primary defined process (note that this is defined in Chapter 9) has combustion as the only activity (that is, defined process) included as a process factor that is executing in the primary environment. The primary defined process time interval is one hour.

Long Defined Process and Short Defined Implementation

On the other hand, what happens if the firewood is not in the pit and must instead be purchased from the store. We can approach this by using a long time interval primary defined process and a short time interval defined implementation.

Figure 7-3 depicts what a long time interval primary defined process and a short time interval defined implementation strategy would look like. The primary defined process has four activities (defined processes) included as process factors and has an associated time interval of two hours, 15 minutes, and 30 seconds. The defined implementation still only requires a single defined process implementation factor of getting into a car so we can start the defined process of driving to the store to purchase the firewood. The time interval implementation factor is only a short two minutes.

However, look what happens to the size of the primary environment. Remember, the primary defined process must execute in a single primary environment. Therefore, the size of the primary environment increased from the fire pit only in Figure 7-2 to an area that is now bounded by the fire pit on one side and the store on the other side.

As a side note, Figure 7-3 also represents another good example of how to address the hierarchy of change discussed above. We could have broken down the activity/defined process of "purchasing the firewood from the store" into smaller incremental defined processes (for example, an individual defined process to reflect starting the car, driving the car right on one road and left another road, parking the car, and so on). However, while the breakout of these activities might be accurate, such a breakout adds no value (that is, no relevancy) to our analysis. Instead it would only increase the amount of our analysis and effort without adding any benefit. So unless there is something unique or unusual associated with the purchasing of the firewood, we can treat this capability as a constant condition in this environment and greatly simplify our analysis and discussion.

Short Defined Process and Long Defined Implementation

A second strategy to the above case of having to purchase the firewood from the store would be to use a shorter primary defined process time interval and a longer defined implementation time interval. Figure 7-4 depicts such a strategy. The defined implementation now has four activities (defined processes) included as implementation factors and has an associated time interval of one hour, 17 minutes, and 30 seconds. The primary defined process has been reduced to the single activity/defined process of combustion with an associated time interval of one hour just like the first situation described in Figure 7-2.

In addition, by using a strategy of a shorter primary defined process time interval and a longer defined implementation time interval, we were able to introduce a secondary environment (from the store to the fire pit) in which the defined implementation could be executed. This, in turn, greatly reduced the size of the primary environment back down to just the fire pit.

Some of you might be saying who cares given that this is a continuous execution cycle represented by the same total time interval in both cases of two hours, 17 minutes, and 30 seconds. In everyday life I would agree with you. However, do not lose focus on what is important here. The take-away should be an understanding that two different options/strategies do exist and that there are what, why, and how ramifications of the differences between these two strategies.

In addition, in many if not most cases in everyday life, change, in fact, does not tend to take place over a continuous execution cycle. Cognitively-influenced change especially tends to be forward looking with breaks in the time interval associated with the execution of obtaining the desired defined change we are looking for. Figure 7-5 is just such an example.

Lack of a Continuous Execution Cycle

In Figure 7-5 we introduce some new dynamics to our example:

1. The bonfire is not scheduled until a week from now.

2. There will not be time to purchase the firewood on the same day as the fire. Therefore, the firewood needs to be purchased in advance.
3. While there is a cover on the fire pit so that the paper does not get wet if it should happen to rain, the cover is not big enough to also cover the firewood. Therefore, the firewood needs to be stored in the garage until it is needed for the bonfire.

Given these new dynamics, it should be obvious to you that a strategy of using a large primary defined process that incorporates all of these activities (defined processes) together with a long period of time of no activity into a single continuous cycle within the primary environment would not be the best choice. Instead, as depicted in Figure 7-5, leveraging off of the inherent capability and flexibility associated with a longer defined implementation is the better strategy.

There is a clear advantage to using multiple environments (for example, house to store, garage to fire pit, and a primary environment of just the fire pit) that do not have a requirement of continuous execution. In addition, the flexibility associated with execution increases. For example, there is flexibility as to when you purchase the firewood given that you could just as easily have a sequence that starts with "no activity" followed by "purchase firewood" and then another time interval of "no activity."

In conclusion, while there are no hard and fast given structures, generally it is better to look at the continuous cycle of change in the context of "incremental" defined processes. Therefore, when determining the beginning and ending points of a defined process, it is usually a better strategy to use smaller shorter time interval primary defined processes with an associated larger long time interval defined implementation than it is to use primary defined processes that are large and/or have long time intervals that must have continuous execution in a single primary environment.

With an understanding of these basics of a defined process in place, we can now move on to Chapter 8 and explore the actual selection of a defined process.

Figure 7-2
Single Defined Process and Single Defined Implementation

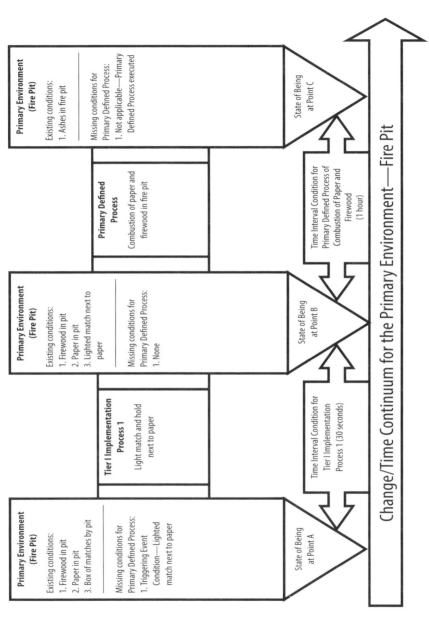

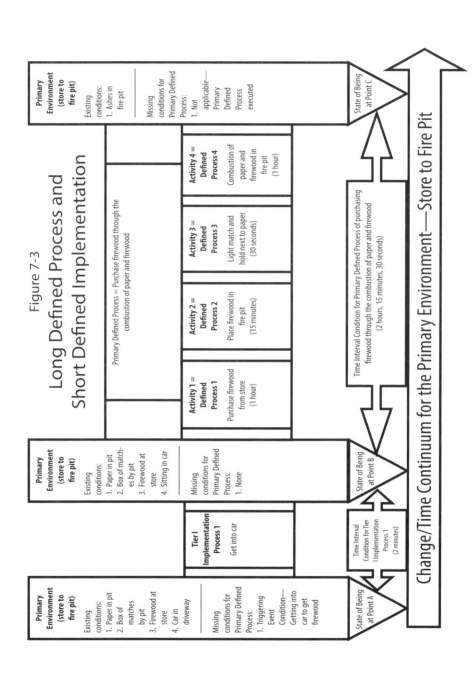

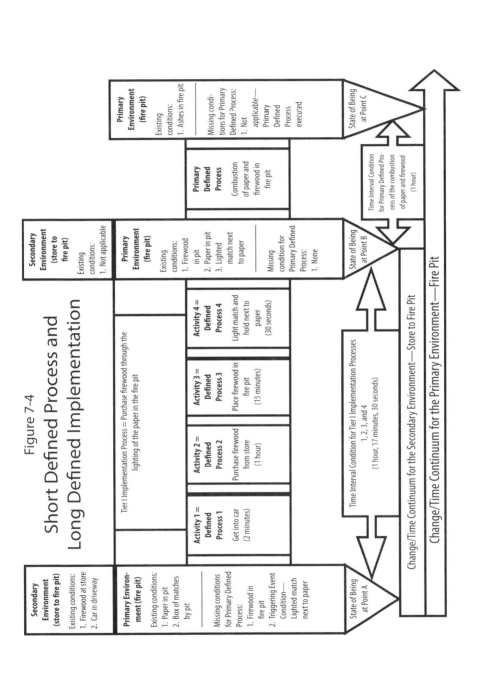

Figure 7-4
Short Defined Process and Long Defined Implementation

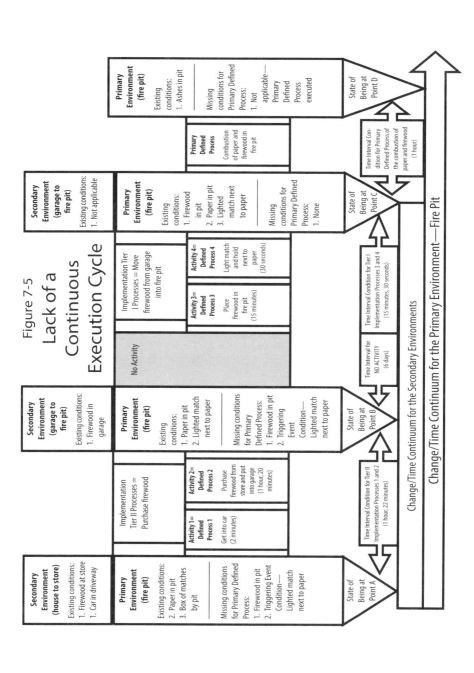

CHAPTER EIGHT

Defined Processes Part II: Selection of Defined Processes

Knowledge is Power.

SIR FRANCIS BACON IN 1597

Now that we have established in Chapter 7 the basics associated with defined processes, it is time to turn our attention to the actual selection and development of defined processes. We will do this by first developing an understanding of some general considerations that should be taken into account when selecting defined processes.

PROCESS SELECTION CONSIDERATIONS

Imagine that you live out in a rural area and it takes approximately an hour to drive to the nearest grocery store. You need to go to the grocery store to get certain items, one of which is a bag of ice. So the defined change is to move a bag of ice from the grocery store an hour away by car to the freezer in your house. The defined process is straightforward in that you are going to drive your car to the grocery store, buy the bag of ice, place the bag of ice in your trunk, drive home for an hour, and move the bag of ice from your car to your freezer.

Logic tells you that this is probably a common straightforward solution. And when I tell you that your house is in northern Minnesota in the middle of winter when the temperature outside is 5 degrees below freezing, you would still not have any concerns at all relative to the defined process. However, if I tell you that your house is located in the middle of the Arizona desert in the middle of summer and the temperature outside is more than 100 degrees, you might start to feel some trepidation about whether you have picked a viable defined process.

Of course, this is an example of the environmental override principle that we should all know by heart by now.

But is the environmental override principle the only reason why we are unable to obtain a desired defined change? Is there only one best defined process to select for any given defined change? If there are alternative defined processes to choose from, how do we determine which one to select?

Reasons a Defined Process Can Fail

As we would expect, in addition to the environmental override principle, there are other reasons why a defined process will fail to produce both a naturally-occurring defined change and/or cognitively-influenced defined change. Some of the other reasons include:

1. Conflicts with the laws of science. Given the laws of science, the defined change is impossible no matter what defined process is selected.
2. An erroneous defined process. The defined process selected is erroneous and, therefore, cannot produce the expected results required to obtain a successful defined change.

3. A conflicting relevant condition or conditions. As discussed previously, there can be situations in an environment in which all the conditions exist to support the required process factors for a given defined process. However, there are conflicting conditions in that environment that will negate or disrupt the execution of that defined process. For example, if you throw a piece of paper into a burning bonfire, you can have all the required process factors of heat, combustible material, and oxygen available, but the execution can become disrupted if a gust of wind (that is, a conflicting relevant condition) blows the paper back out of the fire.
4. An erroneous defined implementation. The defined implementation selected is erroneous, and, therefore, the defined process will never execute even if the defined process is legitimate.
5. No available defined implementation that will work. Given the change dynamics and environmental dynamics at play, there is not an available defined implementation that will work so the defined process will never execute even if the defined process is legitimate.
6. The time interval required to support the defined process. The defined process is valid and the environmental conditions exist in the primary environment to support the required process factors. However, the interval of time required to support the defined process exceeds the stability in the primary environment to support the process factors over the change/time continuum. As already discussed, the longer the time interval, the more likely the stability of the primary environmental conditions required to support a specific defined process will not exist (that is, the ability to have continued matching of environmental conditions to process factors).
7. The number of process factors that are associated with the defined process. Obviously, the more process factors we have,

the greater the risk that the primary environmental conditions do not exist and/or the stability of those conditions will not exist to support those required process factors.

8. The availability of a primary environment within the time interval required to implement the defined process. You can have a legitimate defined process with a legitimate defined implementation. However, if the interval of time required to obtain a suitable primary environment exceeds the time interval required to execute the defined implementation, the defined process will not execute on time.

In other words, the environmental override principle is continuously at play *during the time frame* associated with obtaining the desired defined change. Note, however, it would be inappropriate to conclude that there is not necessarily a defined implementation that will work to support the defined process at a different time frame along the change/time continuum.

A simple example is to imagine there is an unfortunate deep sea diver that experiences a severe case of the bends. He needs to be placed into a hyperbaric chamber to be cured. Therefore, we have a legitimate defined process (recompression in a hyperbaric chamber), a legitimated defined implementation and associated triggering event (transportation to and placement in a hyperbaric chamber), and a known primary environment that will support the defined process (the hyperbaric chamber itself). Unfortunately, if the time interval required to transport the diver from his existing location exceeds the time interval available before the diver experiences permanent physical damage, or even death, then the defined process will not work. This is because the ability to access the required primary environment in the time interval required to implement the defined process is inadequate.

9. The magnitude of the defined change. For our purposes, *magnitude* will represent the degree of change associated with a defined change relative to alternative defined changes that use a common basis of measurement.

For example, the defined change of losing 50 pounds of weight is of a greater magnitude than a defined change of losing 20 pounds of weight. Or, the defined change of communicating a new corporate policy to 50,000 employees is of a greater magnitude than a defined change of communicating that same corporate policy to only five employees.

The larger the magnitude of a defined change, the more likely a specific defined process will fail. In essence, the larger magnitude indicates that one of the reasons a defined process will fail described above will occur. If you think about it:

- A larger magnitude will probably require a much longer time interval in order to execute the defined process.
- The number of process factors will more likely increase as the magnitude becomes larger.
- The number of implementation factors and/or time interval will more likely increase as the magnitude becomes larger.

The above list is, of course, not all-inclusive, but it does provide a good representation of why a defined process can fail. We should also keep in mind that the above list impacts both naturally-occurring change and cognitively-influenced change. Therefore, when we are selecting defined processes, we must focus on the following important considerations.

Validity, Efficiency, Effectiveness, and Reliability

In order to help in the selection of an appropriate defined process, change science introduces four new terms: validity, efficiency, effectiveness, and reliability.

The first two reasons listed above as to why a defined process will fail are as basic and fundamental as you can get. If you try to use a defined process that conflicts or is not supported by underlying laws of science, then it is impossible to obtain the desired defined change using that defined process. Likewise, if the defined process is erroneous for any reason (for example, some of the assumptions and/or process factors are incorrect so it will just not work), then once again it will be impossible to obtain the desired defined change using that specific defined process.

Validity

This then leads to our first new term: *validity*. In change science, a defined process is considered "valid" or has "validity" when it will execute to yield its associated desired defined change if and/or when there are environmental conditions that match all the required process factors and there are no conflicting relevant conditions that exist in that environment.

Put simply, there is validity to a defined process if it is known to work in providing a specific defined change, all other things being equal. If a specific defined process has never been used before or if we do not know for sure if a given defined process will work to provide a given defined change, then the validity of that defined process is in question. Obviously, the risk of a defined process conflicting with the laws of science and/or being erroneous for other reasons increases when the validity of the defined process is in question.

Efficiency

The *efficiency* of the defined process selected is defined as the ability to obtain a specific defined change with a minimum expenditure of time and other process factors when compared to alternative defined processes.

Based upon this definition, in the science of change the measurement of efficiency requires at least two or more alternative defined processes to select from. It focuses on the comparison of the amount of effort (as indicated by the process factors associated with each alternative defined process) and the comparison of the specific process factor of the required time interval for each alternative.

For clarification, we recognize that the term "effort" can have different meaning to different people and that in physics it has the specific meaning of an applied force acting against inertia. For the purposes of change science we will allow room for a little more subjectivity.

In change science the concept of *effort* should be based upon all the process factors associated with a defined process other than the time interval process factor, which, as we shall see, needs to stand on its own. Effort can and should be analyzed from several different perspectives:

- The number of process factors associated with a defined process. Chances are, the more process factors we have, the greater the effort involved in executing the defined process. For example, driving from one location to another location on side streets with multiple turns and numerous stop lights (each turn would be a process factor) would probably be considered by most as more effort than using a single street that has no traffic lights on it.
- The type of process factors involved. Obviously, there are going to be certain process factors (including any associat-

ed laws of science) that to the average person would require more effort than other types of process factors. For example, riding a bicycle between two locations would probably be viewed by most as requiring more effort than driving a car. However, even this can be situational in that if the two locations are only one block apart, then walking might trump both a bicycle and a car.
- Situational conditions. For example, using a process factor of sand to treat ice-covered streets might represent little effort to a community in close proximity to sand and gravel quarries but could represent much more effort to a community that needs to transport the sand in from a long distance away.
- Finally, cost based on the evaluation of effort relative to efficiency. In day-to-day life, cost/benefit can often be the major driver as to why one defined process is selected over another alternative. In many cases, cost would represent the requirement of a monetary exchange, and this is easily acceptable when considering it as a process factor.

  However, cost and effort are sometimes considered one and the same since cost can represent more than just the requirement of monetary exchange (that is, it can have intrinsic components like expenditure of work). For example, it is not unusual to see effort included within the definition of cost. *In the end, the inclusion of cost and/or cost/benefit is an extremely acceptable process factor and/or reflection of effort.*

Once again, it is critical that judgment and logic should prevail in determining effort levels across alternative defined processes. Sometimes, the thought process itself can be as useful as the actual conclusion we reach. Of course, keep in mind that the more significant the defined change is, the more analysis and consideration we should apply.

As a side note, while we will focus on efficiency strictly as it relates to defined process here in Chapter 8, we will learn in Chapters 9 and 10 on implementations and systems that efficiency also applies to defined implementations and systems. In that context, we will find out that while it is important to determine the efficiency of a given defined process, in many cases the reliability of the defined process and/or overall efficiency and complexity of the *combination of the defined process together with the defined implementation* will be the overriding consideration when selecting a final course of action to obtain a desired defined change. However, for now we are going to remain focused on efficiency as it strictly relates to defined processes.

Many of you might be asking an obvious question: is a defined process that requires more process factors but a shorter interval of time on the change/time continuum more or less efficient than a defined process that requires fewer process factors but a longer interval of time? To answer this question, we need to introduce effectiveness.

Effectiveness

Effectiveness in change science is the ability to obtain 100 percent of the desired defined change through the execution of a specific defined process.

For example, let's assume we have a container of acid that we wish to neutralize by combining it with an appropriate quantity of base. If the combination of the two is interrupted for some reason (for example, the stability of the required conditions in the primary environment is inadequate) and we do not obtain 100 percent neutralization, then the defined process is not effective.

Therefore, a defined process can only be effective if we accomplish 100 percent of our objective (that is, 100 percent of the desired defined change). So let us now return to our question:

Is a defined process that requires more process factors but a shorter interval of time on the change/time continuum more or less efficient than a defined process that requires fewer process factors but a longer interval of time?

In change science, effectiveness helps answer this question. The process factor associated with the interval of time for a given defined process is only adverse to accomplishing 100 percent completion of a defined change if its length exceeds the interval of time available to obtain an effective defined change (that is, time required exceeds actual time available). Assuming the comparison of two alternative defined processes, this can be summarized as follows:

1. If both processes are effective (that is, their required time intervals are less than or equal to the actual time available to accomplish 100 percent of the desired change), then the defined process that has fewer process factors (that is, less effort) will probably be considered more efficient. In essence, even though the defined process with the fewest process factors might require a longer time interval, the length of the time interval becomes immaterial given that the defined process will still be 100 percent effective.
2. If one defined process is not effective and the other defined process is effective, then the defined process that is effective is the only true option available, and the number of process factors associated with each alternative becomes immaterial.
3. If the amount of actual available time (that is, stability of the conditions in the primary environment) is difficult to determine or has a high degree of risk associated with it, then the defined process with the shortest time interval process factor is probably the most prudent defined process to select. This is probably true even if the number of associated process fac-

tors/effort exceeds those of the defined process that has the longer time interval associated with it.

Reliability

Finally, even though it can be more subjective in nature, reliability is another concept that can be beneficial in our discussion of defined processes. In change science we define *reliability* as the extent or expected likelihood that a given defined process will yield the same defined change over multiple executions.

For example, let us assume that you coach a baseball team and you are in a game that has a tied score in the bottom of the ninth inning with your team up to bat, two outs, and no one on base. You decide that the defined process you wish to use to win the game (that is, the desired defined change) is to try to have your next batter hit a home run. You have two possible batters, Sam and Peter, who have a history of hitting home runs. However, Sam's history of hitting home runs exceeds that of Peter. Therefore, Sam has more reliability than Peter, and you use Sam in your defined process instead of Peter.

In this example, both the defined process of hitting a home run using the process factor of Sam and the defined process of hitting a home run using the process factor of Peter are valid since you know both of them have a history of hitting home runs if all the environmental conditions support each defined process. However, you use Sam because the likelihood of his hitting a home run based upon past experience is greater (that is, the defined process of hitting a home run and obtaining the desired change of winning the game using the process factor of Sam has a greater reliability).

As indicated above, these rules do not take into consideration dynamics associated with defined implementations, which will be discussed in Chapter 9; however, they are still extremely important concepts as we stay focused on the selection of a defined process.

FINAL SELECTION OF A DEFINED PROCESS

Leveraging off of the above discussion can help us to conclude what defined process we should select relative to any desired defined change. However, the selection procedure is influenced by the context of our examination, which tends to fall into one of three categories:

1. Selecting a defined process that explains why a certain defined change has already occurred.
2. Selecting a defined process that explains a defined change that we expect will occur in the future.
3. Selecting a defined process that will yield an effective desired defined change that we want to obtain.

Selecting a Defined Process That Explains Why a Certain Defined Change Has Already Occurred

Ever think about how we learn? We learn by examining and understanding why the experiences (that is, defined changes) we and/or others have had occurred in the manner they did (that is, what defined processes and defined implementations were executed).

From birth on we start to recognize cause and effect (that is, what defined processes lead to what kind of results/defined changes). Of course, much of this learning takes place subconsciously while other learning takes place through planned exercises. But no matter how it occurs, the result is that we are analyzing/selecting after the fact what defined processes, when executed, have led to what sort of defined changes so as to build an experience base for potential future use.

So how does this all occur? While it might be hard to imagine that the thought process we are about to explain takes place, in reality, the following mental exercise/assessment is at work:

1. You recognize that a defined change has occurred, and you quantify exactly what you believe that defined change is. Through this exercise you have also indirectly identified in your mind the starting and ending points of the defined process.
2. Since the defined change has already occurred, you have also determined the primary environment in which the defined process was executed. From here you follow one of two analytical paths depending on your existing experience base and general analytical skills:
    A. In the first analytical path you assess the primary environment in which the defined change occurred in an attempt to determine:
        i. What relevant conditions existed in order for the defined change to take place.
        ii. What laws of science were at play at some level and in some context in order for the defined change to take place. As described above, the level and context you use to determine these laws of science are predicated on the knowledge and level of understanding you have regarding what laws of science exist that might be associated with the defined change.
        iii. You then attempt either to:
            a. Correlate those relevant conditions and laws of science to the process factors associated with defined processes you are already familiar with looking for a match, or
            b. Link what you believe to be all those relevant conditions and laws of science into a set of corresponding process factors that

you then label in some way as a new defined process.

    c. In both cases you are leveraging off of the fact, **in reverse**, that in order for a defined process to execute, all the required process factors associated with that defined process must exist as conditions in the primary environment.

B. In the second analytical path you perform an analytical exercise that actually starts with an assumed defined process. In other words, starting with the defined process that you assume is at play:

    i. You identify the required process factors and laws of science associated with an assumed defined process.

    ii. You then perform an analytical exercise that verifies that the process factors and laws of science associated with that assumed defined process were, in fact, present as conditions in the primary environment during the time interval associated with the defined change.

        a. If they match up, then you recognize that you have accurately determined the appropriate defined process.

        b. If they do not match up, then you either:

- Select a new defined process as your assumption and start the analytical process over, or
- You default to the first path above and start in reverse using the known environmental conditions as your starting point.

This overall assessment process of determining the appropriate defined process at play has additional dynamics that also need to be taken into consideration. First, your ability to perform either one of these analytical approaches can be greatly influenced by the level of observation you have available to you. Obviously, the ability to determine what defined process was associated with a given defined change is greatly influenced by the data and information that are available. It is difficult to determine environmental conditions without data and information that, in turn, are based upon observation.

Generally, data/information you receive from the direct observation of the defined change are the best, especially if they can be substantiated through multiple consistent observations and/or by the direct observations of others. The next best set of data and information comes from the direct observations of others, again especially if it is substantiated by multiple observations/methods and/or by you through secondary observation. Finally, secondary observation may provide sufficient data and information but is, of course, far less reliable than direct observation.

Bottom line, the weaker the data and information you have available to you, the more assumptions you will most likely have to make relative to the environmental conditions that existed. This then leads to a greater potential for error in the selection of the appropriate defined process; in other words, the more the validity is called into question relative to the defined process you have selected.

Let's take a quick look at a simple example. Assume that someone crosses the street at a busy intersection that has a controlled crosswalk. We see the individual on one side of the street one moment and on the other side of the intersection a few moments later, but we do not directly observe him or her crossing the intersection.

So the defined change is the change in location for that person from one side of the intersection to the other side of the intersection. Thus, we have a clear determination of the defined change and the primary environment in which the defined change took place. However, without any sort of direct observation by us or someone else to rely on, we can only guess as to the exact conditions that existed during the time interval of the defined change.

Therefore, the accuracy of the defined process that is selected becomes questionable. If the environmental conditions include a "Walk" signal and the individual was not in a hurry, then the defined process used was probably walking across from one side to the other. On the other hand, if the environmental conditions were such that the individual was in a hurry and/or the "Do Not Walk" sign was on at the time he or she crossed, then the defined process of running across would be a strong possibility.

Without any data and information available to us, our best conclusion as to the defined process associated with the defined change would be either the process of walking or the process of running. But the selection of a specific defined process would have questionable validity.

A second dynamic that should be taken into consideration is that the analytical path people pick (either consciously or subconsciously) generally depends on their existing experience base and depth of known defined processes. If an individual, organization, or society has an extensive experience base, there is probably a propensity to assess starting with an assumed defined process and verifying that required environmental conditions were present. On the other hand, if the experience base is limited or nonexistent, then an analytical assessment that starts with the determination of the environmental conditions is more likely to be utilized.

For example, if an individual with an illness (a defined change) goes to a seasoned doctor, that doctor will probably start with a probable defined process (a process that he or she knows through experience is responsible for 80 percent of this type of illness) and verify that the conditions exist that support the required process factors associated with that assumed defined process. However, a new doctor or emergency room doctor without such an experience base will more likely start by determining the existing conditions and selecting the defined process causing the illness with an assessment that started with those conditions.

The final dynamic we need to recognize is that an assessment process does not have to be executed by us. In fact, if we take a class in school or learn something from other people's experiences (that is, other people's defined process assessment), we are learning about cause and effects (that is, defined processes that lead to defined changes) through the experiences and the associated assessment procedures of others.

More importantly, this does not automatically mean that this assessment procedure and associated conclusions (whether performed by us or by others) are always correct. It also does not mean that the defined process selected is the most efficient defined process available to obtain the defined change under examination. This is important to understand for several reasons:

1. As described above, validity and reliability are usually built upon repetition and the ability to show that a defined process will consistently provide an expected defined change. Therefore, through repetition, a selected defined process is either refined or its validity and reliability are substantiated.
2. The more experiences we are exposed to (either directly or through communication with others) in which the same defined change is obtained through alternative defined processes, the greater our ability to start broadening our selection procedures to include an assessment of efficiency and effectiveness. Remember that in order to determine efficiency, we must have two or more alternative defined processes

to select from. An analysis of effectiveness will also be more limited when we are only dealing with a single known defined process.

> For example, if we only know one way to drive to work (that is, a single defined process), the effectiveness (the ability to obtain a 100 percent success of reaching work in a desired amount of time) of that defined process will be consistently dependent upon the ever-changing environmental conditions we are dealing with.
>
> On the other hand, if we know two or more ways to drive to work (that is, alternative defined processes), then we can leverage off of our knowledge of the effectiveness and efficiency of those alternative defined processes relative to the actual environmental conditions that exist at any point in time on the change/time continuum. This, in turn, will increase our likelihood of obtaining an effective defined change in the most efficient context available.

3. Finally, the more significant the defined change, the more significant validity and reliability of the selected defined process become. Therefore, awareness that the assessment to determine a selected defined process might be flawed becomes more important as the significance of the defined change increases.

I am fascinated at times in this regard with some of the human behavior that exists:

A. There are those who would fight to the death defending their assessment of a selected defined process even when proof of validity and reliability is weak or when efficiency and effec-

tiveness are called into question relative to alternative defined processes.
B. Then there are others who will not defend their assessment of a selected defined process even when proof of validity and reliability is strong and/or when efficiency and effectiveness relative to alternative defined processes have been established.
C. But the behavior of most concern is how prevalent it is for people to accept both the assessment of a selected defined process and claims that its effectiveness and efficiency are superior to other alternatives just because the individual who has done the assessment is purported to be an expert. I once again want to stress that when examining the claims of others (experts or otherwise), always make sure you have a clear understanding of the underlying assumptions associated with their assessment. This is especially true relative to assumptions and/or validity as they relate to the environment or environments in which the expert's selected defined process was executed.

Bottom line, selecting defined processes to explain defined changes that have already taken place is an ongoing assessment process. It is central to our ability to learn as individuals, organizations, and a society. The concepts of validity, reliability, effectiveness, and efficiency allow us to constantly refine the assessment and selection process. Most importantly, as the significance of the defined change increases to us, our organization, or our society, the more we need to place focus and attention on the validity, reliability, effectiveness, and efficiency of the defined process we have selected.

Selecting a Defined Process to Explain a Defined Change That We Expect to Occur in the Future

There is a reason that we started our discussion on how to select a defined process by focusing first on the selection of a defined process associated with a defined change that has already occurred. It is because the ability to predict/select future defined change and its associated defined process is greatly enhanced when based upon the foundation of experiences that exists for an individual, organization, or as a society.

The more prior experience we have (that is, knowledge about the relationship between what defined change has occurred because of the execution of defined processes in various environments), the more likely it is that we can predict what defined processes will execute in the future resulting in an associated defined change.

For future reference, in change science we will consider an *experience* as the knowledge we have derived of a defined change resulting from a specific "defined process-to-environment relationship."

Therefore, the more experiences (that is, known defined changes "resulting from specific" defined process-to-environment relationships) we can draw on, the greater the likelihood that we will be able to select what defined process will execute in the future resulting in a given defined change. What are some sources for these experiences?

1. Expertise in a specific subject matter is a good source. I know I have cautioned you over and over again about the claims of purported experts. But that does not mean that expertise does not exist. What we need to be cautious about is when a given defined change is significant to us; make sure that all the assumptions (for example, process factors and environmental considerations) associated with the experts' defined

process and claims make sense in the specific context (that is, environment) that we will be operating in.

In any case, *expertise* is derived from the accumulation of an extensive amount of experiences (either directly experienced or learned from others) in a particular subject matter. In other words, over time, an expert in a particular subject matter is exposed to numerous defined process-to-environment relationships and their resulting defined change. This, in turn, creates a knowledge base that increases the likelihood (that is, reliability) that he or she can predict/select what defined process—compared to others—will execute in the future in a particular environment resulting in a specified defined change.

It is important to note that one does not need a Ph. D to be an expert. For example, parents can be experts relative to their children since the parents' ability to predict the future actions of their children (that is, the defined processes the children will execute) is higher given the extensive historical set of experiences (that is, knowledge) parents have in dealing with their children.

2. A second source of experiences occurs with a broadened base in the number of individuals associated with selecting the future defined process that is expected to execute. The old saying that "two heads are better than one" has merit. This is due to the fact that there is a high probability that the level of experiences, and therefore knowledge, increases as the number of individuals involved increases.

It is unlikely that even an expert has experienced every possible defined process-to-environment relationship. So unless we have an expert who can select with a high degree of probability what specific defined process will execute (which is not an impossibility), leveraging off of the broadest group of experiences possible provides the best potential of selecting a future defined process. Note, however, that there can be a decreasing or even negative return to this approach based upon the ability to manage the group dynamics associated with an ever-increasing collection of individuals.

3. The final source of experiences to discuss is intuition. While not as powerful as 1 and 2 above, intuition is still a viable source of potential experiences.

In change science we will consider *intuition* to be the ability to establish an expected defined process-to-environment relationship and the resulting defined change based upon similar but not exact experiences.

We see examples of this all the time in our daily lives. We expect a certain future defined process and resulting defined change to take place not because we have directly experienced it in the past but because we have had similar experiences, and our intuition helps us to reach that expectation. Intuition can be used when we do not have any direct experiences to rely on or, in some cases, as reinforcement of experiences we have actually had.

EXPERIENCE/CHANGE/POWER EQUATION

The saying "knowledge is power" is generally attributed to Sir Francis Bacon in 1597. It is not unusual to see this concept in various forms promoted over the years in literature, movies, politics, and general philosophy. It is also often a fundamental principle underlying discussions regarding the dynamics of the "Information Age" or "Age of the Internet."

In change science, the concept of knowledge representing power goes beyond the philosophical and into the substantive. We start with the question of how do we derive knowledge? In this chapter, we emphasize how important it is to develop and leverage off of our experience base and the experience base of others. We stress this because experience provides data and information that, in turn, are at the heart of the knowledge we have as individuals, organizations, and societies.

At the center of our ability to determine the defined process that yields a specific defined change is our direct and indirect experience base. This experience base, in turn, provides the source of the data and information we use relative to the knowledge base we have developed and/or that we have access to pertaining to the change dynamics and environmental dynamics we are dealing with.

So it is our experiences and/or the experiences of others that provide the data and information relative to the interrelationships that exist between certain defined processes and their associated environments that have resulted in specific defined changes.

Now that we have established in change science the relationship we have between our experience base and the knowledge base we possess and/or have access to, how do we make the leap to the concept that knowledge equals power? We start by exploring more deeply what it means to exert cognitively-influenced change.

As already established, humans are constantly both consciously and subconsciously creating cognitively-influenced defined change. However, just because we are all producing cognitively-influenced defined change in one context or another does not mean we are always obtaining the effective defined change that we desire.

Power can be defined as the ability of doing or accomplishing something. It should be obvious at this point that in change science we equate this to obtaining a desired defined change. However, the desired defined change of one individual, organization, or society can be in conflict with the desired defined changes of others. For example, if two organizations are both providing a product to a potential end customer, then the desired defined change of both is to have that customer choose their product. These are conflicting desired defined changes.

Therefore, when viewed in an environment that contains conflicting desired defined changes, power can also represent the ability to have our desired defined change trump the desired defined changes of others. In order for us to obtain this type of power, we must have the ability not only to select effective defined processes and defined implementations but also to select "superior" defined processes and defined implementations when confronted with the conflicting desired defined changes of other individuals, organizations, and/or societies.

Thus, we have now closed the loop between experiences, change, and power that explains a substantive basis for the expression that "knowledge is power." It can be summarized in an equation as follows:

Experience = data and information = knowledge = increased ability to select within any given environment superior defined processes and defined implementations = increased probability to obtain a superior effective and successful desired defined change = power.

In change science we refer to this as the *experience/change/power equation*.

This experience/change/power equation can have ramifications that might far exceed the initial level of significance we place on it. It is important to consider the following:

1. As individuals, organizations, and societies we all want to obtain as much desired defined change as possible. This desire multiplies as the significance of the desired defined change increases. We have spent a lot of time trying to develop an understanding of the scientific aspects of change. We have done this in order to not only enhance our ability to obtain the defined change we desire but also to better deal with the desired defined change we do not obtain.

    The experience/change/power equation provides one more tool to use in our development of this understanding. Recognizing the significance of experience and knowledge when managing change can be invaluable. It gives us a focus when:

    a. We face the selection of a defined process and/or defined implementation.
    b. We struggle trying to figure out why the desired defined change we were looking for did not occur.
    c. We want to understand the basis of some of the change that is occurring all around us.

    Bottom line, the experience/change/power equation teaches us that we need to concentrate on how to leverage off of our direct experience and knowledge base and/or the experience and knowledge base of others when attempting to obtain the desired defined change we are looking for or when we are attempting to understand why a defined change under examination has occurred. Finally, the equation also teaches us the importance of an increase in research, testing, and analysis when the accomplishment of obtaining or understanding a specific defined change increases in significance.

2. The experience/change/power equation helps explain why power exists in the world we live in. This can be useful in increasing both:

    a. Our ability to obtain the desired defined change we want when the environment includes conflicting defined change.
    b. Our understanding of why an individual, organization, and/or society have the power they have.

3. The experience/change/power equation teaches us to look beyond the superficial assertions of others into the actual substance of the experience and knowledge bases they claim to have. *It is one thing to give someone power because his or her defined processes and/or defined implementations, in fact, are superior to other alternatives and quite another thing to give someone power when his or her perceived superiority, in fact, is not.* We must use our understanding of the experience/change/power equation to substantiate that claims being made are predicated in fact, especially as they relate to the environment we are operating in.

4. Finally, the experience/change/power equation teaches us the significance of capturing the experiences and knowl-

> edge of individuals, organizations, and societies in an easily accessible and understandable format. While there definitely can be a point of diminishing returns, in general, when the experiences and knowledge we have is in an easily accessible and understandable context, the more likely it is that we will make better decisions.
>
> The experience/change/power equation helps explain why there is so much discussion regarding the power associated with the Information Age and the Internet. Experience and knowledge that are lost over time or that are not easily accessible reduce the ability to obtain the cognitively-influenced change individuals, organizations, and societies are seeking. In change science, the experience/change/power equation provides proof behind the statement that knowledge is, in fact, power.

So what assessment process should we use in selecting a defined process to explain a defined change that we expect to occur in a given primary environment in the future?

In this situation we should be working with a primary environment that is predetermined and fixed (that is, cannot be altered). So we would follow the following process:

- Determine as best as possible what the conditions will be in that primary environment as of the point in time that execution is to occur.
- Based upon the experience base we are working under as described above, select the defined process or processes and resulting defined change or changes we believe have the highest probability of execution (that is, validity and reliability). In other words, the process factors associated with the selected

defined process have the highest likelihood of being supported by the conditions in that specific primary environment at that point in time on the change/time continuum.

Of course, there is always the possibility that the defined process and resulting defined change we select will not be correct. As described in earlier chapters, given the change dynamics and environmental dynamics associated with any given primary environment, environmental conditions in the primary environment will be subject to unexpected variation when compared to our assumptions. In addition, the defined process selected is still subject to the experience base we are using and our ability to properly match the required process factors to the required conditions in the primary environment.

However, this does not mean we should give up. As seen by our current ability to predict the weather, our capability of selecting what defined processes are expected to execute in a given primary environment, while not perfect, can, in fact, become very reliable. The key is that this capability is a learned capability that everyone can improve at with practice. By understanding the science of change, we will greatly enhance this ability to learn, and our capability to select defined processes that we expect to execute in the future can and will improve.

Selecting a Defined Process That Will Yield an Effective Desired Defined Change That We Want to Obtain

My guess is that many of you have decided to read this book with the major objective of learning how to select a defined process that will yield the effective desired defined changes that you want to obtain. As we would expect, *the selection of a defined process with an objective of obtaining an effective desired defined change* will continue to leverage off of the above discussion that focused on selecting defined processes that explain why certain defined change "has already occurred" and selecting defined processes that explain a defined change that "we expect to occur" in the future.

However, there are two major distinctions that need to be noted. First of all, the two scenarios discussed above are equally applicable to both naturally-occurring change and cognitively-influenced change. However, the discussion we have here regarding our desire to select a defined process with the specific objective of obtaining an effective desired defined change assumes some level of cognitive influence associated with the selection.

In our earlier discussions on environments, we noted that we have two choices when attempting to obtain a specific desired defined change. We can do nothing and leave our attempt 100 percent contingent upon the environmental and change dynamics associated with naturally-occurring change and the cognitively-influenced change of others (if any). Or we can attempt to influence this naturally-occurring and external cognitively-influenced change by using our own cognitively-influenced change.

However, here we are attempting to actually "select" a defined process to obtain the desired defined change. Therefore, we are saying cognitive influence must be involved. This is true even if the result of that cognitive influence is to do nothing and leave it 100 percent contingent upon the environmental and change dynamics associated with naturally-occurring change and the cognitively-influenced change of others. *This is because your expectation is that the selection of this expected defined process will yield the results you desire.*

The second distinction that must be noted is that the objective here is to obtain an "effective" desired defined change. In the above two scenarios no special consideration is given to the defined change that is either observed or contemplated. The defined change associated with the examination of a defined change that has already occurred is assumed to be effective to whatever level the selected defined process had actually executed.

Likewise, the defined change associated with selection of a defined process that is expected to execute in the future is also considered effective to whatever level of execution is obtained.

In this scenario, where we want to obtain a specific desired defined change in the future, effectiveness is important. The objective is to obtain 100 percent effectiveness, so selecting a defined process that does not yield 100 percent effectiveness is not an acceptable option. If your desired defined change is to move from one side of an intersection to the other side of the intersection, you surely do not want to select a defined process that leaves you stranded in the middle of the intersection (that is, the defined change is not 100 percent accomplished).

So what assessment process should we use in selecting a defined process that will yield an effective desired defined change that we want to obtain? The answer depends on whether the primary environment has already been selected for us or whether we also have the ability to select the primary environment in which the defined process will be executed. For example, if the desired defined change is for you to lose weight, then the primary environment (your body) is fixed and selection of a different primary environment is not possible.

However, if the desired defined change is to move from your current location in Chicago in the middle of winter to somewhere in the world that is 70 degrees or warmer, then there are multiple environments to select from, and the selection of a primary environment or environments becomes part of the assessment process associated with the selection of the defined process.

Therefore, if the primary environment is predetermined and fixed, then we can use the following assessment procedure:

1. Determine as best as possible what the conditions will be in that primary environment as of the point in time that execution is to occur.
2. Select all the defined processes we believe have the highest probability of execution (that is, validity and reliability) to a level of 100 percent effectiveness based upon the experience/knowledge base we are working under as described above. In other words, the process factors associated with the selected defined processes should have the highest likelihood of being supported by the conditions in that specific primary environment for the interval of time required on the change/time continuum in order to reach 100 percent effectiveness.
3. If multiple alternative defined processes exist, then select the defined process that we determine to be not only the most efficient but also has the highest degree of validity and reliability.

In cases in which we are not only selecting a defined process but also the primary environment to execute in, we as individuals, organizations, and/or societies have the option to follow two different assessment procedures:

1. In the first option we focus on the selection of the primary environment in conjunction with the selection of the defined process:

    a. From the universe of potential primary environments, select those environments that have the greatest level of interest.
    b. For each of the potential primary environments, determine as best as possible what the conditions will be, including any possible conflicting relevant conditions, in each potential primary environment as of the point in time that execution is to occur.

c. Based upon the experience/knowledge base we are working under as described above, select all the defined processes that have the highest probability of execution (that is, validity and reliability) to a level of 100 percent effectiveness for each potential primary environment. In other words, select the process factors associated with each selected defined process that have a high likelihood of being supported by the conditions in their respective primary environment for the interval of time required on the change/time continuum so as to reach 100 percent effectiveness.

d. If multiple alternative defined processes exist in any of the potential primary environments, then select the single defined process for each potential primary environment that not only is the most efficient in that primary environment but also has the highest degree of validity and reliability in reaching 100 percent effectiveness.

e. Finally, select the combined primary environment and associated selected defined process that are not only the most efficient among all the combinations of primary environments and associated defined processes but also have the highest degree of validity and reliability in reaching 100 percent effectiveness.

f. The end result of this assessment process is the selection of the combination of a primary environment and associated defined process that should yield the highest probability of obtaining the effective desired defined change.

2. In the second option, the individual, organization, or society selects a "preferable defined process" first and then an associated primary environment:

a. Based upon the preferable defined process selected, determine the required process factors, including any scientific laws (as described earlier in this chapter) and any associated time frame constraints.
b. Given the required process factors that include any scientific laws and time frame constraints, assess the primary environments within the universe of available environments to determine if any of them are expected to have all the required conditions necessary to support the required process factors. Make sure to also take into consideration any possible conflicting relevant conditions in your analysis.
c. From these potential primary environments, select the single primary environment that not only is the most efficient among all the potential primary environments but also has the highest degree of validity and reliability in reaching 100 percent effectiveness.
d. If there is not a discernible primary environment within the universe of environments that you believe will be successful, then select a new defined process and start the assessment process over again. You will probably be able to leverage off of the understanding you have already developed regarding the conditions that exist within the various primary environments under consideration to help you with the selection of an alternative defined process to examine.
e. The end result of this assessment process is the selection of a primary environment that supports a specific preferable defined process and yields the highest probability of obtaining the effective desired defined change.

TESTING ONE, TWO, THREE

We have all been there: just sitting in our chairs waiting for a presentation or speech to begin, and someone comes up to the microphone and says: "Testing, one, two, three." At that time I am sure you probably did not think of this in the context of change science. In reality, however, "testing one, two, three" is the person's attempt to "validate" the defined process of magnifying the upcoming speakers' voices by testing the amplifier system in advance.

As simple as this example is, do not underestimate the power of testing when attempting to select a defined process. It does not matter what context or reason there is associated with the selection of a defined process: testing can be an invaluable tool. This is especially the case as the significance of the desired defined change increases. For example, if we have a critical meeting to attend at a location we have never been to, it is not unusual for us to test our route in advance of the meeting date just to make sure we know how to get there so that we do not arrive late.

Assuming we have sufficient time available to us and assuming the selection of the properly defined process is of a sufficient significance to support the effort, testing the defined process or processes under consideration can be beneficial for several reasons:

1. As indicated in our example, testing can be used to validate in advance the defined process or processes under consideration.
2. Testing can also be used to determine the efficiency, effectiveness, and reliability of a defined process or to compare alternative defined processes.
3. Finally, there will be situations in which the experience base available to us is limited, and we are not sure where to start or how exactly to proceed in selecting a defined process. Testing alternative thoughts, ideas, and/or concepts might be the

only way we can develop a context to improve our ability to select an appropriate defined process short of just guessing at one.

In the end, if the significance of the selection of an appropriate defined process justifies the effort associated with testing in advance, and assuming there is sufficient time available to perform suitable testing, then we should utilize testing whenever possible in our selection of a proper defined process.

As a conclusion to this discussion on selecting a defined process that will yield an effective desired defined change that we want to obtain, all the assessment procedures noted above are focused strictly on defined processes. Therefore, to some extent, there is an underlying assumption that the conditions that exist in any given environment are fixed in context. In the next chapter on defined implementations, we will expand our discussion to include the possibility of changing these conditions through the use of defined implementations.

Therefore, now that we have solid understanding of defined processes, we can move on to defined implementations.

However, based upon the above discussion, this is a good time for me to once again climb on my soapbox relative to how significant the study and understanding of change is to all other scientific and behavioral disciplines in order to stress the need to treat change as a science. Everything that has, is, or will occur is some type of defined change. *All these other disciplines in their own way are built and predicated upon explaining why these defined changes have or will occur the way they do relative to a specific discipline's focus (that is, what are the defined processes and defined implementations that are at work).*

Therefore, a clearer understanding and development of change as a science will only help enhance the expansion of these other disciplines. More importantly, I hope that other disciplines will examine the change science concepts found in this book in order to bring their disciplines to bear for the continued development, refinement, and augmentation of the science of change.

CHAPTER NINE

Defined Implementations

When you can't change the direction of your wind—adjust your sails.

H. Jackson Brown, Jr.

While I have never performed specific research and, therefore, do not have actual data to substantiate this point, my educated guess is that the topic of implementations commands the most attention in the world of change management. My conclusion is based upon all the attempts that exist in the world to get individuals, organizations, and societies to use something (a new defined process) that is not currently being used. If you think about it, in order for this to happen successfully, an implementation needs to take place and, therefore, whoever is doing the promoting generally needs to provide instruction on how to make change happen (that is, how to implement it).

Examples are plentiful. Think about how all the different business systems being promoted almost always come with some sort of suggested implementation assistance. The same can be said about the booming "how to" and "self-help" industry. Even political strategy usually incorporates an associated implementation strategy.

Of course, in many cases, proponents of a change stress how easy it will be to implement. As indicated several times already, if you do fail in the implementation, it most likely is due to a lack of commitment.

But before I steer you too far toward the negative, I need to stress that implementations are, in fact, a critical aspect to change. However, from a change science perspective, the ability to understand, develop, and execute a successful implementation often requires a much deeper knowledge base about change than these promoters are either suggesting or providing. We are frequently disadvantaged in obtaining a successful implementation because of an insufficient understanding of how these implementations interact with, and are impacted by, change dynamics and environmental dynamics. As we have seen, the more significant the change is, the more critical this can be to us, our organization, or our society.

Of course, given all the change constantly occurring around us, many implementations are common, routine, and subconscious. Everything from medicine and food to the purchase of a new hairdryer comes with directions and instructions that are, in essence, guideline implementations of the change associated with these products. Then there are all the routine implementations taking place automatically without any thought on our part. When we decide to change our location in a room, we just automatically trigger (implement) the defined process of walking.

So while some implementations can be simple (for example, limited to just a triggering event) and others can be extremely complex, all change requires the third change element of a defined implementation. This, of course, is not limited to just cognitively-influenced change but also holds true for naturally-occurring change.

KEY POINTS OF DEFINED IMPLEMENTATIONS

So far in the various chapters of this book we have continued to build an understanding of defined implementations. For ease of reference, let us take a few moments to summarize some of these key points:

1. A defined implementation is the third element of change and represents what conditions must exist in order for the actual execution/implementation of the defined process to take place and how those conditions will be obtained.
2. A defined implementation represents the specific activities, dynamics, actions, variables, elements, and any other factors (all of which we have defined as implementation factors) required to match the conditions in a given environment to the process factors required so as to have a successfully executed defined process and, therefore, have the associated defined change successfully obtained.
3. All defined implementations occur along the change/time continuum as a part of the chain of events that is associated with the primary environment selected for the defined process under examination. Therefore, a defined implementation describes the chain of events that has occurred, or needs to occur, in a given environment or environments in order for a specific defined process to successfully execute somewhere along the change/time continuum.
4. All defined implementations require one or more defined processes to explain how the conditions (including the condition representing the triggering event) in a primary environment *have* (in the case of a defined process that has already executed) or *will* (in the case of a defined process that we want to execute) change so as to support the specific defined process under examination.

5. Because all defined implementations require at least one or more defined processes to be incorporated as an implementation factor, all the concepts described in Chapters 7 and 8 on defined processes will apply to any and all the defined processes incorporated into any given defined implementation.
6. There are two facets to a defined implementation.
    a. The first facet is that of defining the specific condition that must exist in an environment in order for the specified defined process to execute in that environment. This condition was defined as the triggering event. The triggering event is the part of the defined implementation that describes the final how the defined process will be executed. The rest of the defined implementation works backward from the triggering event and represents the second facet of an implementation. Therefore, the triggering event represents an ending condition in the environment produced from the implementation that is the starting condition of the defined process. In other words, it is the formal handoff between the defined implementation and associated defined process!
    b. The second facet of a defined implementation describes the "how" of changing the conditions in a given environment from a state of lack of support for a defined process to one of a state of conditions that supports the execution of the defined process. Given that the only way to change the conditions in a given environment is through a defined process, in essence this facet of the implementation defines what process or processes need to take place (or have taken place) in order for the execution of a defined process in a given environment to be successful.

7. Differences between a defined implementation versus a defined process:

    a. A defined implementation, answers the how, why, and when questions as they relate to the "conditions" within the primary environment required to support the specific process factors associated with the selected defined process.
    b. A defined implementation can execute in multiple environments simultaneously and/or sequentially along the change/time continuum.
    c. A defined process focuses on answering the questions of how, why, and when as it relates to the "defined change" under examination.
    d. A defined process executes in a single primary environment during an interval time on the change/time continuum.

8. Defined implementations are equally relevant to both naturally-occurring change and cognitively-influenced change. It does not matter if the change under examination is naturally-occurring change or cognitively-influenced change; there will always be an implementation associated with the change.

BASICS OF AN IMPLEMENTATION PLAN

We are going to discuss how to develop and select a defined implementation. However, before we do that, we need to introduce the use of an implementation plan and how an implementation plan is different from a defined implementation.

It is one thing to understand what a defined implementation is and an entirely other thing to be able to analyze and/or create one.

In change science we will learn to use an implementation plan to help us in our attempt to create these successful defined implementations.

An *implementation plan* will be a detailed description of a defined implementation and will include not only a definition of all the required implementation factors but also any details related to underlying strategies, assumptions, and potential conflicting relevant conditions associated with the defined implementation.

As we have seen, change dynamics and environmental dynamics in a primary environment are complex and often unpredictable, especially as the length of the time interval associated with a defined implementation increases. The challenge is that a defined implementation is created at a specific point in time on the change/time continuum based upon the relationship that exists at that point in time between the conditions in the primary environment and the required process factors associated with the defined process we intend to execute.

Therefore, we are forced to formulate strategies and, even more importantly, assumptions regarding the impact we expect from all the other change dynamics and environmental dynamics (including the potential for conflicting relevant conditions) that we know will transpire in the primary environment during the time interval associated with the selected defined implementation. In addition, since defined implementations can execute in multiple environments, these strategies and assumptions must also take into consideration the change dynamics, environmental dynamics, and potential conflicting relevant conditions in these other environments (that is, secondary environments).

It is the inclusion of strategies and assumptions that differentiates an implementation plan from the defined implementation itself (that is, from the implementation factors). This is an important concept to understand. *All other things being equal*, the definition of the required implementation factors associated with a defined implementation would be sufficient to obtain the successful execution of a defined implementation. The implementation factors include everything we need to know in order to fully execute the defined implementation including the specific incorporated defined processes and associated process factors, the sequence of execution of these incorporated defined processes, and the time interval required.

Unfortunately, *because we are developing the defined implementation at a specific point in time on the change/time continuum, all other things are not always equal and are often unpredictable.*

Therefore, we are developing the defined implementation based upon the change dynamics and environmental dynamics *we expect to occur* during the defined implementation time interval. As a result, *we make assumptions and strategies* relative to these change dynamics and environmental dynamics as they relate to the defined implementation. This is true even if we consciously or unconsciously exclude any consideration of future impacts from change dynamics and environmental dynamics in the primary environment since, in essence, we are making a no impact assumption.

So an implementation plan goes beyond just capturing all the required implementation factors associated with a given defined implementation. It also captures the strategy and assumptions relating to that given defined implementation relative the change dynamics and environmental dynamics that are expected to occur within the primary environment and other associated environments (if any) during the time interval required to execute the defined implementation.

IMPLEMENTATION SELECTION CONSIDERATIONS

Before we explore in more depth how to select a defined implementation, there are some dynamics associated with defined implementations that need to be taken into consideration.

Reasons a Defined Implementation Can Fail

The following is a list of some of the major reasons a defined implementation can fail. You will notice that many of the reasons for the failure of a defined implementation are similar to the list we developed for defined processes:

1. Conflicts with the laws of science. Given the laws of science, it is impossible to determine a defined implementation for the associated defined process.
2. An erroneous defined implementation. The defined implementation selected is erroneous and, therefore, cannot produce the expected results required to obtain a successful execution of the associated defined process.
3. A conflicting relevant condition or conditions. We have an accurate defined implementation, but there are conflicting conditions at play that will negate or disrupt the execution of the defined implementation. For example, let's assume that the primary defined process is to hand everyone a presentation book in advance of their sitting down at a conference that starts at 8:00. Your defined implementation includes:

   - Defined process (A) of having printed presentation books delivered to the lobby.
   - Defined process (B) of opening the doors to the lobby at 7:45 so the participants can pass through the lobby to the conference hall where they will be seated.
   - The primary defined process of handing each participant a presentation book as he or she walks into the conference hall.

   Obviously, the defined implementation requires that the defined process (A) needs to happen sequentially before the defined process (B). However, if there is a conflicting relevant condition represented by a traffic jam that delays the delivery of the presentation books until after the start of the conference, then the execution of the associated primary defined process of handing presentation books to the participants as they pass through the lobby fails even though both defined processes (A) and (B) were in fact executed.

4. One or more erroneous defined processes within the defined implementation. If one or more of the defined processes incorporated into the defined implementation are erroneous for any reason, the defined implementation will fail.

5. The time interval required to support the defined implementation is longer than the actual time available. We can have a defined implementation that is valid, but if the interval of time required to support the defined implementation exceeds the actual time available, the defined implementation will fail. The longer the time interval associated with a defined implementation, the more likely that an inability to fully execute the defined implementation will exist.

    We will discuss later how this situation is more common than is often recognized. My guess is that if we think hard enough, almost everyone will remember how a desired change failed to happen because there was just not enough time available to execute a valid defined implementation. This is very common when defined implementations require long periods of time such as in the implementation of business software or the recovery from an injury.

6. A large number of implementation factors (like defined processes) that are associated with the defined implementation. The discussion on process stacking that is to follow is a good representation of this exposure since risk of failure will tend to increase as the number of implementation factors, such as incorporated defined processes, increases.

As with defined processes the above list is not intended to be all-inclusive but one that summarizes a number of more common reasons why a defined implementation will fail. Given the continuous array of defined implementations that are constantly occurring, I am sure you will encounter variations of the above list and develop new reasons for implementation failures.

In Chapters 11 and 12 we will explore risk in more detail and provide concepts and tools to help address these exposures to failure. In the meantime, increasing our ability to recognize and understand these exposures will improve our overall ability to obtain and/or understand the change that is occurring.

Tiered Implementation Processes

As already stated, a defined implementation is composed of one or more defined processes. These defined processes need to execute along the change/time continuum in order to produce a future state of being of conditions (including the triggering event condition) in a given environment that matches all of the process factors required for a given defined process to execute.

It is important to understand that a defined implementation represents the activity (that is, execution of a defined process or processes) that executes over a future time interval ending in a future state of being. This only makes sense given that if a given environment were to contain all of the conditions, including a triggering event condition, required by a defined process in the current state of being, then that defined process would execute immediately and a defined implementation would not be required (that is, a defined implementation has already been executed).

In addition, a defined process, including the defined processes incorporated into a defined implementation, executes in a single environment (the primary environment) over a continuous time interval on the change/time continuum. However, the defined processes incorporated in a defined implementation can also be structured to execute in multiple environments and in multiple time intervals that are not always contiguous. This is extremely important to understand and can be summarized as follows:

1. Environmental dynamics tells us that conditions in any primary environment can be impacted by both internal and external influences.

    External environmental adjustments are environmental adjustments in a primary environment that are partially or completely influenced by the change dynamics that have occurred externally to the selected primary environment (that is, from a secondary environment).

    Therefore, it is not uncommon to have a defined process that is incorporated into a defined implementation execute in a secondary environment and create a change effect representing a required condition in the primary environment. For example, we might have a defined process that is incorporated into a defined implementation that manufactures a required material in a secondary environment that is 1,000 miles away from the primary environment. Once this material is manufactured and transported into the primary environment, it becomes a change effect condition in the primary environment that was derived from the secondary environment in which it was created.

2. Depending on the sequence of activities (that is, defined processes) incorporated into a defined implementation, these different defined processes can and will execute at various points in time on the change/time continuum. In addition, the time intervals associated with the individual defined processes do not have to be continuous or contiguous. Instead, they can also be simultaneous or even have gaps of open time between them on the change/time continuum. In the example above,

we might have to execute the defined process associated with the manufacture of the material months in advance of the execution of the next required defined process that is incorporated into the defined implementation.

It may have become obvious that if we are not careful, it can be difficult to manage the various defined processes that exist in a defined implementation. To address that, change science has established a reference system based upon where the defined processes that are incorporated into the defined implementation are positioned relative to one another on the change/time continuum. As depicted in Figure 9-1, the reference system is as follows:

- The *primary defined change* is the ultimate defined change with which the defined implementation is associated. It is the final defined change in the primary environment that you expect to obtain from the selected associated defined process and defined implementation.
- The *primary defined process* is the ultimate defined process with which the defined implementation is associated. The process factors along with the triggering event condition associated with the primary defined process are the target conditions in the primary environment that the defined implementation is intended to address.
- *Tier I defined process(es)* is/are the defined process or processes that is/are incorporated into the defined implementation that are expected to execute in the time interval on the change/time continuum immediately prior to the point in time on the change/time continuum in which the triggering event starts the execution of the primary defined process. This time interval must be contiguous to the time interval associated with the execution of the primary defined process. You will always have at least one Tier I defined process.

Figure 9-1
Example of Tiered Implementation Referencing

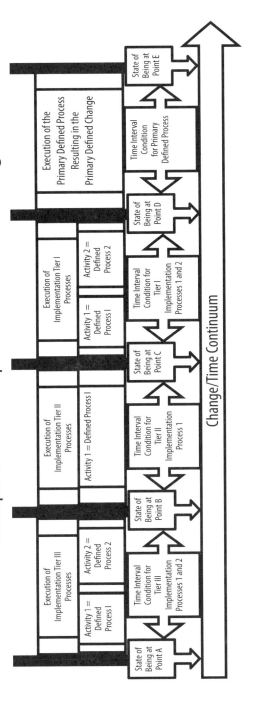

- *Tier II defined process(es)* is/are the defined process or processes that is/are incorporated into the defined implementation that will execute in the first required time interval (although not necessarily contiguous) prior to the Tier I defined process or processes. There can be situations in which a Tier II defined process or processes are not required.
- Depending upon how the time interval associated with Tier II defined processes is configured, we can continue to establish additional tiers (*Tiers III through Tier X+*) as needed in order to manage the sequence of the defined processes that are incorporated into a given defined implementation.

Validity, Efficiency, Effectiveness, Reliability, and Process Stacking

We spent a great deal of time in Chapter 8 on defined processes exploring the concepts of validity, efficiency, effectiveness, and reliability. All of these concepts also apply to defined implementations.

However, it is now time to introduce an additional twist that is referred to as process stacking.

Process stacking represents the fact that whenever the process factors and/or implementation factors have more than one defined process incorporated in them, the validity, efficiency, effectiveness, and reliability associated with that defined process and/or defined implementation are directly impacted by the validity, efficiency, effectiveness, and reliability associated with each one of the underlying incorporated defined processes.

Therefore, the greater the number of defined processes that are incorporated within a primary defined process and/or defined implementation, the greater the potential impact that process stacking has on the validity, efficiency, effectiveness, and reliability associated with the primary defined process and/or overall defined implementation.

So there are two major considerations when determining validity, efficiency, effectiveness, and reliability relative to a defined implementation. The first consideration is directly related to the specific structural nature of the defined implementation. The second consideration is related to impacts associated with process stacking.

Validity, Efficiency, Effectiveness, and Reliability Associated with the Specific Structural Nature of a Defined Implementation

As it pertains to the specific structural nature of the defined implementation, validity, efficiency, effectiveness, and reliability are viewed in the context of the totality of the defined implementation irrespective of any process stacking considerations. This is due to the fact that if the underlying structural nature of a defined implementation has problems, the defined implementation can be invalid, inefficient, ineffective, and/or unreliable even if we have perfectly legitimate and accurate defined processes incorporated into that defined implementation.

For example, if the triggering event condition included in our defined implementation is not accurate or valid, then the defined implementation will not be valid even if the defined processes incorporated into the defined implementation are accurate. Another example is the case in which several defined processes incorporated into a defined implementation are accurate and valid in their own right, but either the sequence of activities (sequence of execution) is not an accurate sequence and/or the time interval implementation factor is too short to execute all those required incorporated defined processes.

So when we analyze the validity, efficiency, effectiveness, and reliability related to a defined implementation, we need to look at the defined implementation in its totality. The best way to do this is to look at the defined implementation in the same way we would look at a single defined process. In this context all the considerations described in Chapter 8 under the section on validity, efficiency, effectiveness, and reliability will also apply in our evaluation of the defined implementation.

In other words, look at the defined implementation as the equivalent of a single defined process treating the individual defined processes that are incorporated into the defined implementation as implementation factors and the end targeted conditions as the defined change we are executing. In this sort of context, all of the discussion on validity, efficiency, effectiveness, and reliability in Chapter 8 will apply equally well in totality to the defined implementation.

Impact Associated with Process Stacking

Process stacking tells us that whenever you have more than one defined process incorporated into a defined implementation, you have the additional dynamic of process stacking to take into consideration when evaluating validity, efficiency, effectiveness, and reliability. *It is important to note that, even though our focus here is on defined implementations, the dynamics associated with process stacking would also apply when you have more than one defined process incorporated into a primary defined process.*

Since a defined implementation can be composed of more than one defined process, then the validity, efficiency, effectiveness, and reliability associated with each individual defined process will also impact the overall validity, efficiency, effectiveness, and reliability of the defined implementation.

Let's take a look at the impact that process stacking has individually on validity, reliability, efficiency, and effectiveness:

1. Validity: Keep in mind that if a single defined process that is incorporated within a given defined implementation fails to execute, then the defined implementation will also fail to execute successfully. Therefore, the more process stacking we have, the more probability that the defined implementation will fail because of the fact that a specific incorporated defined process is not valid in and by itself or is not valid in the context in which it has been incorporated into the defined implementation.
2. Efficiency: In Chapter 8 it was pointed out that efficiency relative to a defined process is only relevant if there are two or more alternative defined processes to select from. The same holds true with regard to defined implementations: efficiency only applies if we have two or more alternative defined implementations to select from. However, the impact associated with process stacking is less obvious given that there is not necessarily a direct relationship between the number of defined processes incorporated in each defined implementation and the overall level of efficiency associated with each defined implementation.

   In other words, the overall efficiency associated with a defined implementation must take into account the efficiency considerations for every defined process incorporated into the defined implementation. This means that, the greater the level of process stacking, the more defined processes we must take into consideration.

   However, the level of overall efficiency does not necessarily depend on the total number of defined processes incorporated into the defined implementation. For example, we can have defined implementation (a) with a single defined process that has a less desirable overall efficiency than alternative defined implementation (b), which incorporates two highly efficient defined processes.

Bottom line, while process stacking can increase the analytical effort and complexity associated with determining the overall efficiency of a given defined implementation, it does not necessarily equate to an overall efficiency that is better or worse than an alternative defined implementation that has a greater or lesser process stacking associated with it. Therefore, it is best to go beyond the size of the process stacking and analyze the efficiency of a defined implementation from the ground up, incorporating the efficiency associated with each individual defined process in the analysis.

3. Effectiveness: In Chapter 8 we defined effectiveness in change science as the ability to obtain 100 percent of the desired defined change through the execution of a specific defined process.

The definition also applies to defined implementations as follows: *the effectiveness of a defined implementation in change science is the ability to obtain 100 percent of the desired conditions through the execution of a specific defined implementation.*

Therefore, as was the case with a defined process, so is the case with a defined implementation: effectiveness is based upon the relationship of the time interval required for 100 percent execution of the defined implementation compared to the actual time interval available on the change/time continuum.

Consequently, process stacking will impact the effectiveness of the defined implementation to the extent the time intervals associated with the individual defined processes that are incorporated in the defined implementation interplay with the overall time interval required to execute the defined implementation.

Process stacking will be considered detrimental if the time interval associated with one or more of the defined processes negatively impacts the overall time interval of the defined implementation relative to the actual time available on the change/time continuum. While an increase in the size of the process stacking may imply an increase in the probability of a negative impact on the effectiveness of a defined implementation, there will be situations in which this is not the case, and a detailed analysis must be performed in order to avoid any incorrect conclusions.

4. Reliability: Like validity, the reliability of a defined implementation is directly related to the reliability associated with each defined process that is incorporated into the defined implementation. Therefore, a general rule is that the more process stacking we have, the lower the reliability associated with the defined implementation since the overall reliability is dependent on the interaction of all the individual reliabilities within the defined implementation. For example, a defined implementation that has only one defined process with a reliability of 80 percent incorporated into it has a greater reliability when compared to a defined implementation that has two defined processes each with a reliability of 80 percent incorporated into it.

SELECTION OF A DEFINED IMPLEMENTATION AND IMPLEMENTATION PLAN

So how do we actually go about selecting a defined implementation and developing an associated implementation plan? At first glance this can appear to be a daunting task. In many cases it is. However, as we have discussed many times already, since change is constantly and continuously occurring, defined implementations are constantly occurring. Whether through the naturally-occurring change cycles, the subconscious thought processes of individuals, or the conscious efforts of individuals, organizations, and societies, defined implementations are continually executing.

To start, we need to recognize that all the discussions associated with defined processes in Chapters 7 and 8 are also relevant when we are discussing defined implementations. Remember, a defined implementation is always composed of a sequence of one or more defined processes executing so as to produce the conditions (including a triggering event) in a primary environment required in order to obtain execution of the primary defined process. Therefore, when we are selecting a defined implementation, we are automatically selecting one or more defined processes.

As we might expect, just like defined processes, our ability as an individual, organization, or society to select an effective defined implementation is greatly influenced by the experiences and learned knowledge we are able to draw upon. As discussed in Chapter 8, even all the subconscious defined implementations we are executing, whether successful or not, are in some context based upon the learned experiences of ourselves or others.

So where do we start? Once again we need to distinguish between the analysis of a defined implementation associated with a primary defined process that has already taken place versus the selection of a defined implementation to obtain the execution of a future desired primary defined process.

Selecting a Defined Implementation That Explains Why a Certain Primary Defined Process Has Already Occurred

Since we already know what the primary defined process is, we also know the primary environment in which it was executed. Therefore, we are able to analyze the associated defined implementation through the following procedure:

1. Determine all the relevant process factors associated with the primary defined process. These process factors detail what conditions we must explain within the primary environment.
2. Determine what the triggering event condition was for the primary defined process.
3. Analyze the chain of events associated with the primary environment working your way backward along the change/time continuum from the point in time that the triggering event existed and the primary defined process under examination executed.

   a. Our objective is to determine what specific defined processes associated with the chain of events for the primary environment executed at what points in time along the change/time continuum and in what environments so as to produce the required conditions necessary for the primary defined process to execute.
   b. We do this until such time as we have satisfactorily determined all of the conditions under consideration including the triggering event condition.
   c. However, note, as discussed in Chapter 7, it is very important to remember that constant conditions that are commonplace do not always need to be traced back to their originating event on the change/time continuum but can be just defined as a given constant condition. By doing so, the analytical procedure can often be greatly simplified.

Just to reinforce this procedure, let's explore a simple example. Assume your neighbors had a bonfire in their yard last night. You are thinking of having a bonfire at your house sometime in the future, and, therefore, you want to understand how they implemented the bonfire they had in their yard. Following the above procedure, you determine the following:

- Primary defined process equals safe combustion of a long-term combustible material
- Required conditions:
  - A fire pit
  - Firewood stacked in the fire pit used as a long-term combustible material
  - Newspaper inserted between the firewood used as an initial combustible material
  - Oxygen to support combustion
  - A triggering event condition of a lighted match held to the newspaper to provide the heat required for the execution of the primary defined process
- The implementation factors associated with the defined implementation your neighbors used working backward through the chain of events:
  - A defined process that lighted a match and applied it to the newspaper (this created the triggering event condition of heat to the newspaper)
  - Oxygen viewed as a constant condition and ignored
  - A defined process that inserted the newspaper between the firewood
  - A defined process that moved the newspaper and box of matches from their house to a location near their fire pit
  - A defined process that delivered precut firewood to a location near their fire pit
  - A defined process that dug a hole and inserted a precast fire pit in the desired fire pit location at their house
  - A defined process that acquired and had delivered a precast fire pit to the fire pit location at their house

You have now developed (that is, learned) how your neighbors obtained the desired change associated with having a bonfire in their yard. If you so choose, you can leverage off of this understanding (that is, experience and knowledge) should you decide in the future to implement a bonfire in your yard.

You can also see that even in a simple example like this, the effort and level of detail associated with a defined implementation can be surprising. This example should also help reinforce just how important the understanding of a defined implementation can be if you want to increase your odds of obtaining successful desired change.

Finally, as indicated before, when examined at this level of detail, you can really appreciate just how routine and normal we have become in our ability as individuals, organizations, and society to integrate defined implementations into our daily lives.

Selecting a Defined Implementation to Obtain the Execution of a Future Desired Primary Defined Process

As already discussed, individuals, organizations, and societies over time develop not only a larger and larger experience base of defined processes but also a larger and larger experience base of defined implementations from which to leverage off of.

These defined process and defined implementation knowledge bases will be derived from both direct experiences and access to the experiences of other individuals, organizations, and/or societies. For example, any time we look a subject up on the Internet, we are, in essence, trying to access and leverage off of the experience and knowledge base of others.

Thus, just as in the case of selecting a defined process as described in Chapter 8, the first place most individuals, organizations, and societies turn to when trying to select a defined implementation is this direct and indirect repository of preexisting experiences/knowledge. As this experience/knowledge base increases, the likelihood that the selection procedure associated with a defined implementation becoming subconscious and/or routine also increases dramatically.

As indicated at the very beginning of this chapter, you can find a significant amount of literature that refers to implementation development, planning, execution, and strategy. Some of the literature approaches the discussion of implementations and/or implementation methodology in a very general context. Other discussions are more focused relative to specific subject matter (for example, how to implement an ERP system at your company or how to implement a specific diet plan).

You will find much of this literature very useful and a possible resource for the expansion of your experience/knowledge base. However, I would still strongly suggest that you use the concepts you have learned from the science of change whenever you are reviewing and/or considering leveraging off of any of the literature under consideration.

Analyzing this literature and methodologies in the context of your understanding of change dynamics and environmental dynamics can often help you avoid unnecessary disappointments. You must always keep in mind that an implementation that works for one individual, organization, or society might not work for another just based upon differences associated with the change dynamics and environmental dynamics that exists between differing scenarios.

There can also be situations where off-the-shelf repeatable change is available that can either completely or partially assist in the implementation of a primary defined process. In this case, you are once again leveraging off of the experience and knowledge base of others by utilizing a predetermined defined implementation that has the potential to implement a primary defined process that will result in the primary defined change you are attempting to obtain.

However, attempting to leverage off of your experience base or the experience base of others does not necessarily guarantee that the defined implementation selected will, in fact, work. When it does not work, or when the available experience base is inadequate, then a more formalized procedure might be required. This is especially the case as the significance of the primary defined process (and the associated primary defined change) increases.

In cases like this, the following selection procedure can be applied.

To start with, Figure 9-2 represents a high-level summary of the various alternative scenarios we need to deal with when selecting a defined implementation.

As Figure 9-2 depicts, the actual number of possible scenarios we have to deal with when determining the selection of a defined implementation is somewhat limited. We will save our discussion on the mitigation of potential conflicting relevant conditions for our future chapters on risk. Therefore, here we will limit our attention to the first four states of being in Figure 9-2.

Figure 9-2
Summary of Possible Implementation Scenarios

State of being	Do existing environmental conditions equal all required process factors?	Do existing environmental conditions equal the required triggering event?	Are there likely to be any conflicting relevant conditions?	Required action
1	Yes	Yes	No	Defined process will execute so no further action will be required.
2	No	No	No	A defined implementation needs to be created for both the process factors and triggering event.
3	Yes	No	No	A defined implementation needs to be created for the triggering event only.
4	No	Yes	No	A defined implementation needs to be created for the process factors only.
5	Yes	Yes	Yes	A mitigation strategy for the conflicting relevant conditions needs to be incorporated into the defined implementation; then 1 above applies. Otherwise need to select a new primary defined process.
6	No	No	Yes	A mitigation strategy for the conflicting relevant conditions needs to be incorporated into the defined implementation; then 2 above applies. Otherwise need to select a new primary defined process.
7	Yes	No	Yes	A mitigation strategy for the conflicting relevant conditions needs to be incorporated into the defined implementation; then 3 above applies. Otherwise need to select a new primary defined process.
8	No	Yes	Yes	A mitigation strategy for the conflicting relevant conditions needs to be incorporated into the defined implementation; then 4 above applies. Otherwise need to select a new primary defined process.

In the case of State of Being 1, all the required process factors and the triggering event conditions exist in the primary environment for the primary defined process. Therefore, "no" defined implementation is required since the primary defined process will begin to execute based upon the triggering event condition and the existence of all the required process factors.

In the case of States of Being 2, 3, and 4, a defined implementation will be required. However, the structural nature of the defined implementation will be different based upon what combination of existing process factors and existing triggering event conditions exist at any particular point in time on the change/time continuum.

In State of Being 2, we need a defined implementation that addresses both the missing required process factors and a missing triggering event condition. On the other hand, in States of Being 3 and 4, we only need a defined implementation that addresses either missing process factors or a missing trigger event condition depending upon which state of being we are starting with.

The selection procedure used for selecting the defined implementation would be as follows:

1. Determine all the relevant process factors associated with the primary defined process. These process factors detail what conditions we must obtain within the primary environment.
2. Determine what the triggering event condition will be for the primary defined process.
3. Analyze the conditions that are present in the primary environment at a specific point in time on the change/time continuum.
4. Determine what required process factors (including the required triggering event) are missing "and/or are likely to be missing" as conditions within the primary environment at the point in time that the primary defined process is expected to execute.

5. Establish a defined implementation composed of a specific defined process and/or defined processes that, when executed in a specified sequence, will create the missing conditions and triggering event required in the primary environment.

Our objective for the above procedure is to determine what specific defined process or defined processes need to be incorporated into the chain of events for the primary environment and at what points in time along the change/time continuum so as to produce the required missing conditions necessary for the primary defined process to execute.

In Chapter 3 on change dynamics, we introduced a tool that was referred to as a change dynamics profile. In change science, the use of a change dynamics profile can be a very useful tool when developing and selecting a defined implementation and/or an implementation plan. To review, we defined a change dynamics profile as follows:

A change dynamics profile *outlines all the specific criteria necessary to try to obtain a specific desired defined change.* It includes such items as:

1. A description of the defined change under examination
2. Environment(s) under consideration
3. The starting state of being in the environment(s) under consideration and its specific position on the time continuum: in other words, what conditions exist in the environment(s) we are considering
4. The length of the time interval on the time continuum (assuming there are restrictions) associated with progressing from the starting state of being to the ending state of being
5. Possible processes under consideration to obtain the desired defined change and how the associated process factors match

up to the relevant conditions that exist in the environment(s) under consideration
6. Some possible implementation strategies based upon the answers to the above questions

If a change dynamics profile for a primary defined change already exists, then there is a high likelihood that much of the information required in the selection procedure outlined above would already be available. All we need to do is focus the change dynamics profile on the specific primary defined change and primary defined process we have already selected and leverage off this information when carrying out the selection procedure associated with the defined implementation.

On the other hand, if we have not yet created a change dynamics profile, we can start our defined implementation selection procedure by creating a change dynamic profile. In this case, the specific primary defined change, primary defined process, and in many cases primary environment have already been selected, so the focus of the change dynamics profile can be based strictly on the selection of a defined implementation.

Let us use an example to better clarify how this whole defined implementation selection procedure might be applied. Let's assume that you are going to have a party at your house. As a part of the party you would like to have a fire occurring (that is, executing) somewhere in a location where your guests can enjoy it. Figure 9-3 represents a possible change dynamics profile that you might develop.

Figure 9-3
Change Dynamics Profile

Description of the Primary Defined Change: Have a fire for a party to be held tonight at the house. Beginning State of Being = No Fire / Ending State of Being = a Fire. Time Interval equals 4 hours starting at 8:00 PM.

Description of the Primary Defined Process: Combustion using firewood as the combustible material. Time interval equals 4 hours.

	Potential Environment	Condition Considerations	Triggering Event (TE) Reference	Possible Triggering Events	Possible Defined Implementation	Comments (i.e., Potential Conflicting Relevant Conditions)	Assumptions and Strategies
Option 1	Fireplace in house (Efficiency For access To drinks and food = 1, Access to firewood = 3, Protections from weather = 1, Number of people = 2 and enjoyment of outdoors = 3) (Reliability = 1)	Limit 20 people / Weather is irrelevant / Cannot enjoy outdoors / Difficult access to firewood	TE-1	Natural gas starter in fireplace (Efficiency of time = 1, Cost = 2) (Reliability = 1)	Move firewood from fire pit area into fireplace area / Place firewood into fireplace / Ignite gas starter / Time Interval = 30 min.	Time availability given everything else to prepare for	A) Rain > 40% / B) Can move enough wood for 4 hours / C) Have time to move wood just prior to getting ready with getting ready being 1.5 hours before start time

Potential Environment	Condition Considerations	Triggering Event (TE) Reference	Possible Triggering Events	Possible Defined Implementation	Comments (i.e., Potential Conflicting Relevant Conditions)	Assumptions and Strategies
		TE-2	Light a match to paper (Efficiency of time = 2, Cost = 1) (Reliability= 3)	Move firewood from fire pit area into fireplace / Place firewood into area / Move newspaper from recycle bin into fireplace / Ignite match and hold to newspaper / Time Interval = 35 min.	Time availability given everything else to prepare for	A) Rain > 40% / B) Can move enough wood for 4 hours / C) Have time to move wood just prior to getting ready with getting ready being 1.5 hours before start time
		TE-3	Light a match to a starter log (Efficiency of time = 3, Cost = 3) (Reliability = 2)	Move firewood from fire pit area into fireplace / Place firewood into area / Go to store to purchase a starter log / Place starter log in fireplace / Ignite match and hold to starter log / Time Interval = 1 hour	Time availability given everything else to prepare for	A) Rain > 40% / B) Can move enough wood for 4 hours / C) Have time to move wood just prior to getting ready with getting ready being 1.5 hours before start time / D) Have time to purchase starter log at store / E) Have money in budget to buy starter log

FIGURE 9-3: CHANGE DYNAMICS PROFILE (continued)

	Potential Environment	Condition Considerations	Triggering Event (TE) Reference	Possible Triggering Events	Possible Defined Implementation	Comments (i.e., Potential Conflicting Relevant Conditions)	Assumptions and Strategies
Option 2	Chiminea on deck (Efficiency for access to drinks and food = 2, Access to Firewood = 2, Protections from weather = 2, Number of people = 3 and enjoyment of outdoors = 2) (Reliability = 2)	Limit 10 people / Weather is relevant / Can enjoy outdoors / Difficult access to firewood	TE-2	Light a match to paper (Efficiency of time = 2, Cost = 1) (Reliability = 3)	Move firewood from fire pit area onto deck / Place firewood into chiminea / Move newspaper from recycle bin into chiminea / Ignite match and hold to newspaper / Time Interval = 30 min.	Potential rainy weather / Time availability given everything else to prepare for / 20 people invited so no room if they are all there at one time	A) Rain > 20% < 40% / B) Can move enough wood for 4 hours / C) Have time to move wood just prior to getting ready with getting ready being 1.5 hours before start time / D) No more than 10 people at party at any given time unless also use house
			TE-3	Light a match to a starter log (Efficiency = 2, Cost = 3) (Reliability = 2)	Move firewood from fire pit area onto deck / Place firewood into chiminea / Go to store to purchase a starter log / Place starter log in chiminea / Ignite match and hold to starter log / Time Interval = 1 hour	Potential rainy weather / Time availability given everything else to prepare for / 20 people invited so no room if they are all there at one time	A) Rain > 20% < 40% / B) Can move enough wood for 4 hours / C) Have time to move wood just prior to getting ready with getting ready being 1.5 hours before start time / D) No more than 10 people at party at any given time unless also use house / E) Have time to purchase starter log at store / F) Have money in budget to buy starter log

	Potential Environment	Condition Considerations	Triggering Event (TE) Reference	Possible Triggering Events	Possible Defined Implementation	Comments (i.e., Potential Conflicting Relevant Conditions)	Assumptions and Strategies
Option 3	Fire pit in backyard (Efficiency for access To drinks and food = 3, Access to Firewood = 1, Protections from weather = 1, Number of people = 1 & enjoyment of outdoors = 1) (Reliability = 3)	Limit 35 people / Weather is relevant/ Can enjoy outdoors/ Easy access to firewood / Distance from the house	TE-2	Light a match to paper (Efficiency of time = 2, Cost = 1) (Reliability = 3)	Move newspaper from recycle bin into fireplace / Ignite match and hold to newspaper/ Time Interval = 5 min.	Potential rainy weather/ Drink and food availability given distance from house	A) Rain <= 20% / B) People willing to walk back and forth to house for drinks and food
			TE-3	Light a match to a starter log (Efficiency of time = 3, Cost = 3) (Reliability = 2)	Go to store to purchase a starter log / Place starter log in fire pit / Ignite match and hold to starter log/ Time Interval = 30 min.	Potential rainy weather/ Time availability given everything else to prepare for / Drink and food availability given distance from house	A) Rain <= 20% / B) People willing to walk back and forth to house for drinks and food / C) Have time to purchase starter log at store / D) Have money in budget to buy starter log

The change dynamics profile depicted in Figure 9-3 indicates a single primary defined change (have a fire for a party to be held tonight at the house) along with a beginning and ending state of being (beginning state of being = no fire / ending state of being = a fire) and a time interval (time interval of four hours starting at 8:00 pm).

In addition, the primary defined process to provide the primary defined change has also been established (combustion using firewood). Therefore, the creation of a defined implementation needs to be addressed to provide the conditions necessary to support the selected primary defined process.

In our example, there are three potential primary environments available at the house that could be used to execute the primary defined process:

1. A fireplace inside the house
2. A chiminea (portable clay fireplace) located on the deck
3. A fire pit located in the backyard

Each of these potential primary environments has different environmental conditions and potentially conflicting relevant conditions to take into consideration including:

A. Accommodation of the number of guests
B. Enjoyment of outdoors
C. Protection from bad weather
D. Location to drinks and food
E. Access to firewood

These differing conditions, in turn, impact the efficiency and reliability of the primary defined process and related defined implementation depending on which primary environment is selected. As summarized in Figure 9-4, the efficiency and reliability for each option can be determined, and "based upon individual preference," these conditions can be weighted in significance. By performing this exercise, we are attempting to use a quantified versus subjective approach to selecting which primary environment option to choose.

Figure 9-4
Change Dynamics Profile—Primary Environment Condition Considerations

			Efficiency Ranking 1 = Best / 3 = Worst		
Priority	Weighting (3=Most Important)	Condition	Option 1 House	Option 2 Deck	Option 3 Fire Pit
1	3	Accomodation of the number of guests	2	3	1
2	3	Enjoyment of outdoors	3	2	1
3	2	Protection from bad weather	1	2	3
4	1	Location to drinks and food	1	2	3
5	2	Access to firewood	3	2	1
		Total Efficiency Ranking	**10**	**11**	**9**
	3	Reliability Ranking	1	2	3
		Total Efficiency and Reliability Ranking	**11**	**13**	**12**
			Weighted Efficieny and Reliability Ranking		
1	3	Accomodation of the number of guests	6	9	3
2	3	Protection from bad weather	9	6	3
3	2	Enjoyment of outdoors	2	4	6
4	1	Location to drinks and food	1	2	3
5	2	Access to firewood	6	4	2
	3	Reliability Ranking	3	6	9
		Total Weighted Efficiency and Reliability Ranking	**27**	**31**	**26**

Note: the lower the number, the better the ranking

However, given the forward-looking aspect associated with the selection of a defined implementation, the strategies and assumptions surrounding the selection of a defined implementation can also play a significant role. Figure 9-5 summarizes some of the strategies and assumptions that have been incorporated into the change dynamics profile we are using to assist in the selection of a defined implementation.

Figure 9-5
Change Dynamics Profile—Possible Strategies

Potential Strategies and Assumptions
A) Check weather 3 hours before party:
   If rain > 40%, then Option 1
   If rain > 20% <= 40%, then Option 2
   If rain <= 20%, then Option 3
B) If Option 2, then utilize house and deck to accommodate more people
C) If Options 1 and 2, need to move enough wood in advance for 4 hours
D) If Option 1 and 2, moving wood is dirty work so move just prior to getting ready for the party

Finally, Figure 9-3 also provides high-level guidance relative to alternative triggering events that can be utilized depending on which primary environment is selected. In our example, there are three potential triggering events that could be used to execute the primary defined process:

1. A gas starter in the fireplace
2. The use of a lighted match held against old newspaper (found in the recycle bin at the house) that has been inserted between the firewood

3. The use of a lighted match held against a starter log (that needs to be purchased from the store) that has been inserted between the firewood.

As was the case with the various primary environments, each of these potential triggering event conditions has different environmental conditions and potentially conflicting relevant conditions to take into consideration including:

A. Efficiency associated with the time to create the triggering event condition within the selected primary environment (that is, the time associated with going to the store to purchase a starter log is greater than using the gas starter in the fireplace)
B. The cost associated with the triggering event (that is, the cost of a starter log is greater than the cost of old newspaper)

Once again, these differing conditions, in turn, impact the efficiency and reliability of the triggering event selected and the related defined implementation which are summarized below in Figure 9-6.

Figure 9-6
Change Dynamics Profile—Triggering Event Considerations

Priority	Weighting (3 = Most Important)	Condition	Efficiency Ranking 1 = Best / 3 = Worst		
			TE 1 Natural Gas Starter in Fireplace	TE 2 Lighted Match to Newspaper	TE 3 Lighted Match to Starter Log
1	3	Efficiency of time	1	2	3
2	1	Cost	2	1	3
		Total efficiency ranking	3	3	6
	3	Reliability Ranking	1	3	2
		Total efficiency and reliability ranking	1	3	2
			Weighted Efficiency and Reliability Ranking		
1	3	Efficiency of time	3	6	9
2	1	Cost	2	1	3
		Total weighted efficiency ranking	5	7	12
		Reliability ranking	3	9	6
		Total weighted efficiency and reliability ranking	8	16	18

Note: the lower the number, the better the ranking

However, probably the most important aspect associated with using the Figure 9-3 change dynamic profile is the ability to start formulating alternative defined implementations and implementation plans for the primary defined process based upon which primary environment and triggering event conditions are selected. Figure 9-7 summarizes these implementation plans that are the combination of each individual defined implementation along with their underlying strategies and assumptions.

Figure 9-7

Alternative Defined—Implementations

Implementation Sequence	Option 1—Fireplace in House		
	TE 1 Natural Gas Starter	**TE 2 Match to Newspaper**	**TE 3 Match to Starter Log**
1	Move firewood from fire pit area into fireplace area	Move firewood from fire pit area into fireplace area	Move firewood from fire pit area into fireplace area 3
2	Place firewood into fireplace	Place firewood into fireplace	Place firewood into fireplace
3	Ignite gas starter	Move newspaper from recycle bin into fireplace	Go to store to purchase a starter log
4		Ignite match and hold to newspaper	Place starter log in fireplace
5			Ignite match and hold to starter log
Time Interval	30 min.	35 min.	60 min.
Strategy and Assumptions	A) Rain > 40% / B) Can move enough wood for 4 hours / C) Have time to move wood just prior to getting ready with getting ready being 1.5 hours before start time	A) Rain > 40% / B) Can move enough wood for 4 hours / C) Have time to move wood just prior to getting ready with getting ready being 1.5 hours before start time	A) Rain > 40% / B) Can move enough wood for 4 hours / C) Have time to move wood just prior to getting ready with getting ready being 1.5 hours before start time / D) Have time to purchase starter log at store / E) Have money in budget to buy starter log

FIGURE 9-7: ALTERNATIVE DEFINED—IMPLEMENTATIONS (continued)

	Option 2—Chiminea on Deck	
Implementation Sequence	**TE 2 Match to Newspaper**	**TE 3 Match to Starter Log**
1	Move firewood from fire pit area onto deck	Move firewood from fire pit area onto deck
2	Place firewood into chiminea	Place firewood into chiminea
3	Move newspaper from recycle bin to chiminea	Go to store to purchase a starter log
4	Ignite match and hold to newspaper	Place starter log in chiminea
5		Ignite match and hold to starter log
Time Interval	30 min.	60 min.
Strategy and Assumptions	A) Rain > 20% < 40% / B) Can move enough wood for 4 hours / C) Have time to move wood just prior to getting ready with getting ready being 1.5 hours before start time / D) No more than 10 people at party at any given time unless also use house	A) Rain > 20% < 40% / B) Can move enough wood for 4 hours / C) Have time to move wood just prior to getting ready with getting ready being 1.5 hours before start time / D) No more than 10 people at party at any given time unless also use house / E) Have time to purchase starter log at store / F) Have money in budget to buy starter log

FIGURE 9-7: ALTERNATIVE DEFINED—IMPLEMENTATIONS (continued)

	Option 3—Fire Pit in Backyard	
Implementation Sequence	**TE 2 Match to Newspaper**	**TE 3 Match to Starter Log**
1	Move newspaper from recycle bin into fire pit	Go to store to purchase starter log
2	Ignite match and hold to newspaper	Place starter log in fire pit
3		Ignite match and hold to starter log
Time Interval	5 min.	30 min.
Strategy and Assumptions	A) Rain <= 20% / B) People willing to walk back and forth to house for drinks and food	A) Rain <= 20% / B) People willing to walk back and forth to house for drinks and food / C) Have time to purchase starter log at store / D) Have money in budget to buy starter log

In conclusion, what sort of concepts and understanding can we derive from this detailed example?

1. You are probably saying to yourself that it is unlikely that anyone would go through this much effort just to determine an implementation plan for something as simple as having a fire at a party. While I would agree with this observation, I choose to use a simple, somewhat commonplace example for two reasons:

   A. While how much documented detailed analysis we use may be unimportant, the example still reflects the reality of the significant amount of information, analysis, and dynamics that are involved when dealing with something as simple as having a fire at a party. The reality is that even if we do not write a single step down on a piece of paper, it is not unusual for us to consciously and/or subconsciously analyze all the information and dynamics outlined in the above change dynamics profile before mentally selecting an implementation plan for our party.

This fact further reinforces what has been continuously stressed in this book. We need to realize that the ability of individuals, organizations, and society to routinely and constantly select and implement primary defined processes to obtain desire change is amazing. Once again, the mind is an incredible thing.

More importantly, the second realization we should have is that the same change dynamics and environmental dynamics are at play no matter how simple or significant the selection of a primary defined process and associated defined implementation is. This should, in turn, reinforce the power that we can obtain through an understanding of the science of change. With the knowledge we derive from the science of change, we will be able to increase our ability to understand and affect the change we are constantly dealing with. **Bottom line, if we do not understand the simple, it is more difficult to tackle the significant.**

B. Using a simple example that we can easily relate to allows us to focus on how the procedures and tools associated with selecting a defined implementation work. Do not overlook the power of the procedures, tools, and thought processes because of the simplicity of the example. We must make sure we fully understand how these procedures and tools work so that we can be comfortable using them in situations where the decisions we are making are more significant.

2. This example clearly depicts how there are often multiple triggering events and multiple defined implementations to select

from, all of which could be utilized in reaching the goal of the same desired defined change. In addition, the availability of these alternative triggering events and defined implementations can be compounded when we also have alternative primary defined processes and/or primary environments to select from.

The take-away is that while there are situations where there may not be any or only one defined implementation available to select from in order to support a given primary defined process, it is also very common to have multiple alternative defined implementations to select from. As we found out when we explored the experience/change/power equation in Chapter 8, the defined implementation selected can often have unexpected ramifications, so we must exercise care as the significance of the desired primary defined change increases.

3. We should notice that these procedures and tools can incorporate both qualitative and subjective facets. There are not always right or wrong selections, and the selection of a specific defined implementation can often be significantly influenced by personal preferences.

    Some individuals might feel compelled to rely heavily on qualitative types of analysis. Others individuals might be far more subjective to their approach, thereby adjusting the strategies they incorporate into their implementation plans to compensate for a lack of quantitative reliance.

    For example, let us assume that enjoying a fire outdoors was subjectively very important to the decision maker. He or she might select the fire pit option no matter what and compensate with a strategy to incorporate the installation of a tent into their implementation plan.

4. Using these procedures and tools can provide powerful "what if" capability. In our example, it was easy to determine the

"what if" impact of weather conditions on the various alternative defined implementations.

We could also quickly determine the "what if" impact of using different strategies and assumptions. For example, based upon the weighting assumptions used in Figure 9-4 in our example, the ranking of the alternative options is as follows:

	Weighted Efficiency and Reliability Ranking		
Condition	Option 1 House	Option 2 Deck	Option 3 Fire Pit
Total weighted efficiency and reliability ranking	27	31	26

However, if we would have adjusted the weighting associated with "Protection from bad weather" from a 2 to a 3 and the weighting associated with "Location to drinks and food" from a 1 to a 2, the ranking of the alternative options would have instead been the following:

	Weighted Efficiency and Reliability Ranking		
Condition	Option 1 House	Option 2 Deck	Option 3 Fire Pit
Total weighted efficiency and reliability ranking	29	35	32

So the "what if" capability shifted our ranking of the options from 3/1/2 to 1/3/2.

5. Using these procedures and tools can help us develop a clearer understanding of the interrelationships that exist when selecting a defined implementation. The whole idea behind using change dynamic profiles is to get, at a minimum, a high-level quick grasp on the interrelationships and dynam-

ics that exist when trying to determine how to obtain a specific desired primary defined change.

Interestingly, these procedures and tools are not always in the context of formal written documentation. You often see individuals jotting down quick notes as part of their thought process, or "talking something through" with another individual, or doing some quick research on a topic. Generally, the more significant the primary defined change is to us, the more formal and detailed we want to be in the procedure used to select a primary defined process and associated defined implementation.

We are now in a position to take our discussion of defined processes and defined implementations to the next level in Chapter 10 with the introduction of systems.

CHAPTER TEN

Systems

Everything must be made as simple as possible, but not simpler.

ALBERT EINSTEIN

Let me start our discussion on systems by saying that I could write this book on change science without even introducing the concept of systems and technically not have any issues. This is due to the fact that all the change around us will follow the same three elements of change and four principles of change irrespective of the concept of a system.

A system does not represent an underlying element, principle, theory, or attribute in change science. Instead, *a system represents a technique/tool of utilizing the underlying technical concepts of change science so as to obtain a specific objective (that is, specific change or set of changes).*

However, even though the subject of systems lacks the change science requirements for inclusion as an underlying element, principle, or theory, the use of systems can be extremely powerful. Therefore, an understanding of systems can prove very beneficial when we are dealing with change.

In addition, the use of the term "system" is common in everyday vernacular. Therefore, clearly defining a system within the framework of change science will help incorporate it properly within the context of the change we are dealing with in our daily lives.

DEFINITION OF A SYSTEM

Up to this point, we have tended to discuss change in more of a singular context. It is true that we have had a great deal of discussion on how a given defined process and/or defined implementation can have numerous defined changes/processes/implementations "incorporated" in them as process factors and/or implementation factors. Nevertheless, we have still been accurately focusing on change as a single discrete combination of a defined process and defined implementation that result in a specific associated defined change.

However, in many cases it might be easier to view/comprehend the ability to obtain a defined change or, more importantly, a set of defined changes in the context of a combination of multiple individual changes. This can especially be true if the execution of the individual changes requires the utilization of different resources for execution (such as, different people performing different individual changes).

For example, if we want to change the location of a piano in a room with no furniture, we can do it with a single process of pushing it from one location in the room to another. But what happens if the change is moving a piano into a room full of furniture and the piano is currently located in a warehouse across town?

We can certainly look at this in the context of one long interval of time with a single defined process operating in a single large primary environment that has many process factors associated with it. However, we can also successfully accomplish this change by breaking it down into multiple defined changes and associated defined processes that are implemented and executed in multiple smaller primary environments with the use of different resources. The series of changes might look like this:

1. Defined change 1 = Change the location of the piano from the warehouse to the house. Executed by the movers in primary environment—warehouse/house.
2. Defined change 2 = Change the doorway by removing the door. Executed by the movers in primary environment—house.
3. Defined change 3 = Change the location of certain furniture in order to provide unencumbered access to the desired location in the room. Executed by the homeowners in primary environment—the specific room in the house.
4. Defined change 4 = Change the location of the piano from outside the house to the desired location in the room. Executed by the movers in primary environment—house.
5. Defined change 5 = Change the doorway by replacing the door. Executed by the movers in primary environment—house.
6. Defined change 6 = Change the furniture back to the original locations. Executed by the homeowners in primary environment—the specific room in the house.

Each one of these changes requires development of a defined change, defined process, and defined implementation in order for us to successfully reach the end goal of changing the location of the piano from the warehouse to a specific location in our room. However, the key is that the amalgamation/combination of all of these changes still represents the accomplishment of the overall defined change of moving the location of the piano from the warehouse to a specific location in our room. It is this amalgamation/combination of multiple defined changes in order to obtain an overall defined change, or set of defined changes, that represents a system.

Therefore, in change science, a *system* (Figure10-1) is defined as the amalgamation and combination of two or more defined changes and associated defined processes and defined implementations that are configured and implemented in such a way along the change/time continuum that when they are executed in their totality, they result in a specific overall defined change or set of defined changes.

So a system allows us to break down the desired defined change into a more manageable and understandable series of defined changes and associated defined processes and defined implementations.

Given this definition for a system, we can also define an *overall defined change* to represent the output from a system consisting of a specific defined change or set of defined changes.

There is an abundance of examples of systems in our daily lives:

- A heating and air-conditioning system creates the overall defined change of heat and/or cool air in a room starting with the defined change/process/implementation associated with the thermostat on the wall and ending with the defined implementation/process/change of blowing the air into the room through a series of ducts.
- A payroll system creates the overall defined change of payment to an individual for services rendered starting with the defined implementation/process/change of accumulating the hours worked and ending with the defined implementation/process/change of the transfer of money to the individual.
- A garbage collection system creates the overall defined change of collecting and disposing of a citizen's garbage starting with the defined implementation/process/change of distributing collection receptacles to participating citizens and ending

with the defined implementation/process/change of delivery of the garbage to the landfill.

Figure 10-1
A System Producing Overall Defined Change

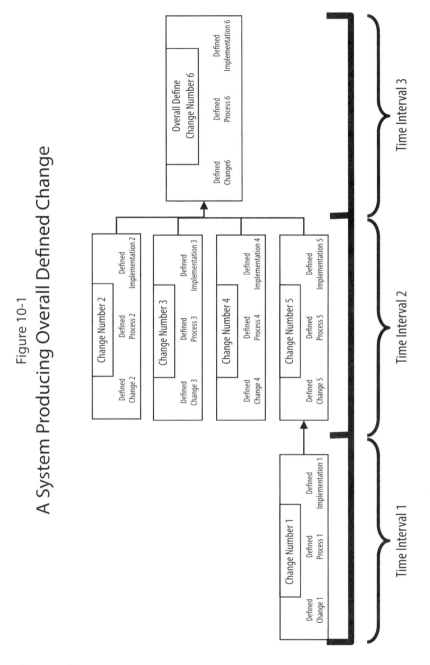

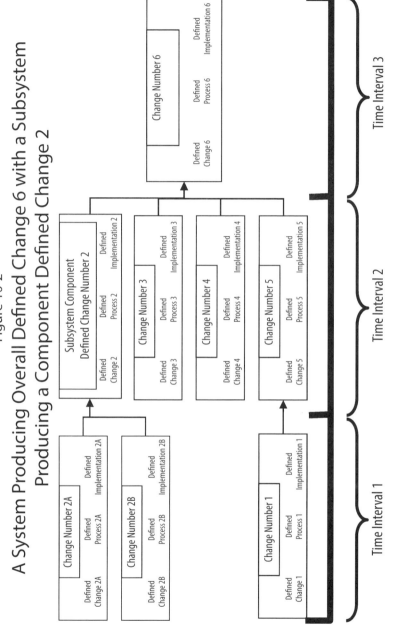

Figure 10-2
A System Producing Overall Defined Change 6 with a Subsystem Producing a Component Defined Change 2

A *subsystem* (Figure 10-2) is defined as a set of defined changes and associated defined processes and defined implementations that represent both a system in and of itself and also a part of a larger system.

Other Characteristics of a System

- It is important to note that, for our purposes, a single defined change will not be considered a system. Therefore, a system in change science requires at least two or more defined changes executing during the change/time continuum, resulting in an overall defined change. It is the delineation of defined changes for a given system that will go to the heart of what represents the makeup of that given system.
- The implementation and execution of the individual defined changes/processes/implementations that are incorporated into a system can occur sequentially and/or simultaneously along the change/time continuum in one or more environments. In our piano moving example above, defined change 3 (change the location of certain furniture in order to provide unencumbered access to the desired location in the room) can be executed by the homeowners "simultaneously" in their primary environment while the execution of defined change 1 (change the location of the piano from the warehouse to the house) is being executed by the movers in a different primary environment.
- Since a system is composed of a set of underlying defined changes/processes/implementations, it is important to recognize that all the concepts already discussed in this book regarding defined changes, defined processes, defined implementations, change dynamics, and environmental dynamics also apply to systems!

- Since a system represents a series of defined changes/processes/implementations for the ultimate accomplishment of the overall defined change, a system also allows us to improve our ability to explore alternative defined processes for each defined change that is incorporated into the system. This in turn increases our opportunity to determine if certain alternative defined processes work better in supporting the overall system.

Types of Systems

We will be exploring discrete systems (one-offs) and repeatable systems (recur in a consistent context and with consistent results at multiple points in time on the change/time continuum) in detail below. However, there are other types of systems that you should be aware of:

1. *Systems can be both naturally-occurring systems and/or cognitively-influenced systems.* Many people probably think of systems strictly in a context of requiring human involvement. However, nature is full of systems including repeatable systems that under the laws of science will naturally occur if conditions in the environment support them. From the tides that occur every day on Earth to a multitude of chemical reactions we see in the environment we live in to the combustion that takes place in the engines of our automobiles, we have come to rely on all sorts of these naturally-occurring repeatable systems.
2. *Personal systems.* These are systems that are specific to obtaining overall defined change at an individual, organizational, or societal level. For example, if you go to work daily, you have probably created a personal system that you follow each day that is unique to your desired defined change. So while other

individuals might also have a system they use to go to work, their system would be unique (personal) to them, and yours would be unique (personal) to you even though you would both have the same overall defined change of going to work in the morning from where you live.

3. *Off-the-shelf/canned systems.* These are systems developed and promoted by individuals, organizations, and societies to provide products, services, or change methodologies across a diverse base of possible users and/or environments. For example:

    - Off-the-shelf/canned service. When you use FedEx, UPS, or the like, you are using a system that these organizations have developed to provide the service of moving items such as packages from one location to another location.
    - Off-the-shelf/canned product. Likewise, when you buy a can of motor oil or a pound of hamburger meat from the store, you are accessing a system or set of systems utilized by organizations that provide these products to you.
    - Off-the-shelf/canned change methodology. If you read a book that explains a certain methodology to obtain a certain defined change (for example, to lose weight or to accomplish a do-it-yourself home repair), you are probably accessing a system that the author has developed. However, not only is it a system to obtain a certain desired defined change, but also it is an off-the-shelf/canned system that can be used by a multitude of people or organizations.

4. *Multi-causal systems.* Most systems are multi-causal in that they either utilize other types of systems or evolve from other types of systems. For example:

- An off-the-shelf repeatable system might depend on and/or incorporate certain naturally-occurring repeatable systems.
- A repeatable methodology system promoted by an author might have been developed from a personal repeatable system he or she originally utilized in his or her personal life.
- An off-the-shelf/canned service, product, or change methodology might be "customized" to some level to become more personal in nature to the individual, organization, or society that is considering using it.

REASONS FOR USING A SYSTEM

Major reasons for using a system include:

1. Systems can play a critical role in our ability to obtain the change we desire.
2. Systems can represent an overall defined change that is broader in context than just a single defined change.
3. Systems can provide an ability to standardize.
4. Systems can improve our ability to control the change that is occurring around us.
5. Systems can represent a path to continuous improvement.
6. Systems can be an excellent technique of capturing and quantifying our experience and knowledge base relative to change.

Systems and Our Ability to Obtain Change

We have already determined that a defined process must execute in a single primary environment over a continuous time interval. We also discussed how increasing the size of a primary defined process (that is, increasing the number of process factors including other defined processes embedded within the primary defined process) and/or increasing the time interval associated with the primary defined process can increase the risk of failure to obtain the desired defined change.

Since a system is made up of multiple defined changes, we can take an incremental approach to obtaining a desired overall defined change. This means that:

1. Each individual defined change incorporated into a system can be executed in its own primary environment. Therefore, as noted above, the execution of these individual incremental defined changes can be sequential and/or simultaneous along the change/time continuum.
2. We increase our ability to reduce the length of the time interval associated each individual defined change.
3. We have the ability to obtain change through a predefined configuration of independent defined changes that, when executed in their totality, provide the overall defined change that we are looking for.
4. A system can incorporate additional defined processes/defined changes that in turn differentiate the overall defined change produced by that specific system from a corresponding underlying desired defined change.

    For example, we can have a primary defined process that can produce an underlying desired defined change of watering our lawn. But what if the ultimate desired defined change also requires watering the lawn only between 2:00 am and 3:00 am in the morning? Then the "time of day" represents a condition that is in addition to the underlying conditions that are required to support the underlying process factors associated with the execution of the primary defined process of watering the lawn.

Therefore, sprinkler systems have been created. These systems produce the capability to have an overall defined change that includes not only (a) the execution of the defined process associated with obtaining the defined change of watering the lawn but also (b) a defined process/defined change to monitor the time of day and water the lawn specifically between 2:00 am and 3:00 am in the morning.

The above flexibility associated with the use of multiple defined changes and multiple primary environments, therefore, can help reduce the risks and broaden the criteria associated with obtaining the desired change we are looking for.

At this point in time you might be asking how does this differ from a defined implementation? It is true that, just like a system, a defined implementation can also have multiple individual defined changes incorporated in it that can execute in multiple environments sequentially and/or simultaneously. However, the objective of a defined implementation is very specific and can be different from the objective of a system.

The objective of a defined implementation is to create the conditions in a specific primary environment necessary to support the execution of a specific defined process. On the other hand, the objective of a system is to obtain a specific overall defined change (that is, a specific defined change or set of defined changes) through the use of two or more defined changes.

At the risk of confusing the issue, this does mean, however, that if an implementation has two or more defined processes that, therefore, represent two or more defined changes, such a defined implementation could, by definition, be considered a system. In this case, the overall defined change would be the creation of the required conditions in the primary environment to support the execution of a specific defined process. Sometimes such an implementation is referred to as an *implementation system*.

However, we must be careful in our thought process and make sure we recognize the following:

1. A defined implementation can only be considered a system if it has two or more defined processes and associated defined changes embedded in it as implementation factors. *Therefore, not all defined implementations are systems.* Any defined implementation with only one defined process as an implementation factor (that is, a triggering event) cannot be by definition a system. For example, if a piece of paper is in the same environment as a bonfire, then throwing the paper into the bonfire represents a single defined process creating the triggering event condition that initiates combustion of the paper resulting in a defined implementation that is not a system.
2. While there are situations where a defined implementation can be considered a system, *not all systems are defined implementations. A system is only a defined implementation when the objective of the overall defined change is the creation of conditions in a specific primary environment to support the execution of a primary defined process (in other words the same objective as that of a defined implementation).* As described in the examples earlier in this chapter, there are obviously many systems that are created with an objective of creating an overall defined change that has nothing to do with the implementation of a specific defined process.
3. Finally, to further cloud the issue, we must recognize that *implementation systems are not the same as a systems implementation.* An implementation system is a specific defined implementation with two or more defined processes embedded in it as implementation factors, that is, in turn, being referred to as a system.

   On the other hand, a *system implementation* is the methodology associated with the implementation of a specific system. In other words, as we will discuss shortly, systems also need to be implemented, which, in turn, is referred to as a system implementation (the implementation of that specific system).

Systems and Overall Defined Change Versus a Defined Change

Systems can represent an overall defined change that is broader in context than just a single defined change. If we so choose, a system allows us to establish an overall defined change that represents multiple defined changes (a set of defined changes) and, therefore, is not limited to a single defined change.

For example, let's say you own a restaurant and one of the items on your menu is a spaghetti dinner composed of spaghetti, meat sauce, and a salad, all of which are prepared fresh and presented simultaneously for each new customer order. On one hand, you can view this as three individual defined changes as follows:

1. Prepare and present the salad to the customer. Takes four minutes to prepare at the salad station.
2. Prepare and present the spaghetti to the customer. Takes 10 minutes to prepare at the cooking station.
3. Prepare and present the meat sauce to the customer. Takes six minutes to prepare at the cooking station.

However, under this context, each order would have to be coordinated as three individual defined changes each time an order for this menu item is received. Therefore, it is more likely that, as the owner, you would prefer to create a repeatable system for this menu item. In this way, when a customer order is received, your staff can follow a specific sequence of a predetermined configuration of defined changes in order to prepare and present this order simultaneously to the customer. In other words, the overall defined change would be the preparation and presentation of a spaghetti dinner composed of a salad, spaghetti, and meat sauce executed upon receipt of a customer order.

In this case, the system might look like this (remember the spaghetti, meat sauce and salad take 10, 6 and 4 minutes to prepare respectively):

Change/Time Continuum	Defined Process	Defined Change
Point in time = 0 minutes		Order received from customer equals the triggering event for the execution of the system
Point in time = 0 minutes	Cook begins execution of preparing the spaghetti	
Point in time = 4 minutes	Cook monitors time starting with the execution of preparing the spaghetti	Time equaling 4 minutes is the triggering event for the execution of the defined process to prepare the meat sauce
Point in time = 4 minutes	Cook begins execution of preparing the meat sauce	
Point in time = 6 minutes	Cook informs salad station that 4 minutes remain	Triggering event for the execution of the defined process to prepare the salad
Point in time = 6 minutes	Salad station begins execution of preparing the salad	
Point in time = 10 minutes	Defined processes of preparation of the spaghetti, meat sauce, and salad have been completed	Spaghetti, meat sauce, and salad all prepared and represents the triggering event for the presentation to the customer
Point in time = 10 minutes	Defined process of consolidation and presentation of spaghetti, meat sauce, and salad to the customer	
Point in time = 11 minutes	Defined process of consolidation and presentation of spaghetti, meat sauce, and salad to the customer has been completed	Customer has received spaghetti, meat sauce, and salad

From this example you should recognize that the end result of the overall defined change is exactly the same as if we viewed this in the context of the execution of three independent defined changes. However by creating a system we gain the following advantages:

- We are able *to create an overall defined change composed of multiple (a set of) interrelated independent defined changes in a meaningful context.* In this example, that context is a specific customer menu item (spaghetti dinner) composed of three independent components (a salad, spaghetti, and meat sauce).
- We are able *to configure the execution and sequence* of the various defined changes so as *to meet specific timing requirements* associated with the overall defined change. This allows us to provide all three components of the meal simultaneously in a more efficient manner.
- We are able *to integrate additional defined changes and defined processes* into the system configuration so as *to establish an ability to repeat the execution of the system* in the future in order to consistently obtain the same overall defined change. The inclusion of the defined processes and defined changes associated with the monitoring of the time and the communication of when to start the salad preparation represents this sort of additional capability provided by a system.
- Finally, by using a repeatable system, we are able *to establish a training tool and execution methodology* that can be used *to reduce direct intervention and coordination.* Once the system is established, the owner no longer has to worry about coordinating the execution of three independent defined processes/changes. Instead, he or she can train the staff on a methodology (system) that would repeatedly provide the overall de-

fined change (spaghetti dinner) without direct intervention or coordination.

Systems and Our Ability to Standardize

Standardization is central to the benefits derived from the use of systems at the individual, organizational, and societal levels and has been a main driver behind the continuous improvement in our standard of living.

For example, a major concern of many fast food restaurants, as well as restaurants in general, is being able to consistently provide the same tasting food and the same quality of food over and over again in both the same environment and across multiple environments. They want their customers to experience a consistent taste and quality no matter how often they eat at the same restaurant or at different restaurants located all around the world.

Early pioneers in the fast food business quickly came to depend on standardized repeatable systems to accomplish this objective. Once a reliable repeatable system was developed, it was standardized and launched as a standard operating procedure at all of their restaurant locations.

Just as in the above example, the system to provide a spaghetti dinner could be executed repeatedly with a high expectation that the same results (that is, desired overall defined change) would be obtained each time. In addition, such a system provides an easy way to document procedures and provide training in both a single environment or across multiple environments.

Systems and Our Ability to Control Change

The ability to configure and integrate multiple defined changes within a system provides an ideal opportunity to create monitoring and control points. This is especially helpful when we are dealing with change that is occurring across multiple environments and/or over different time intervals on the change/time continuum. Obviously, incorporating a capability to adjust the timing and execution of the defined processes that are executing within a system based upon what is actually transpiring within the various environments improves our ability to reduce risk.

Remember that many of the decisions that are made relative to the selection of specific defined processes and defined implementations are based upon the change dynamics and environmental dynamics that "we anticipate will take place" within any given environment or environments. Therefore, having an ability to adjust or modify these selections based upon the exposure to the actual events taking place in these environments greatly increases our opportunity to obtain the desired change we seek.

A good example of this capability can be found again in the above example regarding the system that produces a spaghetti dinner. The defined process of monitoring the time associated with the production of the spaghetti can also be viewed as a control point. By doing so, the cooks executing the defined process associated with preparing the spaghetti can adjust the timing of the execution of the defined process associated with the meat sauce and/or salad. They can do this based upon the actual change and environmental dynamics that exist as the execution of the defined process of producing the spaghetti proceeds along the change/time continuum.

In other words, if the defined process associated with the preparation of the spaghetti is for some reason executing more slowly than expected, the cooks can wait (that is, adjust the timing) before they begin to execute the defined process associated with the meat sauce and before they tell the salad station to begin the execution of the defined process to prepare the salad. Likewise, if there is a new person at the salad station, the cooks may decide to increase the time interval of the defined process associated with preparing the salad by communicating with the salad station earlier than otherwise would be expected.

In Chapters 11 and 12 on risk, we will explore further how the utilization of monitoring and control points can reduce risk when attempting to obtain either a single defined change and/or an overall defined change. For now, the take-away is that the use of a system can often provide an ideal opportunity to leverage off of the benefits that are inherent in the use of monitoring and control points.

Systems and Continuous Improvement

Another important aspect associated with the use of systems is the capability to continually look for improvements in our ability to obtain the overall defined change. These improvements might be in effectiveness, reliability, efficiency, or any combination thereof. As a specific system is repeatedly executed, our ability to observe, to modify, and/or test defined processes/implementations and system configurations increases.

This, in turn, provides the ability to look for continuous improvements in the way a system operates and performs. For example, we can once again look at the above example of the system used to obtain the overall defined change of a spaghetti dinner. Let us say we believe that having a pot of boiling water constantly available might help reduce the time interval associated with the preparation of the spaghetti (that is, the longest lead-time component of the spaghetti dinner). Testing this belief within the system would allow us to determine if the overall time interval associated with providing a spaghetti dinner to the customer would, in fact, improve.

If it does, then such an improvement can be incorporated into the system. If not, then the system remains the same. *The key is that the existing system becomes the benchmark with which we can determine whether or not an improvement actually takes place and by how much.* Without an existing system as a benchmark to measure by, it becomes much more difficult to determine if improvements are real or not and, if so, by how much.

Systems and Our Ability to Capture Experience and Knowledge

We have already continually stressed the importance of experience and knowledge and even introduced the experience/change/power equation. Unfortunately, without adequate documentation that is easily accessible, such experience and knowledge can often be lost.

It is in this regard that repeatable systems can play a vital role in the creation and retention of experiences and knowledge. Through repeatable systems, individuals, organizations, and societies can encapsulate experiences and knowledge, providing an understanding of defined changes, defined processes, and defined implementations. In addition, an understanding is also developed of any ensuing overall defined change that results from a specific configuration of this information.

For example, the system we created to obtain the overall defined change of a spaghetti dinner encapsulates all the information regarding the defined changes, defined processes, and defined implementations necessary in order either to continue to repeat this system moving forward or to share this capability with others on an as needed basis.

While systems are not the only way to capture and share experiences and knowledge, they do provide an invaluable way of doing so. More importantly, while it is always preferential to formally document a system, history and mankind are full of examples in which repeatable systems have been excellent methods for the transfer of experience and knowledge from one generation to another generation even when the system was never formally documented.

DISCRETE AND REPEATABLE SYSTEMS

In our quest to understand systems, it is often helpful to distinguish the various contexts in which systems are used. We have already alluded to systems that can be repeatable in that the system is constructed to be either naturally or cognitively repeatable over time. On the other hand, a system can be discrete in that, while the system can be duplicated, it has not been specifically constructed to be repeated over time.

There are some basics that apply to both discrete and repeatable systems:

- A given system, whether discrete or repeatable, might represent only one approach out of many possible approaches that could be utilized to obtain a given overall defined change. For example, the systems utilized by Fedex, UPS, and DHL all have different characteristics associated with them even though they all have the same objective (that is, overall defined change) of delivering your package from point A to point B. In addition, within each of these organizations there is probably a good chance that they have alternative systems to select from for delivering your package (for example, next day versus three days).
- The understanding and documentation of both the discrete systems and repeatable systems are good ways of capturing experiences and enhancing our knowledge base as individuals, organizations, and societies. This experience and knowledge base, in turn, can be beneficial when selecting specific defined processes and defined implementations as outlined in Chapters 7 through 9.

- Even though it has already been noted above, it is worth emphasizing that since a system is composed of two or more defined changes, then all the underlying principles and concepts related to defined changes and associated defined processes and defined implementations also apply to all systems. This includes the concepts and influences associated with change dynamics and environmental dynamics.

Discrete Systems

Discrete systems represent systems that are intended to obtain an overall defined change that is one-off in context.

Discrete systems are constantly used every day by individuals, organizations, and society. We might create a discrete system to obtain the overall defined change of traveling somewhere special. An organization can create a discrete system to obtain an overall defined change of building a prototype product. And a city might create a discrete system in order to obtain an overall defined change of holding a one-off special event. The common theme is that at the time such a system is developed, it is done to address the need to obtain an overall defined change that is not expected to recur in the future.

Since a discrete system is only expected to be executed one time, discrete systems would always be considered a personal system (that is, specifically oriented to the specific individual, organization, or society that will use it). However, that is not to say that a discrete system cannot be duplicated. For example, if you develop a system to obtain an overall defined change of a fire pit in your backyard, your next door neighbors could utilize that same system to create a fire pit in their backyards, even though your system was originally developed as a discrete system from your perspective.

Discrete systems can also become the foundation for, or transition into, repeatable systems. In our fire pit example, if all your neighbors decided to utilize your system to create a fire pit in their backyards, then the system that was initially discrete to you has now morphed into a repeatable system. In fact, you might determine that there is an opportunity to establish a business of creating fire pits in people's backyards and develop an off-the-shelf/canned repeatable system based upon the discrete system you initially created.

In addition, a discrete system could be incorporated into a broader set of changes such as a subsystem of a larger repeatable system. A good example of this would be a repeatable system used for the next day pickup and delivery of packages. While the structure of an overall repeatable system might be constant in context, the subsystem associated with the actual daily pickup of the packages from customers could be considered discrete.

This is due to the fact that the location of the customers requiring pickup would vary daily. This in turn generates a requirement to create a new discrete system each day in order to obtain the overall defined change of producing a route to pick up all the packages based upon that particular customer mix. Since it is generally unlikely that a customer mix would be the same from one day to the next, this subsystem could be considered discrete from one day to the next.

Finally, discrete systems can be future-focused. For example, let us assume that a city develops an emergency response system to control the overall defined change that is expected to take place if a natural disaster occurs within the community. The anticipation is that the likelihood of executing this system would be low to none, in essence making it a future-focused personal discrete system for that city.

Repeatable Systems

Repeatable systems represent systems that are intended to recur in a consistent context and with consistent resulting overall defined change at multiple points in time on the change/time continuum.

In Chapter 6 we were introduced to the concept of repeatable change and the influence it has had, and continues to have, on us as individuals, organizations, and society. While repeatable change does not have to be represented by a repeatable system, the reality is that much of the repeatable change that has occurred or will occur moving forward leverages off of the use of repeatable systems. Therefore, it would be a good exercise to take a look back at Chapter 6 to recognize the relationship and overlap between the discussion to follow on repeatable systems and our prior discussion on repeatable change.

To start with, much of the change we deal with as individuals, organizations, and societies has a certain amount of routine and repetition connected with it. It does not matter if it is a daily routine we follow when we get up in the morning and get ready to go to work or if it is a machine at work that changes a piece of material into an end product that we sell: there are repeatable systems that we rely on when managing all the change in our lives. These repeatable systems provide ongoing benefits when dealing with the change we face as individuals, organizations, and society.

Therefore, one of the main drivers in the development and use of a repeatable system is the inherent propensity for individuals, organizations, and societies to want to avoid continually conceptualizing over and over again a solution for obtaining a recurring defined change or, more specifically, a recurring overall defined change.

Potential Disadvantages of Repeatable Systems

Repeatable systems have their advantages and disadvantages. *Inherent in repeatable systems are all the advantages already outlined above for systems in general.*

However, there are also disadvantages that need to be taken into consideration when an individual, organization, or society uses repeatable systems:

1. The output from a repeatable system may not fully match up in its ability to provide a specific desired defined change/overall defined change. This can especially be true of a third party off-the-shelf repeatable system.

    For example, if you need to get a package delivered the next day, then using a service provider that has an off-the-shelf repeatable system that can only support a three-day delivery is not acceptable. Likewise, paying an added cost to a service provider that only has a one-day guaranteed off-the-shelf repeatable system also does not make sense if a three-day delivery is an acceptable desired overall defined change for you.

2. Just because you have a repeatable system, there is no guarantee that the desired defined change you are looking for will always be successful. People, organizations, and society often have this false sense of security that a repeatable system they are relying on will always work. However, repeatable systems are subject to the same exposures to failure as any other type of defined change.

    For example, they are susceptible to the change science principle of environmental override in that environmental conditions must still exist that will support the implementation and process factors required in the repeatable system. So even though you use the same repeatable system to drive to work for an entire year without a problem, it does not mean that the next day your repeatable system will not fail if the environment includes a condition of delays because of a traffic accident along your route.

Likewise, even the most reliable of delivery service providers who have spent significant amounts of money on backup and contingency plans can have failures associated with major weather related problems in the environment they must operate in.

3. Many repeatable systems, especially third party off-the-shelf repeatable systems, are provided/promoted by consultants and outside service providers that have a vested interest in a specific off-the-shelf solution or have a skewed preference to a particular theory or methodology. Therefore, if these providers are utilized, they can negatively influence and affect the analysis associated with a particular desired change and the resulting process that is selected to execute the desired change.

This can lead to an unsuccessful desired change. Interestingly, my experience has shown that more often than not, it is the consultant or the vendor of a third party off-the-shelf repeatable system that makes the comment that the implementation of their process is failing because of a lack of commitment.

Do not misunderstand me; I strongly believe that consultants and experts can often improve the odds of obtaining a successful desired change. However, I think this is associated more with their ability to draw on a broad experience base for knowledge transfer and guidance than it is with their necessarily having a perfect fit off-the-shelf repeatable system or change methodology. Just use caution!

4. Finally, a focus on selecting an off-the-shelf repeatable system or specific consultants can often center the attention on

dollars and off-the-shelf repeatable system functionality. This in turn can lead to a lack of proper analysis of the specific requirements associated with obtaining a specific desired change.

While an individual or organization may appear to get the biggest bang for the buck or obtain certain functionality that appears to be appealing, in reality they get a system that will not support a successful desired overall change.

For example, how often have you as an individual or a businessperson been convinced to purchase a third party off-the-shelf repeatable system (for example, a piece of software or maybe a mobile phone) based upon certain promoted functionality or an appealing price point. You did this only to find that, at the end of the day, what you purchased really does not provide the functionality (that is, the desired overall defined change) that you really require.

Maybe it is because the off-the-shelf repeatable system totally lacks the capability to provide the desired overall defined change you require. Or maybe, it is because the environment you are operating in does not contain the conditions required to make it work (for example, a lack of cell tower capacity in the area you most often operate in). In any case, in the end you are disappointed that you are not receiving the result you require.

Favorable Characteristics to Look For in a Repeatable System

So what sort of expectations should we have relative to repeatable systems? For a repeatable system to be beneficial, it should have certain characteristics:

1. That the execution of a repeatable system has validity and reliability to consistently produce an expected overall defined change.
2. That the use of a repeatable system will be effective in producing 100 percent of the desired overall defined change that we require it to provide.
3. That the use of a repeatable system represents an efficient (but not necessarily the most efficient) alternative way to obtain a specific overall defined change.
4. That environmental considerations associated with a repeatable system are understandable and recognizable so as to provide guidance relative to any strengths and/or limitations that might exist when executing the system in alternative environments.
5. That there is the potential for continuous improvement.

It should not be surprising that validity, reliability, effectiveness, and efficiency are at the heart of the expectations and benefits associated with a repeatable system. It would not make sense to continue to use the same system over and over again if it never produces the overall defined change we are expecting (that is, it is not valid).

Nor would it make sense to use a repeatable system that is valid but has a low reliability. For example, if the valid route we use to go to work consistently has construction along it that makes us late 40 percent of the time, we would view it as unreliable and search for an alternative method to go to work (an alternative system) that was both valid and more reliable.

Likewise, a system that tends to be ineffective would be of limited value. For example, let us say that a supplier has a repeatable system that is supposed to produce and deliver 100 pieces of material to you every week. However, if that supplier consistently can only produce and deliver 80 pieces, you would considered their system to be ineffective, and you would probably discontinue using that supplier.

Finally, inherent in the use of a system is some level of expectation of efficiency. While we might not be able to tell if a system is the most efficient, we probably have determined that it is more efficient than other alternatives we have considered. For example, we are relatively certain that using a reputable package delivery service provider would be more efficient than getting into our car and personally delivering the package across the country.

In addition to expectations regarding validity, reliability, effectiveness, and efficiency, there are two other characteristics of repeatable systems that deserve close examination. As pointed out above, one is that repeatable systems are subject to the change dynamics and environmental dynamics in which they are intended to operate. Therefore, while the benefits of a repeatable system might be obtainable under certain environmental dynamics, they might be limited or nonexistent under a different set of environmental dynamics.

For example, delivery system providers that service only a local geographical area would be of no value if they need to deliver a package under the environmental dynamics associated with an international delivery. Consequently, a clear understanding of the environmental considerations associated with a repeatable system can be critical when considering utilizing a repeatable system.

Another characteristic—in addition to validity, reliability, effectiveness, efficiency, and environmental factors—that must be considered regarding repeatable systems is the potential for continuous improvement. There is an old saying that states, "If you build a better mousetrap, the world will beat a path to your door." As already discussed, the use of systems in the context of change science has played a significant role in the advancement of society's standard of living.

This is due in part to the fact that there is often an expectation that systems will tend to improve and advance over time. It is anticipated that systems will leverage off of the existing experience and knowledge in an attempt to look for enhanced structures, thereby driving progress. Therefore, repeatable systems that present opportunities for continuous improvement are generally preferable to those that do not have such a capability or focus.

Repeatable Versus Repetitive

It should be noted that I have intentionally avoided the use of the term *repetitive* system in favor of *repeatable* system. While there can often be circumstances in which "repeatable" and "repetitive" can be interchangeable, it is my feeling that "repetitive" more closely implies adherence to a specific process over and over again. The use of control points, alternative processes, environmental dynamics, and continuous improvement seems less relevant to a repetitive system than to a repeatable system.

The use of repeatable system terminology is intended to focus more on a system that is oriented to consistently provide the same overall defined change. Focusing on the ability to repeatedly and consistently obtain the same overall defined change provides the flexibility necessary to incorporate the use of control points, alternative processes, environmental dynamics, and continuous improvement into the discussion.

DEVELOPMENT AND IMPLEMENTATION OF A SYSTEM

To begin with, it should be noted that the world is already full of books, methodologies, experts, and service providers on how to develop and/or implement systems. Therefore, it is not the intent here to provide a specific how-to approach to system development and/or system implementations. Such a goal is beyond the scope of this book.

Instead, the goal here is to show how change science should interact with and influence the development and/or implementation of a system. In addition, in the next section on the evaluation and selection of a system, we will also explain how individuals, organizations, and society can leverage off of change science when evaluating and selecting the possible systems that are under consideration.

What have we learned from change science that can influence the development and implementation of a system? First and foremost, we have discovered that, by definition, a system is composed of two or more defined changes that, in turn, also represent two or more associated defined processes and defined implementations.

Therefore, everything that we have learned about defined change, defined processes, defined implementations, change dynamics, and environmental dynamics must be taken into account when developing and/or implementing a system. *It is important to remember that if any of the defined changes incorporated within the configuration of a system fails to execute for whatever reason, then the overall defined change associated with that system will not be obtained.*

This means that when a system is developed and implemented, it is critical that both the individual components (that is, the individual defined changes/processes/implementations) incorporated into the system and also the configuration of the system in its totality have validity, effectiveness, and reliability.

This, of course, starts by making sure up front that there is a clear understanding and a definition of what exactly the overall defined change is. Keep in mind that this objective is just like the objective we have expressed regarding an individual defined change. However, with a system, it can be broader in context given that an overall defined change can represent not only a specific single desired defined change but also a set of desired defined changes.

For example, a package delivery service might develop and implement a system that incorporates into its overall defined change two separate desired defined changes. One is the defined change of the movement of customer packages from point A to point B. A second would be the defined change of the movement of an airplane from point A to point B. In this case, the defined change associated with the movement of the packages supports two objectives.

One objective is providing customers the ultimate delivery of their packages. The second objective associated with the movement of the airplane creates a condition in the environment in which the plane is now at a location that can support the execution of a defined process to transport a new set of packages from point B to point C. Bottom line, there is a set of two desired defined changes incorporated into the overall defined change that is related to this system.

Once we have a clear definition of the overall defined change we are looking for, change science next tells us that it is generally best to take an incremental approach when dealing with change. Therefore, the same is true when developing and implementing a system. Breaking a system down into incremental steps (that is, incremental defined changes) allows us to:

- Potentially minimize the process factors and implementation factors and shorten the time intervals associated with each incremental defined change, thereby increasing the likelihood of reducing execution risk.
- Incorporate monitoring and control points within the system. This provides flexibility through the use of alternative defined processes based upon the actual change and environmental dynamics that have taken place within any relevant

environments. Once again, this can help reduce execution risk.
- Leverage off of the use of multiple environments since each individual defined change incorporated within a system can be executed in its own primary environment.
- Leverage off of the sequencing of the execution of the individual defined changes. Given that each individual defined change can be executed independently of one another, taking an incremental approach to the development and implementation of a system allows maximum flexibility in our ability to execute our defined changes. Execution can be either sequential and/or simultaneous based upon the specific execution requirements of that system.

If we closely examine some of the systems we come into contact with, especially complex systems, we will see that they are often designed and implemented in exactly this incremental fashion. This is often most depicted by the modular design found in many systems.

For example, it is common to see a business accounting system with a separate general ledger module, accounts payable module, accounts receivable module, payroll module, and so on. In addition, each of these individual modules is generally further broken down into its own individual incremental modules based upon the specific functionality (that is, specific defined change) it represents. This can be illustrated by looking at the accounts receivable module where we will probably find a separate module to handle the incremental function of invoicing the customer versus the incremental function of collecting and posting the cash received from the customer.

Of course, all this discussion naturally flows into two major change science considerations: change dynamics and environmental dynamics. Consistent with what we have learned about defined processes and defined implementations, it is possible to have a system that has a 100 percent valid configuration and implementation. However, this valid system can still fail because of the change dynamics and environmental dynamics associated with the environment or environments it must execute in. In other words, a system can look great conceptually but be impractical or limited in the environments in which it must execute.

Therefore, when developing and/or implementing a system, strong consideration must be given to the change science concepts associated with change dynamics and environmental dynamics. Failure to do so can lead to the development and/or implementation of a valid system that will not provide the overall defined change you are looking for or that is limited in the environmental scope you desire.

At this point we might ask if it is really necessary to put this level of energy into the development and implementation of every system we come into contact with. The answer is, of course, no. Change science reminds us that the level of effort, including cost, we expend on any given defined change should take into consideration the significance of that defined change.

The same holds true with systems. The more important the ramifications associated with the execution of a system and the accomplishment of the overall defined change, the more the effort we should put forth.

A good example of this is the development and implementation of computer aided design (CAD) systems. Today, there are all sorts of CAD systems available in the marketplace including those that can be used by the average person for such tasks as designing a home or deck. However, originally only the large corporations in the automotive and airplane industries could justify the effort and cost connected with the development and implementation of these sorts of CAD systems. That was because the significance that these sorts of CAD systems represented to these large companies was enormous, thereby justifying the effort and cost required to develop and implement such a system at that point in time.

The last major concept associated with change science to take into consideration when developing and implementing a system is that of leveraging off of experience and knowledge. We have already discussed in prior chapters how the selection of a specific defined process and/or defined implementation is generally heavily dependent on leveraging off of the experience and knowledge base we have access to. As individuals, organizations, and society we often tend to do this subconsciously or inherently within the world of change we are dealing with. This sort of leveraging of experience and knowledge is just as critical when we are developing and implementing a system.

More importantly, the regular use of a system can help us to constantly expand on this experience and knowledge base, providing a source for the continuous improvement we discussed above. This, in turn, leads to an expansion of the overall defined change available to us and continuous improvement in our standard of living.

The real take-away is that an understanding of change science and the concepts it represents enhances our ability to develop and implement a successful system and/or understand why a system fails to provide the overall defined change we are attempting to obtain.

EVALUATION AND SELECTION OF A SYSTEM

Above we outlined some potential disadvantages associated with an individual, organization, or society using a system, especially a repeatable system. An understanding of these disadvantages is a great foundation upon which to begin your procedure for the evaluation and selection of a system. They represent some important concerns to consider when evaluating and selecting a system.

From these concerns we can derive the following procedure for evaluating and selecting a system:

1. First we need to clearly understand exactly what the overall defined change we are looking for (that is, desire) consists of. If we are not sure, we need to spend the time to develop a clear and concise understanding and definition of what our desired overall defined change is all about.

   It can be helpful to expand our knowledge base by leveraging off of consultants and service providers. However, as discussed above, we must make sure to have our antenna up relative to any vested interest they may have or to any attempts to convince us that we do not need certain functionality given any limitations in functionality inherent in their solutions.

2. After we have a clear understanding of the exact desired overall defined change we are looking for, we need to match the specific outputs/results from this overall defined change that we desire against the outputs/results we expect to actually receive from the system/systems we are evaluating. Obviously, the closer the match of the system outputs/results to the desired outputs/results, the more interest we should have in selecting that system. In addition, the level of significance should also be taken into consideration when evaluating this matchup.

3. Once we have narrowed our evaluation down to systems that best match the desired overall defined change we wish to obtain, we need to shift our focus to environmental requirements. In this context, our evaluation should be broad in nature and include such considerations as:

   a. What are the exact environmental conditions that must exist for the implementation and execution of this system, and will the actual environment/environments in which we will be executing support those requirements? If not, can the conditions in the environment/environments be adjusted to support the system, or are there alternative environments that can be used that will be still acceptable?

b. Even if we have a great matchup of system requirements to environmental conditions, we must consider the cost and effort associated with the implementation and execution of the system as part of the environmental requirements. Effort and cost/benefit can often play a major role in the evaluation of a system. In this context, the level of significance, complexity, and control should all be taken into consideration when evaluating the selection of a system.

Remember that no matter how well a system might provide the overall defined change we wish to obtain, the inability of our environment/environments to support the implementation and execution requirements of the system can be disastrous. In addition, evaluating environmental conditions should go beyond just those specific conditions required to support the implementation and execution of the system and should include the conditions of cost and effort.

4. Do monitoring and control points exist within the systems we are evaluating? If they exist, do they match up with the requirements? If they do not, is there an ability to include some monitoring and control points in a context that is acceptable to us?

We have discussed numerous times the benefits of having monitoring and control points together with associated alternative defined processes. Monitoring and control points are common in the systems we use as individuals, organizations, and society in our daily lives.

For example, just think of how many individuals check the weather or traffic reports as part of their system of getting up and going to work in the morning. The weather and traffic reports represent monitoring and control points that allow them to select alternative routes, time intervals, and the types of transportation they will use on any given day as part of their system of getting up, getting ready, and going to work. Therefore, it is important to take the capability of monitoring and control points into consideration when evaluating and selecting a system.

5. Does the system support standardization, the collection, and documentation of actual experiences associated with the use of the system and/or the capability for continuous improvement? Once again, significance will play a role here in our evaluation and selection of a system. However, when relative, standardization, documentation of experience, and continuous improvement should all be considerations when evaluating and selecting a system in order to maximize the advantages of using a system.

We have now reached a point where we can utilize all the information we have discussed thus far in this book and approach in more detail the subject of risk.

CHAPTER ELEVEN

Risk Dynamics Part I: Structural Nature of Risk

Where's the risk?

Tom Somodi

In the Introduction to this book, I indicated that a main driver in my quest to further understand change is the illogical aspect associated with the notion of a lack of commitment that is so often promoted as the main reason for failure to obtain a desired change. As we have demonstrated at various junctures in this book, however, there can be other major reasons for a failure to obtain a desired change that can be far more relevant than a lack of commitment.

As I started to define and refine my understanding of the reasons for successful and unsuccessful change, I realized that there is an underlying focal point that is often skirted, if not totally avoided, when discussing change. That focal point can be summarized in one word: risk!

If nothing else, you should have already come to realize by reading this book that there can be a great amount of risk associated with predicting what change will occur in the future and/or with our ability to obtain the desired defined change we are looking for. I must say that in my opinion, I have seen a favorable trend in the discussion and methodologies associated with risk avoidance and control over the years, especially in the arena of system implementation methodologies.

However, I still see that these discussions often take place after the selection of a defined process or defined implementation methodology. In other words, after the individual, organization, or society has already committed to a specific change implementation and/or execution methodology.

So the obvious question is why is this happening? The answer, in my opinion, is much more straightforward than you might think. It is generally in the *best interest of the individuals and organizations promoting and/or selecting a specific implementation or methodology* to avoid any sort of discussion of risk until after the commitment to the approach/methodologies has been selected. Just look at these questions:

1. What individual or organization, as part of their promotion of a specific implementation or execution strategy for change, wants to stress the risks associated with obtaining a successful result prior to the selection of what they are promoting? Such an approach might jeopardize their ultimate objective of selling their products, services, or strategy, which is what they want to avoid.
2. What individual, organization, or society contemplating spending significant amounts of time, energy, effort, and/or money wants to do so if there is a high degree of predefined risk associated with the specific implementation and/or execution strategy for change they are considering? If individuals, organizations, or societies really realize the amount of risk related to some of their decision-making selections, especially risks associated with time interval requirements or environmental override, their selections and strategies might be significantly different.

This once again would be contrary to the objectives of the individuals or groups trying to sell their products and services. It is also important to note that such information can also even be counterproductive to "individuals internal" to organizations or societies making the selections. It is not unusual for these internal individuals to have some sort of vested interest in, or strategic belief in, obtaining the change under examination no matter what the level of associated risks might be.

3. How often are the individuals, organizations, or societies responsible for selecting a specific implementation or execution strategy for change ill-equipped in their understanding of change and risk, leaving them dependent on less reliable decision-making criteria? Remember that all of the alternatives under consideration will have some level of risk connected with them.

    Therefore, it can often be easier for individuals or organizations to assume that all risk is relatively the same between the alternatives. This allows them to justify an assumption that risk can be ignored completely while rationalizing a focus just on functionality.

4. How often is the significance or the critical nature of obtaining and/or implementing a change felt to be so great that, risk is discounted or ignored because the individuals, organizations, or societies feel they must take the chance no matter what the level of risk?

    In addition, often the time interval associated with making these types of significant selections is short (that is, emergency situations). This can force the decision makers to rely on the experience/knowledge base immediately available to them since there is not adequate time to perform a more comprehensive risk analysis.

The bottom line is that there are multiple reasons for avoiding, discounting, misunderstanding, or even ignoring a discussion of risk connected with the selection of a specific implementation or execution strategy for change. This creates an exposure for unsuccessful change greater than what might otherwise be acceptable. That is why one of the visions of this book is to promote change as a science in the quest to improve our understanding of change and help us increase our chances of obtaining the desired change we are striving for.

Now for the good news: Change science provides concepts and tools to enhance our ability as individuals, organizations, and societies to understand, manage, control, and reduce the risks associated with obtaining the desired change we are looking for. However, before we examine some of these concepts and tools, we need to develop a clearer understanding of what risk is in the world of change science.

DEFINITION OF RISK

In change science, *risk* is defined as the probability that an expected defined change and/or overall defined change will not be obtained.

The greater the risk, the greater the probability that a defined change and/or overall defined change will not be obtained (that is, the result will be unsuccessful change).

Risk factors represent characteristics, situations, circumstances, features, aspects, or other factors that increase the risk/probability that an expected defined change and/or overall defined change will not be obtained.

We have already discussed multiple reasons why a defined change and/or overall defined change will not, or cannot, be obtained. The key is that we now recognize that there is always a level of risk linked to the change we think will take place in the future and/or the desired change we are hoping to obtain.

Change science teaches us that environmental dynamics, change dynamics, and defined process and defined implementation selections inherently present risk in our ability to predict and/or influence the change around us. This is always true no matter what anyone tells us. While change science can show us ways to reduce and manage our exposure to risk, change can never be 100 percent guaranteed.

However, this does not require us to become overwhelmed by risk. Change science has also introduced us to the concept of significance. Significance can help us balance the amount of focus and attention we should be placing on the change confronting us.

While risk always exists with every change that we desire or are exposed to, the "negative impact" on us as individuals, organizations, or societies of this risk is generally "directly related to the significance the change represents to us." This, in turn, allows us to focus on addressing the risk that is linked to the change that is most significant to us at any point in time.

Before we begin our exploration of how to reduce and manage risk, we first need to discuss risk factors.

RISK FACTORS

As already noted, the literature and the world are full of comprehensive discussions, theories, and methodologies regarding the implementation, execution, and management of change. Incorporated into these discussions, theories, and methodologies are often risk considerations. In my opinion, while some of these discussions are really good and some are questionable, it is beyond the intent of this book, and quite frankly beyond the capacity of this author, to perform a comprehensive analytical review of these various perspectives on risks.

Nevertheless, I do believe there is benefit to starting our discussion of risk factors with some observations I have made over the years. It has been common in my experience to see a tendency to focus on three main high-level risk factors associated with obtaining successful implementations and executions associated with change.

In change science, we will refer to these three risk factors as *traditional risk factors and/or tactical risk factors*, which represent a traditional approach to the subject of risk associated with change and/or the implementation of change. The three risk factors are:

1. *Scope*—represents the degree of change and effort to obtain the change that is under consideration.

    The logic goes that the greater the scope (that is, degree) of the change and effort we are dealing with, the greater the risk that the change we desire will not be obtained. The concept of scope can focus on the execution of the change, the implementation of an ability to obtain a change, and/or the combination of both the implementation and execution associated with obtaining a change.

2. *Duration*—represents the length of time associated with the implementation of obtaining a change, executing a change, and/or any combination thereof.

    The logic goes that the longer the length of time associated with implementing and/or executing a change, the greater the risk that the change we desire will not be obtained.

3. *Resources*—represents the amount of time/effort, human capital, financial capital, and other resources an individual, organization, or society must commit to the implementation of an ability to obtain a change, execute a change, and/or any combination thereof.

    The logic usually goes that, assuming the resources are properly managed (which can be a major subject area in and by itself), the greater the amount and/or quality of resources we apply to an implementation and/or execution of a change, the less risk we will have associated with obtaining the change.

It is important to note that while each of these risk factors can be important in its own context, there is also significance to the interrelationship among these three risk factors. In other words, there is a direct relationship among all three risk factors such that an increase or decrease in one leads to direct ramifications on the other two risk factors. For example:

- It is generally assumed that a decrease in resources without a coinciding reduction in scope must lead to an increase in the duration associated with obtaining a change if that change is to be successful.
- It is generally assumed that a decrease in duration must also require either an increase in resources in order to obtain the change as originally expected, or there must be a decrease in scope or some combination thereof.
- It is generally assumed that an increase in scope will require either an increase in resources, an increase in duration, and/or some combination thereof if the change is still to be successfully obtained.

Fundamental Versus Tactical

I believe there is relevance and significance to understanding the three risk factors of scope, duration, and resources in the context outlined above. These three risk factors not only represent legitimate considerations when dealing with risk and change, but they also are a good representation of the traditional way that many approach the subject of risk.

However, I would also look at these traditional risk factors as more tactically oriented. They tend to focus on the "how-to" of obtaining a successful implementation or execution of a project associated with obtaining a change, thereby missing other more fundamental risk factors that exist relative to change.

On the other hand, change science takes us to another level of comprehension regarding risk factors that enhances our ability to understand, control, and manage risk. This can, in turn, increase our ability to successfully attain the change we are expecting to obtain. While we should see some noticeable overlaps between these three traditional risk factors and the discussions presented in previous chapters, the concepts derived from the study of change science can provide a broader and more extensive level of understanding of risk factors.

This fundamental understanding goes well beyond the tactical aspects of having a successful implementation or execution of a change and looks at the underlying reasons why change fails. This deeper level of comprehension will help us to react more fully to the change taking place around us and to increase our ability to obtain the desired change we are looking for. Equally as important, our understanding of the fundamental risk factors of change has the potential to improve our ability to reduce risk even when the change is significant and the time intervals are short.

Levels of Risk Factors

To start, change science looks at risk in the context of having two levels of risk factors summarized as follows:

- Primary risk factors
  1. Invalid defined change
  2. Invalid defined process
  3. Invalid defined implementation

4. Invalid primary environment
  5. Environmental override
- Secondary risk factors
  1. Time interval on the change/time continuum
  2. Conflicting relevant conditions
  3. Complexity

Why are we breaking it out this way?

Because the *primary risk factors* represent the underlying reasons why the change we expect or, the change we desire, will fail to be obtained.

The *secondary risk factors* represent some of the more prevalent risk factors underlying why environmental override can exist.

In other words, the reasons change fails to occur in the context we expect or desire can be captured in one of the primary risk factors listed. However, environmental override can occur because of numerous underlying sources so a further breakout of these risk factors can be extremely helpful when trying to control and reduce risk.

Primary Level Risk Factors

The primary risk factors represent all the underlying reasons why the change we expect or the change we desire will fail to be obtained.

Validity of a Defined Change

You open your newspaper or hear it on the radio: someone just got swindled out of his or her money because of some scam. Or maybe you have overheard someone telling someone else, "If it sounds too good to be true, it probably is." These examples just reinforce the fact that not all defined change is valid.

The reality is that certain defined change is just impossible to obtain, at least based upon the known laws of science and/or capabilities that we have at our disposal. Of course, if the defined change we expect or desire is not valid, then there is also not a valid defined process or valid defined implementation that will produce such a defined change.

So as basic as it might sound, the validity of the underlying defined change represents a primary risk factor relative to obtaining an expected or desired defined change or overall defined change. In general, there are two categories of this type of risk factor:

- The first category is due to the fact that a defined change will not work in any context because it violates or is inconsistent with the known laws of science and/or conditions that exist in the world in which we live. In other words, it is just physically impossible to obtain such a change no matter what. Therefore, the defined change is invalid.
- In the second category, a defined change can be invalid in one specific primary environment because the laws of science and/or conditions that exist within the context of that particular primary environment will not support the defined change. This can exist even though the defined change is valid in an alternative primary environment where the laws of science and/or conditions do support the defined change in that alternative primary environment.

  For example, while the laws of science and conditions that exist allow us to move around in our house without the use of any special equipment or clothing, the same laws of science would preclude us from moving around in outer space without the use of some sort of special equipment. Therefore, the defined change of moving around without the use of special equipment is valid in the primary environment confines of your home but is totally invalid when the primary environment represents outer space.

It is often this second category of validity that catches individuals, organizations, and even societies off guard and opens them up to the risk of not obtaining the change they expect. This is due to the fact that a defined change might be valid in one primary environment so people come to believe that it will also work in the primary environment that is relevant to them.

The key is *to recognize that the laws of science that are at play can differ significantly based upon the primary environment we are dealing with*. Therefore, it is critical that you examine validity of a defined change in two contexts:

1. Is a particular defined change fundamentally invalid because the laws of science and/or conditions preclude it from happening no matter what primary environment is selected?
2. Is a particular defined change invalid because of the laws of science and/or conditions in the primary environment you have selected, even though there are primary environments that are not precluded by these laws of science and/or conditions?

In either case, the validity of the defined change represents a primary risk factor to be taken into consideration.

Validity of a Defined Process and/or Defined Implementation

In Chapter 8 we indicated that a defined process is considered *valid*, or has *validity*, when it is known that *a given defined process will execute to yield the desired defined change associated with that defined process if and/or when the environmental conditions are available that match all the required process factors and there are no conflicting relevant conditions that exist in that environment*. In other words, there is validity to a defined process if it is known to work in providing a specific defined change, all other things being equal.

There are two reasons why a defined process will be invalid. One, consistent with our discussion above regarding defined change, will emerge if you try to use a defined process that conflicts with or is not supported by underlying laws of science and/or conditions. When this situation exists, it is impossible to obtain the desired defined change using that defined process. For example, if you want to move from point A to point B that is 25 feet away from you, using a defined process of jumping is physically impossible and would be considered an invalid defined process.

The second reason a defined process can be invalid is when the defined process is erroneous for any reason (that is, some of the assumptions and/or process factors are incorrect so it will just not work). Once again, it will be impossible to obtain the desired defined change using that specific defined process. For example, let us assume once again that you want to move from point A to point B that is 25 feet away from you. If you choose to walk from point A to point B but head in the opposite direction without turning around, then the defined process would be invalid. It was invalid even though that portion of the defined process associated with walking would have been valid had the process factor of the direction of your travel not been erroneous.

The validity associated with defined implementations is also consistent with this discussion of the validity of defined processes. Just as in the case of a defined process, a defined implementation can be invalid for the same two reasons. One, it conflicts or is not supported by the laws of science; or two, it is erroneous for any reason (some of the assumptions and/or implementation factors are incorrect so it will just not work).

In the end, there is risk associated with the fact that the defined process and/or defined implementation we selected could be invalid. Therefore, the invalidity of a defined process and/or defined implementation represents primary risk factors.

Validity of the Primary Environment

If you have ever been in a hospital you might have noticed the focus the staff places on making sure the treatment they are providing to a particular patient is consistent with what that patient is, in fact, supposed to receive. You can have a valid surgery to remove a gallbladder (that is, a valid defined change, defined process, and defined implementation), but if you remove the gallbladder from the wrong patient, you have made a serious mistake. In essence, the removal of the gallbladder from the wrong patient would represent an example of having an invalid primary environment.

The doctor performing the surgery has a valid and successful defined change, defined process, and defined implementation. However, the primary environment being the body of the wrong individual having the gallbladder removed would be an invalid primary environment.

I like to use this as an example because some people find it hard to believe that executing a defined change in the wrong primary environment can happen. But in reality it does. We have all heard about situations in which a knee surgery was performed on the wrong knee, a letter from an office was sent to the wrong address, a customer received product that was not theirs, or a repairman serviced something at the house of a relative with the same last name instead of at our house.

These examples represent cases in which a valid defined change, defined process, and defined implementation were successfully executed in the wrong primary environment. Therefore, it is clear that the potential to have an invalid primary environment is a risk factor that should be taken into consideration as part of the potential risk that is associated with obtaining an expected or desired change.

Environmental Override

I would be surprised if you have never heard someone say, "It happened because the conditions were just right." In reality, change science teaches us that all change occurs because the conditions are just right.

It was explained in Chapter 2 that if you had to choose only one concept to understand and take away from this book, it would be the change science principle of environmental override. Simplicity prevails once again within the discipline of change science. We are reminded that all of the change that is occurring within any given environment in the universe is based upon the execution of defined processes in which the associated required process factors are supported by the conditions that exist at that point in time on the change/time continuum within that given environment.

Therefore, assuming we have a valid defined change, valid defined process, valid defined implementation, and a valid primary environment, then the change science principle of environmental override is the only primary risk factor remaining that will stop us from obtaining an expected or desired defined change.

This is extremely important to understand. The risk associated with obtaining an expected or desired change centers around the five primary risk factors we have outlined above. However, *even if we satisfy the first four primary risk factors by having a valid defined change, valid defined process, valid defined implementation, and valid primary environment, the execution of a defined process will still not take place until the process factors required by the defined process are supported by the conditions that exist at that point in time on the change/time continuum within that primary environment—in other words, until the environmental override within the primary environment no longer exists.*

The best way to understand and ultimately attempt to control environmental override risk is to examine more closely some of the main underlying factors associated with this risk. We have defined these as secondary risk factors.

Secondary Risk Factors

As noted above, the three major secondary risk factors include:

1. Time interval on the change/time continuum
2. Conflicting relevant conditions
3. Complexity

We differentiate these as secondary risk factors because they represent underlying exposures as to why the risk of environmental override will exist. In other words, while the risk factor of environmental override is sufficient to explain why a certain defined process will not execute, there are underlying structural considerations that increase the probability that environmental override will be present at the time of the execution of the defined process.

These are, in turn, considered secondary risk factors since they do not directly inhibit the execution of the defined process. Instead, they contribute to the existence of the primary risk factor of environmental override that ultimately stops the execution of the defined process from taking place.

Time Intervals

One of the concepts indicated by the change/time continuum principle of change science is that the potential amount of total change that takes place within any given environment increases as the time interval on the change/time continuum increases. This, of course, is reinforced by what we have learned regarding the chain of events principle, change dynamics, environmental dynamics, and the hierarchy of change. This change can be naturally-occurring change, cognitively-influenced change, or some combination thereof.

The ramifications related to the traditional risk factor of duration explained above generally focus on tactical aspects of implementing and executing change such as expectation setting, resource commitment, and cost estimations. Remember that in many cases duration can impact the costs of a quote for services or the expectation of completion. Therefore, in this context, the risk can often center on the ramifications of these estimates being incorrect.

From a change science perspective, the real underlying risk associated with the length of the time interval centers around the level of unpredictability of the change that will occur in a given environment because of naturally-occurring change and the cognitively-influenced change of others taking place during that time interval. In this case, the underlying risk is how all this ancillary change increases the potential of creating unexpected and/or undesirable environmental override relative to the defined change we are expecting or that we want to obtain.

So the length of the time interval related to any given defined change represents a secondary risk factor through the potential influence it has on the primary risk factor of environmental override.

The secondary risk factor of the time interval reflects the fact that *the potential to have environmental override increases as the time interval associated with a defined change increases.*

The time interval risk factor for a defined change includes more than just the *implementation time interval* associated with the execution of the defined implementation and the *process time interval* associated with the execution of the defined process.

The time interval risk factor also includes the *total time interval* available between the point in time that the defined change/process/implementation "is selected" and the point in time on the change/time continuum when the desired defined change "is expected to be effectively obtained."

We must be careful not to confuse the time intervals associated with a defined process and defined implementation with the actual total time interval available on the change/time continuum between the point in time we select the defined change/process/implementation and the point in time we expect to have obtained an effective defined change. The time interval risk factor for the defined process and defined implementation focuses on the dynamics that can cause environmental override to occur during those specific time intervals in which the defined process and/or defined implementation are actually executing.

The time interval risk factor for the total time interval available for the defined change focuses on the dynamics that can cause unexpected and/or undesirable conditions, which represent environmental override in an environment, that are "inconsistent with the assumptions made" when the defined process and defined implementation were selected.

In essence, these types of risk negatively impact or even negate the ability to obtain an effective execution of the defined implementation and/or defined process selected. In other words, if we would have known at the time we selected the defined process/implementation that the environmental conditions creating the environmental override were going to exist, we would have modified the design and/or selection criteria used when initially selecting our defined process/implementation in an attempt to eliminate the impact of this environmental override.

Bottom line, in earlier chapters we focused most of our attention on the time intervals associated specifically with defined processes and defined implementations, and the time interval risk factor definitely applies in these cases. However, we also now need to stress that having a large amount of "total time" available is not necessarily your friend either.

The amount of ancillary change occurring in all of the environments we are dealing with (remember a defined process must execute in a single primary environment, but a defined implementation can be executed in multiple environments) can be significant. This, in turn, makes the design and selection of a defined process and defined implementation to obtain a defined change all the more difficult and open to the primary risk of environmental override.

Conflicting Relevant Conditions

There are times where all the conditions exist in a primary environment to support a defined process, but execution does not occur because there is a conflicting relevant condition or conditions that override the triggering event condition of the defined implementation. These conflicting relevant conditions represent environmental override in that the conditions in the primary environment do not support the final execution of the defined process.

The most easily understood examples of the secondary risk factor of conflicting relevant conditions are those in which dominant conditions exist in the primary environment. Weather conditions such as hurricanes and tornados represent conflicting relevant conditions in that they prevent what would otherwise be successfully executing defined processes from taking place had they not been located in the primary environment.

However, there are numerous other examples of conflicting relevant conditions, and, in fact, many a movie has been made around just such a theme. I am sure many of you have seen a movie where someone or the world could be saved, but someone or something stands in the way of executing what needs to be done. In essence, what needs to be done to save the world represents the execution of a defined process, and whatever stands in the way of the execution of that activity represents a conflicting relevant condition.

We can also see examples in our everyday life. It might be at the office where our ability to do something we want to do is available to us (that is, all the required environmental conditions exist), but the boss says no (the boss represents a conflicting environmental condition that stops the execution). Another example could also be an attempt to start a fire with a match only to have a strong wind constantly extinguishing the match before we can light the fire. All the conditions exist to start a fire, but the strong wind represents a conflicting relevant condition.

What is interesting about conflicting relevant conditions is that they often are not what we would normally consider a risk to the defined change we are expecting to obtain. This is because in many cases we would actually consider them irrelevant conditions during our design and selection of the defined process and defined implementation. They only become relevant and conflicting when they become the basis for environmental override.

So if the boss is normally a good person who goes along with what we recommend, then his or her approval could easily be considered an irrelevant condition by us. It is not until the boss says no that environmental override takes place and the lack of approval became a conflicting relevant condition. Likewise, we may have lighted our match hundreds of times when there was wind occurring around us. Therefore, it would not be surprising for us to consider the wind an irrelevant condition until such time as the strength of wind reaches a level that represents a conflicting relevant condition and environmental override kicks in.

Bottom line, the risks related to conflicting relevant conditions can sometimes be greater than anticipated, and recognizing these risks can often be difficult given that they can be derived from conditions that we might normally consider irrelevant.

Complexity

The concept of complexity has already been alluded to several times in this book. In a general context the definition of complexity is pretty straightforward.

Complexity is considered by most as something composed of many interrelated parts or components that can be complicated to understand, control, and/or manage. Given how change is taking place all around us from multiple levels on the change hierarchy to multiple environments throughout the universe, this underlying definition of complexity obviously applies to change.

In the context of risk, most people would inherently consider the level of risk associated with the ability to obtain a given change to increase as the level of complexity increases. However, in change science, complexity from a perspective of risk also has a context of relativity to it.

For example, a change that is considered complex to one person, organization, or society might not be considered complex to another person, organization, or society. This can occur because of underlying differences between the environmental conditions, change dynamics, environmental dynamics, and implementation and execution strategies with which the alternative individuals and/or groups must contend. A case in point might be differences in an environmental condition represented by the variation in the experience and knowledge base that exists between two different individuals or groups of individuals.

Therefore, change science includes the notion of relativity in the concept of complexity and explores complexity in the context of underlying drivers of the risk that is connected with our ability to obtain change.

So in change science, *complexity* is defined as certain conditions that are measured in relative terms, can be interrelated, are complicated to understand and manage, and can represent underlying secondary drivers that increase the probability that the primary risk factor of environmental override will exist to negate the ability to obtain a desired defined change or desired overall defined change. Five major underlying conditions of complexity include:

1. Magnitude
2. Disconnect or difference in existing and required environmental conditions
3. Experience and knowledge
4. Control
5. The degree of unpredictability of future environmental conditions

We can try to solidify our understanding of complexity as it relates to change science by looking at some examples. Let us start with a desired defined change of creating a cake. Now let us look at some situations that can alter the complexity associated with obtaining this desired change:

- If the cake we wish to obtain is a multi-tiered highly-decorated wedding cake, then the complexity associated with this cake would be greater than that of a simply decorated single-layer birthday cake. This is an example where the "magnitude of the desired change" can influence the complexity associated with the desired change.
- If the ingredients and cooking equipment required to obtain this defined change already exist in the primary environment we are operating in, then the complexity is less than that which would exist if the primary environment did not already have some or all of these ingredients or equipment. This is an example of how "existing environmental conditions can influence the level of complexity" associated with the desired change.
- If we are master pastry chefs by training, then the complexity associated with obtaining this defined change would be less than that of someone who had no formal training and had to rely strictly on following the instructions from a cookbook. This is an example of how an individual or organization's "ex-

perience and knowledge base can influence the complexity" associated with the desired change.

- If we are required to write down the instructions on how to produce this cake that, in turn, would be used by a group of individuals in the actual preparation of the cake, this would represent more complexity than if we can directly produce the cake ourselves. This is an example of how "control can influence the complexity" associated with the desired change.

- If we are required to produce the cake outdoors where we have to contend with an extended array of unpredictable environmental conditions such as weather or insects, this would represent more complexity than the ability to produce the cake in an indoor kitchen. This is an example of how the "unpredictability of future environmental conditions because of the change dynamics, environmental dynamics, and conditions associated with the selected primary environment can influence the level of complexity" associated with the desired change.

- The above five situations are not necessarily mutually exclusive but, in fact, can and will exist in an interrelated context. For example, the cake could be a multi-tiered highly-decorated wedding cake (more complexity) produced indoors in a well equipped kitchen (less complexity) that did not have all the necessary ingredients (more complexity) by a master pastry chief (less complexity) directing the efforts of a group of students remotely (more complexity) via a live audio and video link (less complexity). It is apparent that this overall scenario can be broken down into interrelated independent components, each representing a different level of significance relative to the overall level of risk connected with obtaining the desired change of producing a cake.

We can now use these examples to help further expand our understanding of these five underlying conditions representing complexity:

1. *The magnitude of the defined change or overall defined change.* A greater magnitude of change usually requires more process factors and/or implementation factors. It also often increases the length of the time intervals associated with the defined process and/or defined implementation. Both of these dynamics increase the likelihood that the change dynamics and environmental dynamics will negatively impact the conditions that exist in the environments that the defined implementation and defined process are executing in, creating environmental override and the inability to obtain the desired change.
2. *The relationship of the conditions that already exists in the environments* that the defined implementation and defined process are executing in to the required process factors and implementation factors at the point in time on the change/time continuum that the defined process and defined implementation are selected.

   Assume that the defined process and defined implementation are selected at point A on the change/time continuum. Then the level of difference (which we define as disconnect) between the conditions in the environments and required process and implementation factors as of point A on the change/time continuum represents the degree of change that needs to take place through the execution of the defined implementation and within the execution of the defined process in order to avoid environmental override and obtain the defined change.

   Obviously, the larger the disconnect (difference) between the existing conditions as of point A and the required imple-

mentation/process factors, the greater the likelihood that the change dynamics and environmental dynamics will negatively impact the conditions that exist in the environments that the defined implementation/process are executing in, creating environmental override and the inability to obtain the desired change.
3. *The level of, or access to, experience and knowledge.* The better the level of, or access to, experience and knowledge, the greater the likelihood that the defined process/implementation selected will be successful. In contrast, lower levels of experience and knowledge will tend to increase the likelihood that the selection and execution of the defined process and defined implementation will be subject to environmental override, creating an inability to obtain the desired change.
4. *The level of control that exists over the selection and execution of the defined process and/or defined implementation.* A lack of direct control usually leads to an increase in the potential for a poorer selection of the defined process and/or defined implementation. It also tends to increase the potential for errors in the execution of the defined process and/or defined implementation. Both of these situations will tend to increase the likelihood that the defined process and/or defined implementation will be subject to environmental override, creating an inability to obtain the desired change.
5. *The degree of unpredictability of future environmental conditions.* The level/amount of change dynamics, environmental dynamics, and existing conditions associated with the environments in which the selected defined process and defined implementation must execute can greatly influence the degree of unpredictability in the conditions during the "total time interval" associated with the desired change. This increases the likelihood that the defined process and/or defined

implementation will be subject to environmental override, creating an inability to obtain the desired change.

6. *The interaction of the five underlying conditions of complexity.* As discussed above, these underlying complexity conditions do not just exist in a singular context but, in fact, interrelate with one another. Consistent with the standard definition of complexity discussed above, this interaction can be complicated to understand, control, and/or manage, which increases the likelihood that environmental override will interfere with the ability to obtain the desired change.

These examples and discussion should help us understand how the secondary risk factor of complexity represents underlying conditions that can increase the probability that the primary risk factor of environmental override will continue to ultimately negate the ability to obtain the desired defined change or desired overall defined change.

It is important to note that *magnitude, disconnect, experience and knowledge, control, and the degree of unpredictability of future environmental conditions represent conditions that exist at a specific point in time on the change/time continuum as they relate to the particular change that is under consideration.*

Therefore:

a) The measurement and significance of these conditions are only relative to the specific change and, therefore, the defined process and defined implementation under consideration.

b) These conditions can and will vary over time so that complexity can and will vary as we proceed along the change/time continuum.

c) These conditions are often most relevant at the point in time that the defined process and defined implementation are being selected or modified.

d) Complexity can and will vary between alternative defined processes and/or defined implementations.
e) These five characteristics are not meant to be all-inclusive but represent some of the more major characteristics leading to complexity that are relevant across a broad range of change.

With this background in risk and risk factors, we are now in a position to move on to Chapter 12 and examine how change science can help to manage, control, and reduce the risks associated with the change we are dealing with in our daily lives.

CHAPTER TWELVE

Risk Dynamics Part II: Concepts and Tools to Control Risk

*Living at risk is jumping off the cliff
and building your wings on the way down.*

Ray Bradbury

We have finally reached the point that many of you have probably been waiting for. Are there ways to leverage off of change science to increase our chances of obtaining the change we desire and/or expect?

The answer is, of course, yes. We will not fall into the trap of telling you that the change you desire or expect can be 100 percent guaranteed. However, there are concepts and tools that, when coupled with what we learned through the study of change science, can improve our potential to manage, control, and reduce risk, thereby increasing our chances to obtain the change we desire and expect.

It is in this context that we will explore the following concepts and tools:

1. Significance and probability

2. Controllable and uncontrollable risk—eliminate and mitigate
3. Disconnect analysis
4. Energy/effort hump theory
5. Time interval considerations
6. Control, monitoring, feedback, and adjustment
7. Validity testing

To start, we need to think in general terms, initially focusing on significance and recognizing the fact that not all risk is created equal.

SIGNIFICANCE AND PROBABILITY

Significance

We have already had numerous exposures to how the concept of significance plays a role in many aspects of dealing with change. From the role significance plays in the amount of anxiety and frustration we encounter; to how significance tempers our efforts when developing process maps; to the role significance plays during the evaluation and selection of defined processes, defined implementations, and systems—the concept of significance is integrated throughout our discussions.

So it should be no surprise that significance also plays a role when attempting to manage, control, and reduce the risk associated with a change under consideration. Interestingly, when it comes to the subject of risk, significance must be addressed from two different perspectives.

The first perspective focuses on determining the amount of attention and/or effort we should expend in our attempts to analyze and control risk based upon the significance a particular change has to us as an individual, organization, or society. This perspective is more of a global perspective that is very similar to many of the earlier discussions we have already had relative to significance.

The second perspective is more of a micro perspective that examines the amount of attention and/or effort we should expend on any individual explicit risk that might exist relative to obtaining a specific desired change.

Let's look at each of these perspectives in more detail.

The Global Perspective of Significance

While there can be exceptions, as a general rule: the level of effort and focus placed on the evaluation and attempted management of risk associated with a given change will increase as the level of significance increases to us as an individual, organization, or society.

Here are some rules related to significance that should be a starting point for dealing with the risk associated with a given change that is under consideration:

1. The level of effort for managing and reducing risk can be minimal to nonexistent if a given change represents little to no significance. However, this does not mean that we should not learn from the experiences associated with these changes and the risk incurred.
2. The level of analysis and effort expended on the evaluation and control of risk should expand as the significance associated with a given change increases.
3. Whenever a given change is considered important or critical, then the level of effort and concentration we place on analyzing how to manage, control, and reduce risk should be substantial and well thought out.

While the rest of our discussion in this chapter on managing, controlling, and reducing risk can be applied to any change under consideration, it is really most applicable to change that is considered important or critical in significance. The reality is, that unless unusual circumstances apply, the time and effort involved to execute many of the concepts and tools we are about to discuss are difficult to justify unless the level of significance of the change warrants the effort.

In addition, as discussed in Chapter 6, people, organizations, and societies have inherently learned how to deal with the routine change they have on a daily basis, greatly reducing the need to apply many of these concepts or tools.

Bottomline, the overall significance of a given change should play an instrumental role in determining how much time and effort should be expended in managing, controlling, and reducing the risk associated with a given change.

Micro Perspective of Significance

What is the significance to obtaining a change if a particular risk takes place? Note that this is not the significance to "us" as discussed above. This is the significance (that is, impact) a "specific risk" has on obtaining the particular change we are looking at. The impact of a specific risk on a given change can be different depending on what the particular risk is.

For example, assume a delivery of some material we need during the execution of our defined implementation has the potential to be delayed by one day (a risk). This delay would in turn impact the timing of completing our execution by a day. However, if our interval of time associated with the defined implementation can easily be extended by one day because the actual total time available is longer than the execution time required, this risk of a one-day delay becomes somewhat insignificant. However, if the delay in receiving the material turns into weeks, then the level of significance/impact of this risk increases substantially.

The advantage of assessing what the impact will be from the various specific risk exposures we face is that it helps filter out the risk that has low significance while focusing on the risk that signifies the greatest potential significance/impact on the change we want to obtain.

Probability

What is the probability that a particular risk will take place? Just like significance, the level of probability that a specific risk will, in fact, occur can influence the level of effort and concentration we want to place on that particular risk.

For example, if the execution of our defined implementation is sensitive to weather conditions and is required to execute outdoors over a four-week time interval, the probability that weather could be a risk to the execution would most likely be high.

However, having a risk that has a high probability in and by itself may not be an issue. This is due to the fact that unless the probability of a risk is also associated with the significance of that specific risk, it will be difficult to determine the true ramifications associated with the probability.

The table in Figure 12-1 depicts the interrelationships between probability and significance along with some suggested potential high-level actions.

Figure 12-1
Risk Assessment

	Probability of a Specific Risk = High	Probability of a Specific Risk = Medium	Probability of a Specific Risk = Low
Significance of Risk = High	Requires high level of attention and a detailed eliminate/mitigate action plan	Requires high level of attention and a detailed eliminate/mitigate action plan	Eliminate/mitigate risk where cost justified and monitor closely during execution
Significance of Risk = Medium	Requires high level of attention and a detailed eliminate/mitigate action plan	Requires high level of attention and a detailed eliminate/mitigate action plan	Eliminate/mitigate risk where cost justified and monitor closely during execution
Significance of Risk = Low	Eliminate/mitigate risk where effort is minimal	Eliminate/mitigate risk where effort is minimal	Little to no attention or effort

- A significance of High means an inability to obtain the change.
- A significance of Medium means the potential for a major disruption including the possibility that the change will not be obtained.
- A significance of Low means minor disruption to the ability to obtain a change, which is anticipated to be easily correctable if the risk occurs.

CONTROLLABLE AND UNCONTROLLABLE RISK— ELIMINATE AND MITIGATE

A big mistake is looking at risk in a homogeneous context. In actuality, as already pointed out above, not all risk is created equal! One of the easiest ways to manage, control, and reduce risk is to separate and analyze it into two categories: controllable and uncontrollable.

Controllable Risk

Definition

It is a sad situation when we do not obtain a desired change only to find out that if we had done something differently, the reason (risk) that the change failed would not have occurred. Unfortunately, I have seen this situation transpire more times than I want to count. That is why I stress to people and organizations the need to analyze risk from the perspective of being controllable and uncontrollable.

A *controllable risk* is any risk that has the potential to be subject to a direct influence through the action and/or actions (that is, cognitive influence) generated by individuals and/or organizations that in some way have a vested interest in obtaining the given change under consideration.

Depending on the specifics of any given situation, controllable risks can include the selection of people (for example, experienced versus inexperienced), the selection of the primary environment, the use of a particular piece of equipment or resource, the timing of a project, and the list goes on.

Functionality Trade-off

It should be noted that controllable risk can also be related to an important but more subtle risk exposure that we will refer to as functionality trade-off.

Functionality trade-off represents situations in which a change requires a selection between two alternative functionalities, both of which have a level of desirability but which are interconnected in such a way that you cannot obtain the functionality of one alternative without sacrificing the functionality of the other alternative.

Functionality tradeoffs can be very common within software installations where selecting a software configuration that provides functionality to one department sacrifices the functionality the software will provide to another department. It can also be seen in our personal lives where we might purchase a piece of equipment (like a phone, computer, or car) and buy into a functionality that we later find is obtained through the diminution of the level of functionality we were originally looking for.

Bottom line, functionality trade-off is often more common than we think in personal and organizational change initiatives.

So what does functionality trade-off have to do with controllable risk? The answer lies in the basics of change science. We must remember that the first element of change is clearly defining what the change we are looking for will be.

Therefore, the selection of functionality in most cases can be considered a controllable risk. So if the choices made during functionality tradeoffs are not focused on the ultimate defined change we are looking for, there is a risk that we will not receive the desired defined change that we initially expected to get. This is a controllable risk that can be eliminated if it is recognized and the functionality is selected based upon what best reflects the ultimate desired defined change.

Elimination of Controllable Risk

The first question we should always ask when dealing with controllable risk is: are there ways to eliminate the controllable risk associated with the change we want to obtain?

Since by definition, controllable risk is a risk that is subject to influence, controllable risk should be eliminated whenever possible. This should apply not only to highly significant and probable risk but also to any controllable risk that can be justified from a time, effort, and cost perspective.

There are not necessarily any specific guidelines to follow in how to eliminate controllable risk. The issues, dynamics, and approaches are generally very situational. The key is to make sure you recognize all the controllable risk that exists and analyze it for possible elimination whenever the effort and cost associated with the elimination can be justified.

The elimination of controllable risk is often low hanging fruit and represents an easy way to reduce the risk we face when trying to obtain a desired change. However, there are situations in which the elimination of a controllable risk can be more complicated in nature. This can especially be true when functionality trade-off issues are involved.

It is important to note that in cases in which a controllable risk should be eliminated but is not because of the issues surrounding such an elimination, it is important that all critical parties connected with the given change recognize the ramifications and exposures associated with the decision not to eliminate the specific risk.

Uncontrollable Risk

Unlike controllable risk where the potential for some sort of direct influence exists, no such capability exits in the case of uncontrollable risk.

Therefore, *uncontrollable risk* represents any risk for which direct influence is outside of the control of the individuals and/or organizations that in some way have a vested interest in obtaining the given change under consideration.

Many of you will immediately and accurately think of the risk associated with various naturally-occurring changes (such as, the weather or an earthquake) as being uncontrollable risk. However, uncontrollable risk can also be associated with the actions of others that do not have a vested interest or even have a conflicting vested interest, relative to the change you want to obtain.

For example, the actions of your competitors can be considered uncontrollable risk when you introduce a new product in anticipation of changing customer buying habits. A competitor could drop its prices in response to your new offering, which would be an uncontrollable risk since it is totally outside the realm of your influence.

Mitigation of Uncontrollable Risk

The sad situation with uncontrollable risk is that individuals and organizations often just assume that because a risk is uncontrollable, there is nothing they can do and they just must live with the ramifications. However, if we want to manage, control, and reduce risk, then this perspective is not acceptable, especially in cases where the risk is of high significance and moderate to high probability.

Instead, the proper perspective should be one of mitigation. While certain risks might be outside of our direct control (for example, the weather and the actions of other people or organizations), that does not mean that there is not an opportunity to mitigate the risk if it should occur.

I like to refer to this as *change protectionism,* which is developing a plan that, if executed, has the potential to counter the impacts of an uncontrollable risk if and when it occurs.

Examples of change protectionism can include the use of life insurance (it mitigates the uncontrollable risk of an unexpected loss of life), the use of a backup generator at work (it mitigates the uncontrollable risk of an unexpected loss of power at your organization), and even the availability of a tent at an outside party (it mitigates the uncontrollable risk of unexpected bad weather).

Thus, while change protectionism is not uncommon, it is often underutilized when we address the risk associated with a major change. The key is the upfront assessment and planning for uncontrollable risk.

As you might expect, many mitigation efforts can be straightforward and simple to conceive of. For example, if you have a heart condition, you might mitigate the ramifications associated with the potential risk of an unexpected heart attack by not traveling to places where medical resources are not readily available, by having a defibrillator in your home, or by having your loved ones trained in CPR.

Of course, there are also situations in which mitigation efforts are not so simple or straightforward. In these cases, you might want to leverage off of the expertise or experiences of others, become creative in your thought process, or look for ways to adjust the defined process/implementation you selected to see if there are ways to mitigate some of the risk.

Finally, even though we will discuss monitoring and feedback in more detail below, it is important to recognize here that leveraging off of monitoring and feedback when dealing with mitigation efforts can be crucial to the avoidance of the ramifications associated with uncontrollable risk. If you do not monitor the actual change and environmental dynamics that are occurring, then your assessment of the significance and probability of an uncontrollable risk will potentially become stale and outdated.

Therefore, monitoring and feedback of uncontrollable risk should be built into every mitigation plan and thought process that you have.

Eliminate and Mitigate

In summary, the concept of eliminate and mitigate can be summarized as follows:

> *Eliminate and mitigate* is the concept that risk can be viewed in the context of risk factors that are controllable and risk factors

that are uncontrollable. If you have a risk factor that is controllable, then that risk factor should be eliminated provided the significance of the risk factor justifies the time, effort, and cost of elimination. However, if the risk factor is uncontrollable, then that risk factor should be mitigated provided the significance of the risk factor justifies the time, effort, cost of mitigation.

The major take-away from the above discussion is that categorizing and analyzing risk in the context of controllable and uncontrollable and then applying the concept of eliminate and mitigate can be a great first step in reducing the risk associated with a given change. While these efforts will not 100 percent guarantee a successful desired change, they can definitely increase the odds that a successful desire change will be obtained.

Therefore, I cannot stress to you enough how beneficial the exercise of assessing risk in the context of controllable and uncontrollable can be. At a minimum, it provides a method of potentially eliminating the significant controllable risk connected with a change while helping to define and prepare in some context (mitigate) the significant uncontrollable risk.

So the next time you are dealing with a major change in your life or your organization, just remember these two words: *eliminate* and *mitigate*!

DISCONNECT ANALYSIS

Here is a simple premise in change science with major ramifications: *if a change does not already exist in a given environment, then there is a disconnect between the conditions that exist in that environment and the factors required to obtain the change.* This disconnect in essence represents the specifics as to why environmental override exists.

So *disconnect analysis* is defined as the concept that if a change does not already exist in a given environment, then there is disconnect between the conditions that exist in that environment and the factors required to obtain the change, and, therefore, disconnect analysis attempts to quantify the disconnects in order to reduce risk.

Understanding the degree and structural nature of this disconnect can play a pivotal role in helping manage, control, and reduce the risks involved with obtaining any given change (both a defined change and an overall defined change). It is incredibly common for individuals, organizations, and societies to select valid defined processes and defined implementations only to fail to obtain the expected change because the defined process and/or defined implementation did not adequately address, or even work within, the disconnect context that existed relative to the required primary environment they were executing in.

We have been repeatedly saying that environmental override is a powerful risk to contend with when the desire to obtain a specific change is high. This has been further substantiated when we identify the number of secondary risk factors that can influence the probability of facing environmental override.

Why do these dynamics continue to happen and why is attention/effort toward defining the disconnects ignored? There can be numerous reasons why, but two of the more noteworthy reasons, in my opinion, are:

- There is an inherent propensity for individuals, organizations, and societies to believe that if it works for someone else, it should also work for them. Therefore, disconnects are either not quantified or there is an assumption that any disconnects that exist will automatically be somehow taken care of.
- The authors, product suppliers, service providers, and consultants either truly believe or, in some cases because it is in

their best interest, just want to make you incorrectly believe that their solutions have broader applicability than they really do. Therefore, the relevancy of disconnects is not determined or is ignored.

In the end, the reason is irrelevant, and what is crucial is that you do not fall into the trap of ignoring the importance associated with analyzing the disconnect between the conditions that exist and the factors that are required in order to obtain a successful change.

When performing disconnect analysis, here are some important considerations to remember:

1. Disconnect between the conditions in an environment and the required factors to obtain a change is measured as of a specific point in time on the change/time continuum. Therefore, the level and structure of the disconnect can and will vary as we move along the change/time continuum toward the point in time that the ultimate desired change is required to be obtained.
2. The variation in disconnect from one point in time and a future point in time on the change/time continuum can be a product of two sets of activities. One is the cognitive influence that we are attempting to apply through the defined process and/or defined implementation we select.

    The second is the naturally-occurring change (naturally-occurring change dynamics and environmental dynamics) and/or the cognitive influence change of others simultaneously taking place along the change/time continuum in the pertinent environments.
3. The disconnect is directly related to the defined process and defined implementation that are selected to obtain the de-

sired change. In other words, alternative defined processes and/or defined implementations should yield differing disconnects given that the process and implementation factors will be different between the various alternatives.

Furthermore, even though the defined process must execute in the primary environment, defined implementations can simultaneously and/or sequentially execute in multiple environments. So the disconnects can also vary based upon the pertinent environments associated with each set of alternative defined processes/implementations under consideration.

4. Therefore, if we want to maximize the potential to reduce risk we should:

   a. Perform the disconnect analysis in conjunction with the selection of a defined process and defined implementation in order to leverage off of the knowledge obtained regarding the levels and structural nature of the disconnect among alternative defined processes/implementations. We can reduce risk by attempting to select the defined process/implementation that has the least amount of disconnect risk or other structural types of risk associated with it.

   b. Look for controllable and uncontrollable risk as part of our disconnect analysis and incorporate the concepts of eliminate and mitigate into our selection of the defined process/implementation.

   c. Continue to monitor the disconnect associated with the selected defined process and defined implementation over the course of execution along the change/time continuum. This continued monitoring will help detect and, where possible, respond to any unexpected deviations or issues as close to the point of occurrence as possible, thereby further providing an opportunity to reduce risk.

Let us use some examples to show what a disconnect analysis might look like. In Example 1, we keep everything straightforward and less technical.

In Example 2, while the example will still be straightforward, we will get more technical regarding what the steps associated with a disconnect analysis might consist of. This second example will be for those of you interested in a more technical explanation. Therefore, Example 2 incorporates the use of the appropriate technical terminology. While it might appear to be overkill for such a straightforward example, I am doing it intentionally to help reinforce some of the change science concepts we have already learned.

Example 1—A Boat Ride with Skiing

Let us say that you want to take the family on a boat ride and water skiing this weekend. You will be using the boat that is currently in your garage and launching it onto a nearby lake.

This outing is very significant to you since it is your wife's birthday and everyone is looking forward to it. Therefore, you want to make sure nothing is forgotten so you create the following list of activities/actions you need to perform:

- Check the gasoline in the boat.
- Make sure the water skis are moved from storage in the shed to the boat.
- Reserve a launch time at the dock on the lake.
- Make sure to pay the launch fees when reserving launch time.
- Make sure you have the keys to the boat.
- Check that there are five lifejackets in the boat.

- Make sure you know the location of the trailer-ball and wrench for attachment to the hitch.
- Check the weather.

While not necessarily very technical, this list and your thought process in fact represent the basis for a change dynamics profile including an implementation plan, a controllable/uncontrollable risk analysis, and a disconnect analysis. If we formalize it slightly, it might look like this:

1. The primary defined change is taking the family boating and skiing on the lake.
2. The primary defined process is to use the boat that is located in your garage.
3. The primary environment is the lake.
4. The required primary process factors include:

    a. The boat located on the lake (controllable risk)
    b. Gasoline in the boat (controllable risk)
    c. Skis in the boat (controllable risk)
    d. Lifejackets in the boat (controllable risk)
    e. Keys to run the boat (controllable risk)
    f. Good weather (uncontrollable risk)

5. The "initial" anticipated primary defined implementation is (each one of these is an incorporated defined process/implementation factor into the primary defined implementation):

    a. Verify there is gasoline and lifejackets in the boat (this eliminates these controllable risks).
    b. Move the skis from storage to the boat (this eliminates this controllable risk).
    c. Locate the trailer-ball and wrench (this eliminates this controllable risk).

    d. Place keys in advance into the boat (this eliminates this controllable risk).
    e. Establish a launch time at the dock (time availability is a potential uncontrollable risk).
    f. Pay launch fee by charge card when scheduling a launch time (this eliminates this controllable implementation risk).
    g. Connect the trailer-ball to the hitch using the wrench.
    h. Transport boat to the dock.
    i. Launch the boat onto the lake.
    j. Start the boat with the keys (this is the triggering event).

6. In your mind, you might also have these additional implementation factors included:

    a. Check weather report the day before (this is an attempt to monitor this uncontrollable risk).
    b. Check flexibility of family to move date if weather conditions are bad (this is an attempt to mitigate this uncontrollable risk).
    c. Immediately call dock for a launch time (this is an attempt to mitigate the uncontrollable risk of the availability of time to launch the boat).

It is important to recognize that we have labeled number 5 an "initial" defined implementation. This is due to the fact that the disconnect analysis is not complete until the status of the gasoline, lifejackets, and trailer-ball/wrench have been established. Based upon the results of these implementation activities, the primary defined implementation might have to be adjusted to reflect additional activities (that is, additional implementation factors).

For example, if upon inspection it is determined that you need more gasoline, then the primary defined implementation would need to be adjusted for an additional implementation factor of a incorporated defined process to purchase additional gasoline.

Example 2—A Bonfire

Let us assume you want to have a bonfire in your backyard. Figure 12-2 represents what the change dynamics profile including an implementation plan and a disconnect analysis might look like.

Figure 12-2
Bonfire Example of Steps Included in a Disconnect Analysis

DISCONNECT ANALYSIS STEPS	CHANGE DYNAMICS PROFILE/IMPLEMENTATION PLAN
1 - Determine a specific defined change (i.e., the primary defined change) and the primary environment in which we want this desired primary defined change to take place.	Primary Defined Change = Bonfire Primary Environment = Fire pit in backyard
2 - Select a primary defined process that is composed of one or more relevant internally incorporated defined changes. When these internally incorporated defined changes/processes/implementations are executed as part of the primary defined process, they will result in the primary defined change we are looking for.	Primary Defined Process = Combustion Primary Process Factors (includes internally incorporated defined changes) = • Relevant internally incorporated defined process = rapid chemical reaction of oxidation of wood (this is the applicable law of science) • Oxygen (constant condition) • Wood • Fire pit • Initial heat source (triggering event)
3 - Determine primary process disconnect.	Existing Conditions In Primary Environment = • Fire pit • Oxygen (constant condition) Primary Process Disconnect = • Wood in fire pit • Initial heat source (triggering event)

Figure 12-2
Bonfire Example of Steps Included in a Disconnect Analysis (continued)

DISCONNECT ANALYSIS STEPS	CHANGE DYNAMICS PROFILE/IMPLEMENTATION PLAN

4 - Determine primary implementation plan that is composed of one or more relevant internally incorporated defined changes.
 	
The objective of the primary defined implementation is to (a) eliminate any disconnect that exists that will not be eliminated as part of the execution of the primary defined process and (b) create a triggering event condition in the primary environment that will start the execution of the primary defined process.
	Primary Implementation Plan =
	• Move wood, newspaper, and matches from garage and place into fire pit
	• Light match and hold against newspaper to provide initial heat source (i.e., triggering event)
	
	Primary Implementation Factors (includes internally incorporated defined changes) and Associated Environment =
	• Move wood, newspaper and matches from garage to fire pit
	  • First-degree Secondary Environment = Garage/Backyard
	  • Implementation Process Factor Time Interval = 1 hour before bonfire
	• Light match and hold against newspaper in fire pit
	  • Primary Environment = Fire Pit
	  • Implementation Process Factor Tier I Time Interval = Immediately prior to execution of Primary Process

5 - Determine primary implementation disconnect.	Existing Conditions in First-degree Secondary Environment Garage/Backyard = • Newspaper • Matches • Insufficient wood Primary Implementation Disconnect = • Insufficient wood in garage

Figure 12-2
Bonfire Example of Steps Included in a Disconnect Analysis (continued)

DISCONNECT ANALYSIS STEPS	CHANGE DYNAMICS PROFILE/IMPLEMENTATION PLAN

6 – If required, adjust primary implementation plan.	Adjusted Primary Implementation Plan =
	• Purchase wood from store and place in garage
	• Move wood, newspaper, and matches from garage and place into fire pit
	• Light match and hold against newspaper to provide initial heat source (i.e., triggering event)
	
	Primary Implementation Factors (includes internally incorporated defined changes) and Associated Environment –
	• Purchase wood from store
	  • Second-degree Secondary Environment = Store/Garage
	  • Time Interval = 2 days before bonfire
	• Move wood, newspaper, and matches from garage to fire pit
	  • First-degree Secondary Environment = Garage/Backyard
	  • Time Interval = 1 hour before bonfire
	• Light match and hold against newspaper in fire pit
	  • Primary Environment = Fire Pit
	  • Tier I Time Interval = Immediately prior to execution of Primary Process

7 – Determine adjusted primary implementation disconnect	Existing Conditions in Second-degree Secondary Environment Store/Garage = • Automobile • Wood at store Existing Conditions in First-degree Secondary Environment Garage/Backyard = • Newspaper • Matches • Insufficient wood Primary Implementation Disconnect = • None

Step 1 depicts the selection of a desired primary defined change and the selected primary environment in which we want to obtain this desired change.

Step 2 is the selection of a valid primary defined process that we believe will yield the change we desire. The selected primary defined process will have primary process factors (including a primary process time interval) associated with it that must be supported by the conditions that exist within the primary environment.

Step 3 shows the difference between the conditions that exist in the primary environment at the point in time that we select the primary defined process and the required primary process factors that, in turn, represent the primary process disconnect. This primary process disconnect, in essence, is a representation of exactly what the environmental override consists of. The desired primary defined change cannot be successfully obtained until this disconnect is eliminated (that is, environmental override no longer exists).

While not depicted in this example, it should be noted that at this point we do have the option to try to modify the selected primary defined process (that is, look at alternative primary defined processes) in an attempt to either eliminate the disconnect as part of the execution of the primary defined process or in an attempt to create an improved structure relative to the level of disconnect that exists.

We can do this either by increasing or decreasing the number of primary process factors or by using alternative primary process factors that are incorporated within the selected primary defined process. However, any such modification will have an impact on both the length of the primary process time interval and the level and structural nature of the disconnect. At some point in time the option to modify the primary defined process can no longer be realistic and must be stabilized (that is, a primary defined process must be selected).

Once you have stabilized and selected a primary defined process, then a primary defined implementation must be created as indicated in Step 4. The objective of the primary defined implementation is (1) to eliminate any disconnect that exists that will not be eliminated as part of the execution of the primary defined process and (2) to create a triggering event condition in the primary environment that will start the execution of the primary defined process.

As shown in Step 5, primary implementation disconnects (that is, insufficient wood) can continue to exist between the primary implementation process factors and the conditions in the environments in which the primary defined implementation will execute. Therefore, if these primary implementation disconnects are not corrected, we will fail to obtain the desired primary defined change.

So in Step 6 the primary defined implementation is adjusted in response to the primary implementation disconnect.

Step 7 represents a final analysis to determine if any possible disconnect still exists. If there are no further primary process/implementation disconnects that exist at this point in time on the change/time continuum, then the primary defined implementation is ready to be launched with an expectation that the desired defined change will be obtained.

However, keep in mind that new disconnects can arise as we progress along the change/time continuum because of the change dynamics and environmental dynamics occurring within the relevant environments. Therefore, as we will come to discuss shortly, when a desired change is high in significance, we are probably going to want to attempt to incorporate monitoring and control points within the primary defined process/implementation in order to reduce the risks associated with any of these new disconnects.

Before we move on, there are some other points that can be derived from the example in Figure 12-2:

1. As we presented in Example 1, a disconnect analysis can also be a good time to analyze controllable and uncontrollable risks associated with obtaining the desired change. We can then look for ways to eliminate and mitigate as part of the development and selection of our primary process/implementation.

   For example, by examining the above disconnect analysis, we might determine that there is a risk that the particular store we go to is out of wood. The fact that the store could be out of wood could be considered an uncontrollable risk. We can mitigate this risk by adding a defined process to our primary defined implementation that determines what other stores in the area carry wood just in case the particular store we normally go to is out of wood when we need it.

   Likewise, the above example assumes the wood is already stored in the garage. However, if we assume that the wood is not stored inside the garage but outside in a woodpile, then there could be a risk that the wood could get wet from the weather between now and the time we want to use it. This would be considered a controllable risk that can be eliminated by adding a defined process that moves the wood into the garage and/or covers the wood well enough in advance of the bonfire to ensure the wood is dry when it is needed.

2. The example in Figure 12-2 focuses on a single primary defined process. However, a disconnect analysis can and should be used to select between potential alternative primary defined processes/implementations. By analyzing how the various available alternative primary process/implementations address any disconnects that exist, we increase our opportunity to reduce risk.

We should be selecting a primary process/implementation in which the degree and structural nature of the disconnect is smaller and/or more conducive to obtaining a successful primary defined change compared to other alternatives.

For example, let us say we want to produce a product. The product can be built using two alternative primary defined processes. One primary defined process uses Material A and the other one uses Material B. The product (that is, desired primary defined change) is acceptable no matter which material we use.

When we perform the disconnect analysis, we determine that Material B is already available in the primary environment whereas Material A is not and must be ordered. Therefore, the primary defined process that uses Material A has a disconnect whereas the primary process that uses Material B does not have a disconnect. In this case, all other things being equal, the primary defined process that uses Material B should be selected since there is less risk associated with it.

3. We should be selecting a primary process/implementation where the disconnect associated with the primary process/implementation time intervals is the most conducive to obtaining a successful primary defined change compared to other alternatives.

While we will explore the risk factor of time intervals in more detail shortly, the following should be noted here: the total time interval in the primary environment represents a condition in the primary environment. Therefore, there can be a disconnect represented by the difference between the total time interval available and the combination of the primary process and primary implementation time intervals (that is, the total of the time required to execute the primary defined process/implementation).

If any of the alternative primary defined process/implementations have a total time required to execute the primary defined process/implementation that exceeds the available total time interval (a negative disconnect), then they must be eliminated since the risk of failure is imminent.

ENERGY/EFFORT HUMP THEORY

We have determined earlier in this book that change requires energy and that, in fact, scientifically all change is nothing more than the transformation of one form of energy to another form of energy. In Chapter 7 on processes we also discussed the concept of effort as it applied to the science of change, noting that effort can be represented by the level of process factors associated with a given process. Given our recent introduction to the concept of disconnect, we have an opportunity to expand on our discussions of energy and effort.

If we take a step back to think about it, we should realize that the disconnect that is associated with any given defined process/implementation is a reflection of the amount of energy and effort it will take to accomplish a desired change by executing that particular given defined process/implementation. In essence, the number and structure of the process/implementation factors are not only a direct reflection of the disconnect but also a reflection of the amount of energy and effort that will be needed to eliminate this disconnect and obtain the desired change.

Just to close the loop, we have already shown how this measurement of effort, together with other intrinsic variables associated with a given defined process/implementation, can be used as a measure of efficiency when attempting to compare one alternative defined process/implementation against another alternative defined process/implementation.

However, there is another aspect (disconnect) linked to the amount of energy and effort required to execute a defined process/implementation that most often gets lost in the context of the dynamics related to complexity. It is this additional disconnect that the Energy/Effort Hump Theory centers its attention on with the intent of focusing on reducing risk.

The *Energy/Effort Hump Theory* states that the difference in the amount of energy/effort related to a given defined process/implementation compared to the actual amount of free available energy/effort that exists within the pertinent environments associated with the given defined process/implementation represents a disconnect (a Hump Theory disconnect).

If the disconnect is negative (that is, the amount of energy/effort related to a given defined process/implementation is greater than the actual amount of free available energy/effort that exists within the pertinent environments), then the defined process/implementation will fail, and the desired change will not be obtained. This disconnect exists not just at the macro level of the primary defined process/implementation but also at the micro level of the individual process/implementation factors.

I refer to it as a hump theory because the energy/effort required by the execution of a new defined process/implementation can be viewed as a "hump" along the change/time continuum in the energy/effort relative to the existing energy/effort levels that are in place for any given resource in the environment.

It is important to understand that these existing energy/effort levels that are in place for any given resource represent a condition in that environment. That is why we have a hump theory disconnect because there is a required process/implementation factor (that is, the required energy/effort) and there is an existing condition (that is, available energy/effort capacity) in the environment. Figure 12-3 is a presentation of just such a hump.

Figure 12-3

Energy/Effort Hump Theory

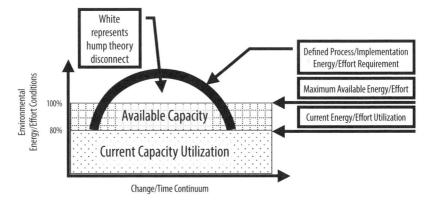

There are many examples of the Energy/Effort Hump Theory that are easy to understand. For example, let us say that the amount of gasoline in our gas tank (that is, available energy/effort) is less than the amount of gasoline required to reach our destination (that is, the desired defined change), and there are no places to obtain additional gasoline along the way.

The defined process of using our car to go from our current location to our final destination will fail, and we will be stranded somewhere in between, unsuccessful at obtaining our desired change. This is an example of a negative hump theory disconnect where the amount of gas available in the environment is less than the amount of gas required by the defined process/implementation.

While these sorts of obvious hump theory disconnects are not usually difficult to recognize when performing a disconnect analysis, there are more subtle hump theory disconnects that are very common and are missed, creating environmental override and a failed ability to obtain a desired change. The logic and issues look like this:

1. It is common for individuals, organizations, and societies to recognize upfront that there is energy/effort associated with a defined process/implementation. However, they often do so either (a) assuming an availability of an adequate or unlimited amount of energy/effort (that is, unlimited resources), (b) ignoring the availability all together, or (c) assuming that somehow things will work out and if a negative hump theory disconnect exists, it will somehow work its way out on its own.
2. Product providers, service providers, authors, and consultants often make the argument that as long as they adequately tell us upfront what their estimate of the required energy/effort is, it is our responsibility to make sure there are enough available resources (available energy/effort) to reach a successful execution of their defined process/implementation. As a side note, this is often the basis for why a claim of "lack of commitment" is made.
3. In reality, my experience indicates that because a negative hump theory disconnect can be very subtle, poorly understood, and/or undefined, it is often not adequately addressed as part of the defined process/implementation selection process. It, therefore, represents a major risk to the successful execution of the defined process/implementation, and the desired change is either compromised or never attained.

I am promoting the Energy/Effort Hump Theory because besides helping to define an often overlooked disconnect, it embraces a missing link in the analysis that individuals, organizations, and societies perform when selecting and executing a defined process/implementation.

The missing link is the reality that in most cases, "the resources to provide the energy/effort required to execute" a defined process/implementation "already have capacity considerations" that need to be evaluated and adjusted for in order to obtain the level of available energy/effort necessary to accommodate these "new" defined process/implementation requirements.

This is not a heavy-duty concept but is based upon everyday observation and common sense. For example, most people, both in their personal lives and in their business lives, are busy and/or have existing commitments. Therefore, if we add additional commitments associated with the execution of a new defined process/implementation, the result is an immediate negative hump theory disconnect that exists, assuming the energy/effort required exceeds any available excess energy/effort that the individual might have.

If this negative hump theory disconnect is not evaluated, and if a plan is not created to address the issues associated with it, then the available energy/effort required by the individual to execute the defined process/implementation will not be sufficient and the desired change will not be obtained.

Think of it this way. Let's say that our organization at work has a department in which the employees are already putting in an average of 60 to 70 hours per week. Thus, it is unlikely that this department has any excess capacity (energy/effort) that it can make available for the execution of a new defined process/implementation.

Assuming this department represents a critical resource to the execution of the defined process/implementation, the negative disconnect related to this department will create an environmental override that will cause the execution of the defined process/implementation to fail unless other accommodations (changes) are incorporated into the defined process/implementation that address this negative hump theory disconnect.

The Energy/Effort Hump Theory goes beyond just defining the issue and provides some tools to use that can potentially help reduce the risk of a hump theory disconnect:

1. As part of the disconnect analysis we perform for any given defined process/implementation, we should include an assessment of the amount of energy/effort that is required at both a macro (overall) and micro (individual process factor) level within the defined process/implementation.
2. Based upon this assessment, we should perform a focused hump theory disconnect analysis "for critical resource requirements" to determine if any negative hump theory disconnects exist. For example, within a business organization, a negative hump theory disconnect can exist based upon critical resources at the individual, department, or even the organizational level.
3. If a negative hump theory disconnect exists, we must either (a) modify the defined process/implementation to reduce the amount of energy/effort required in order to eliminate the hump theory disconnect, (b) include additional process/implementation factors to address the available energy/effort capacity condition within the environment, and/or (c) use some combination of both.
4. Potential alternatives to address a negative hump theory disconnect can include:
    a. Making sure all existing excess capacity is appropriately consumed
    b. Eliminating some of the current energy/effort requirements that exist within the environment (that is, eliminating workload)
    c. Transferring some of the current energy/effort requirements within the environment to a different environment (that is, transferring workload)
    d. Outsourcing some of the current energy/effort requirements that exist within the environment to a new environment (that is, using external versus internal resources)

e. Increasing the maximum amount of available energy/effort levels within the environment (that is, increasing-capacity)

TIME INTERVAL CONSIDERATIONS

We have had numerous discussions regarding time intervals, and hopefully you have developed an appreciation as to just how important they can be relative to obtaining the change you desire. It is critical to note that there can often be a great deal of flexibility in the time intervals that are related to change.

This includes not just flexibility in the time intervals incorporated as process and implementation factors within the selected defined process and defined implementation. It also includes the total time interval available from the point in time of selecting the defined process/implementation you want to use to the point in time when you expect the defined change to be 100 percent effective (that is, fully obtained).

Unfortunately, this flexibility also leads to a great deal of opinions and options as to how best to structure time intervals leaving the ability to create hard and fast rules difficult at best. For example, I have met individuals and service providers who strongly believe that it is better to have long process/implementation time intervals. Their logic is that total time intervals in excess of the process/implementation time intervals related to the selected defined process/implementation are desirable so that there is time available to react to the unexpected (risks).

I have also been involved with individuals and organizations that believe in shorter process/implementation time intervals and total time intervals in order to limit the time exposure to all the ancillary change (risks) that can take place.

Then there are philosophies that tend to lean toward long time interval defined processes with associated short time interval defined implementations. On the other hand, some philosophies and methodologies lean toward short time interval defined processes with associated long time interval defined implementations.

Interestingly, I have seen all these philosophies succeed and all these philosophies fail. In addition, I have often seen situations in which there is little choice as to the time intervals available. This is because of either the critical nature of the change (emergency situations) or the fact there is a very limited, or even only a single choice, in the selection of a defined process/implementation that can yield the desired change (a limited number of known valid options).

So where does this leave us in attempting to manage, control, and reduce the risk connected with time intervals? It leaves us relying on the basics we have learned from change science and trying to focus on those concepts that might help.

Once again, unfortunately there are no hard and fast rules, and every situation needs to be evaluated in its own context. However, as presented in Figure 12-4, there are change science concepts that, when arranged into a certain perspective, I think do support some opportunities that increase the odds of reducing risks, depending on the context.

Figure 12-4
Time Interval Scenario Analysis

Context	Time Interval Considerations (Rule of Thumb)	Rationale
1 - Change that needs to occur or naturally occurs quickly	Shift activity into the primary environment and toward the defined process. This represents more process factors and a longer process time interval and limited implementation factors (i.e., a focus on the triggering event only) and a short implementation time interval.	Since the change either must execute or naturally executes quickly, it is best to keep all the activity executing in a continuous stream within the primary process and concentrated within the primary environment. This allows us to concentrate on creating the most efficient and effective defined process possible.
2 - Change where gaps of open time exist between activities (i.e., between internally incorporated defined processes/defined process/implementation factors)	Shift activity away from the defined process. This represents as few process factors as possible with a short process time interval and an expanded defined implementation and implementation factors and longer implementation time interval.	Given that a defined process should be executed in a continuous sequence of activity, gaps of open time are accommodated more successfully as part of the defined implementation. This allows better utilization of multiple environments and more flexibility breaking the implementation activities (i.e., internally incorporated defined processes) into smaller incremental activities within the implementation time interval. It also provides increased opportunity to use control/monitoring points.
3 - Change that can leverage off of multiple environments	Shift activity away from the defined process. This represents as few process factors as possible with a short process time interval and an expanded defined implementation and implementation factors and longer implementation time interval.	Given that the primary defined process must execute 100 percent in the primary environment, activity should be shifted toward the primary defined implementation in order to best leverage off the use of multiple environments and the ability to execute both sequentially and simultaneously.

Figure 12-4
Time Interval Scenario Analysis (continued)

Context	Time Interval Considerations (Rule of Thumb)	Rationale
4 - Change that we want to use control and monitoring points in	Shift activity away from the defined process. This represents as few process factors as possible with a short process time interval and an expanded defined implementation and implementation factors and longer implementation time interval.	Given that a defined process should be executed in a continuous sequence of activity, the stopping points/gaps of open time associated with control and monitoring points are accommodated more successfully as part of the defined implementation. Therefore, activity should be shifted toward the primary defined implementation. This allows better utilization of multiple environments and more flexibility breaking the implementation activities into smaller incremental activities within the implementation time interval which, in turn, increases the flexibility and effectiveness of using the control/monitoring points.
5 - Lack of stability in the primary environment —change where there is a great deal of change/environmental dynamics occurring in primary environment	Shift activity away from the defined process. This represents as few process factors as possible with a short process time interval and an expanded defined implementation and implementation factors and longer implementation time interval.	It is important that the primary defined process is 100 percent effective so the longer the primary defined process must execute, the more likelihood that the ancillary changes associated with change/environmental dynamics within the primary environment will create environmental override and a failed primary defined process. Therefore, activity should be shifted toward the primary defined implementation. This allows better utilization of multiple environments and more flexibility breaking the implementation activities into smaller incremental activities within the implementation time interval. It also provides increased opportunity to use control/monitoring points in order to better react to the ancillary changes associated with change/environmental dynamics.

Figure 12-4
Time Interval Scenario Analysis (continued)

Context	Time Interval Considerations (Rule of Thumb)	Rationale
6 - Lack of stability in all environments—change where there is a great deal of change/environmental dynamics occurring in most/all of the environments (i.e., primary environment and any secondary environments used for the defined implementation)	The key here is to keep the overall time interval associated with the primary defined process/implementation as short as possible *no matter how large the total time interval that is available.* To increase the probability that we obtain a 100 percent effective primary defined change, we will probably shift activity away from the primary defined process toward the primary defined implementation. We also might want to use control and monitoring points that would also represent a shift in activity away from the defined process. This represents as few process factors as possible with a short process time interval and an expanded defined implementation and implementation factors and longer implementation time interval.	Rapidly occurring change dynamics and/or environmental dynamics are a representation that a lot of ancillary change (i.e., change occurring outside of the change associated with your defined process/implementation) is taking place. While much of this ancillary change might be irrelevant, the greater the amount of ancillary change, the greater the probability that some of the ancillary change will be relevant conflicting change that will lead to environmental override. In short, it represents a lack of stability in the environments, which increases risk. Therefore, we want to execute the primary defined change as quickly as we can which would require a primary process time interval and primary implementation time interval that is as short in length as possible. These short execution time intervals should be irrespective of the total time interval that might be available unless early execution of the primary defined change is not an option, in which case, the execution of the primary defined change should be delayed but the primary process/implementation time intervals should still remain as short as possible. Consistent with Example 3, we will probably also want to keep the primary defined process as short as possible by shifting activities toward the primary defined implementation in order to increase the likelihood of obtaining 100 percent effectiveness. If the amount of ancillary change is really dramatic, we should also consider using control and monitoring points in order to react to the rapidly occurring ancillary change even though it might require increasing the time interval associated with the primary defined implementation.

Figure 12-4
Time Interval Scenario Analysis (continued)

Context	Time Interval Considerations (Rule of Thumb)	Rationale
7 - Change where there is the requirement to use critical resources that have large amounts of demand on them (i.e., limited capacity)	The key here is to keep the overall time interval associated with the primary defined process/implementation as short as possible *no matter how large the total time interval that is available.* We also might want to use control and monitoring points, which would represent a shift in activity away from the defined process. This represents as few process factors as possible with a short process time interval and an expanded defined implementation and implementation factors and longer implementation time interval.	This example is extremely similar to the lack of environmental stability in Example 6 in that limited capacity can often equate to excessive demands (i.e., rapidly occurring change/environmental dynamics) on a certain resource (i.e., an individual). However, it can also represent situations like a temporary requirement for a piece of equipment that is already running at or near capacity. In any case, we want to execute the primary defined change as quickly as we can, which would require a primary process time interval and primary implementation time interval that is as short in length as possible. These short execution time intervals should be irrespective of the total time interval that might be available unless early execution of the primary defined change is not an option in which case the execution of the primary defined change should be delayed but the primary process/implementation time intervals should still remain as short as possible. The reasons for these short execution time intervals center around two factors. One, the ability to provide some level of flexibility if the extra demand is only for a short period of time (i.e., as in the case of a piece of equipment already running at or near capacity). Two, the fact that the change/environmental dynamics associated with the critical resource creates a lack of stability so the shorter the time interval, the less exposure to stability risk. If the amount of ancillary change is really dramatic, we should also consider using control and monitoring points in order to react to the rapidly occurring ancillary change even though it might require increasing the time interval associated with the primary defined implementation.

Figure 12-4
Time Interval Scenario Analysis (continued)

Context	Time Interval Considerations (Rule of Thumb)	Rationale
8 - Total time interval is long compared to process/implementation time interval requirements	Lengths and structure of time intervals should first be determined based upon the situations in Examples 1 through 7. However, the primary process interval and primary implementation time interval should always be as short as possible unless there are obvious risk factors that would justify longer primary process/implementation time intervals. Execution of the primary process/implementation to obtain the primary defined change should be based upon when the primary defined change needs to be obtained but must take into account the limiting condition of the actual total time interval available at the point in time that the primary defined change and primary environment are selected. Allocation of activities and therefore time intervals between the primary defined process and primary defined implementation should be shifted toward the primary defined implementation and away from the primary defined process unless there are obvious risk factors that would indicate otherwise.	It should be noted up front that not everyone will agree with this position. However, the secondary time interval risk factor indicates that the greater the length of the time interval associated with executing and obtaining a defined change, the greater the probability that the ancillary change occurring during that time interval because of change/environmental dynamics will create environmental override. Therefore, unless there are other conditions or potential conditions (such as other risk factors) to the contrary that need to be taken consideration, it is best to keep the execution time intervals associated with a primary change as short as practically possible. With regard to the allocation of activities between the primary defined process and primary defined implementation, except in cases like Example 1 where rapid execution is required or cases where risk factors would dictate otherwise, an allocation of activity toward the primary defined implementation provides more flexibility and capability to leverage off of such considerations as: • The use of multiple environments • The use of simultaneous and/or sequential execution • The use of smaller incremental internally incorporated defined changes (i.e., smaller incremental implementation factors) • The ability to accommodate gaps of time between the execution of the incremental implementation factors • The use of control and monitoring points Finally, shorter primary process time intervals also decrease time interval/environmental override risk relative to obtaining a 100 percent *effective* desired primary change.

Figure 12-4
Time Interval Scenario Analysis (continued)

Context	Time Interval Considerations (Rule of Thumb)	Rationale
9 - Total time interval is short compared to process/implementation time interval requirements	This represents a risk of imminent failure. If the primary process/implementation is not modified so that the execution time interval is reduced, the defined change will fail for certain given that there is not enough total time available to obtain a 100 percent effective primary defined change.	This is another example of the secondary time interval risk factor where the execution time interval to obtain a desired primary defined change exceeds the available total time interval. The total time interval represents the time interval from the point in time on the change/time continuum where the defined implementation starts execution and the point in time on the change/time continuum where the primary process completes execution and a 100 percent effective desired primary defined change is obtained. Since a negative time interval disconnect exists, the defined process/implementation must be modified or replaced so as to reflect any time restrictions associated with the total time interval that is available.

Before we leave this section on time interval risk considerations, I want to discuss risks associated with emergency situations. People will say that emergency situations are often the cases in which the critical nature of the change is the highest, risk is high, the time intervals are the shortest, and the ability to apply change science concepts associated with risk is limited at best.

While I could not agree more with this assessment, that does not mean we should just give up. Because the time intervals are so short in emergency situations, the best way to approach risk reduction is from a perspective of uncontrollable risk.

In essence, an emergency situation is usually the result of some sort of unexpected uncontrollable risk. Therefore, the best chance of reducing risk is through mitigation. In fact, there are all sorts of examples of just this sort of emergency risk mitigation. Fire extinguishers and sprinkler systems, portable first aid kits and defibrillators, EMTs and specialized trauma centers all represent uncontrollable risk mitigation (change protectionism).

There is obviously no way we can extend mitigation to every potential emergency situation we face. The key is to focus our attention on emergency situations that have the greatest applicability to us as individuals, organizations, or societies.

We need to remember that change science teaches us that experience and knowledge represent a powerful advantage when selecting a defined process/implementation. Therefore, developing an experience/knowledge base in advance can help us determine proper actions in cases of an emergency and can be a great way to help mitigate risk for any potential emergency situations that represent the greatest exposures to us as individuals, organizations, or societies.

Likewise, environmental conditions should be taken into consideration as part of our mitigation. For example, people with a major health condition probably do not want to live in a location where the environmental conditions include few if any medical facilities.

Bottom line, if there is a possibility that an emergency situation has a higher than normal likelihood of occurring, some efforts focused on risk mitigation should be something we can and should explore.

CONTROL, MONITORING, AND ADJUSTMENT POINTS

If we want to reduce risk and we do not have any time interval constraints, then using control and monitoring points can be a powerful tool.

As already discussed, *control and monitoring points* represent stopping points embedded within our defined process/implementation that allows us to:

1. Evaluate actual progress status versus expectations
2. Modify defined process/implementation
3. Update risk and disconnect analysis
4. Provide feedback

The above capabilities all help us reduce the potential for risk. Central to the use of control/monitoring points is a recognition that many of the decisions that are made relative to the selection of specific defined processes/implementations are based upon the change dynamics and environmental dynamics we are anticipating/expecting to take place within the pertinent environments.

Control/monitoring points provide an ability to adjust or modify these selected defined processes/implementations based upon the events (that is, change/environmental dynamics) that actually transpire in these environments. In other words, they provide us an opportunity to adjust and compensate for any new risks that might have arisen.

A big advantage of control/monitoring points is an ability to revisit our risk and disconnect analysis. Given that disconnects are only relevant as of the point in time on the change/time continuum that the disconnect analysis is performed, control/monitoring points provide an opportunity to update the list of disconnects. This, in turn, provides the ability to look for new "eliminate and mitigate" opportunities and/or, as noted above, adjust the selected defined processes/implementations to compensate for any disconnects that are new or that are no longer applicable.

Another advantage of control/monitoring points is an increased opportunity for feedback. It should be recognized that it is often difficult to derive desired feedback because of the pace of execution and structural nature connected with certain defined process/implementations. Therefore, control/monitoring points can provide opportunities to derive and communicate feedback based upon actual data.

Finally, some people will challenge the logic of increasing the process/implementation time intervals through the inclusion of control/monitoring points. While there is a definite trade-off to be considered, it is not unusual for control/monitoring points to actually reduce process/implementation time intervals.

This is due to the fact that there are often alternative defined processes/implementations that we can incorporate into the overall primary defined process/implementation at these control/monitoring points. Because we have the ability to modify our selection of executing defined processes/implementations on the fly at these control/monitoring points, the overall primary process/implementation time interval could be positively or negatively impacted. However, the key is that any such impact will be in response to the actual conditions that currently exist and, therefore, in the end represents a reduction in risk.

VALIDITY TESTING

You may be scratching your head wondering why we are addressing validity at the end of this chapter when the validity of the defined change, defined process, defined implementation, and the selected primary environment is considered a primary risk factor. The answer is very simple: if we perform the other risk reduction exercises already discussed, many of issues associated with validity should become apparent.

For example, one of the outputs from performing a disconnect analysis should be a determination as to whether a particular primary defined process/implementation will even work. If it does not work, then it is not a valid defined process/implementation, at least within the context of that primary environment. As in the example of the gallbladder surgery, we can also leverage off of the use of controllable and uncontrollable risk analysis for the validation of the selected primary environment.

Likewise, if we cannot find any primary defined process/implementation that will yield the primary defined change we desire, then we have at least an indication that those primary defined changes might not be valid. However, we must take care here because of the fact that the inability to find a primary defined process/implementation that will work could be more of a reflection of our capability to determine one based upon our experience/knowledge base rather than on the fact that the primary defined change is structurally invalid.

This brings us to another aspect to consider when trying to determine the risk associated with the validity of the defined change, defined process, defined implementation, and the selected primary environment. The depth and strength of our experience/knowledge base needs to be a definite consideration. The deeper the level of experience/knowledge we have, the more we can rely on it to determine validity, especially when it is utilized in conjunction with the other risk reduction exercises.

Therefore, if our experience/knowledge base leaves something to be desired and validity is an issue, we should attempt to increase our experience/knowledge base either through research and/or, if possible, through the testing of some alternatives.

However, I will caution you one last time, even if your experience/knowledge base, research, and/or testing indicate that you have a valid defined change, defined process, defined implementation, and selected primary environment, you should still perform at a minimum a disconnect analysis and any other risk analysis necessary to verify that the validity is maintained within the context of the pertinent environments in which the execution will take place.

FINAL THOUGHTS

This is a good time to revisit the quandary regarding lack of commitment. I have reached the conclusion that while there are times where a lack of commitment is the basis for a failure to obtain successful change, more often than not, lack of commitment has nothing to do with it.

Over the years I have come to realize that much of the change that fails is really because of a lack of a fundamental understanding of how change works together with a lack of attention to risk.

By reading this book you should have come to realize that change is not just some mystical notion that we are forced to live with and that only a selected group of people have mastered. Instead, change operates in very specific ways that can be understood through a scientific approach using definitions, principles, and concepts.

More importantly, change will naturally occur with or without our influence in ways that can often be too intricate and complicated for us to fully predict. Therefore, there is risk associated with obtaining the desired change we are looking for, and it is this risk that is generally ignored when explaining why the change we are expecting does not take place.

So in order for the concepts and tools that we have explored to have the greatest potential to help us obtain the change we are looking for, I am not asking you for your unwavering commitment. Instead, when dealing with a change that is significant to you as an individual, organization, or society, you need to recognize that risk exists and do the best you can to address it head-on, leveraging off of the knowledge that exists within the science of change.

EPILOGUE

What We Have Discovered

The change around us is transformed from the mystical to the practical through the science of change!

Tom Somodi

I doubt if, prior to reading this book, many of you have thought about the subject of change in the same context as I have. But I am relatively certain most people have experienced frustration, anxiety, and even excitement relative to the change that has occurred in their lives. I also believe that many, if not most of you, have been confused and/or even suspicious of what you have read, heard, or been taught about the change taking place for you as an individual, at your place of work, or in the world in which you live.

In the introduction to this book I described how I too, became more and more suspicious about the approaches, promotions, methodologies, and understandings that I was exposed to surrounding the subject of change. A major tipping point in this suspicion centered on the common reference to a lack of commitment to explain the failure of an individual, organization, or society to obtain the change they desired and were working toward. While at times a lack of commitment might have been an accurate reflection of fact, more often than not, such a conclusion did not appear to be supported by the actual facts at hand and therefore, was erroneous.

As discussed in the two chapters on risk, I also came to realize that more often than not, a proper perspective and analysis of the risks associated with obtaining a desired change were missing. On top of that, if and when risk was incorporated into the dialog and/or methodology, it all too often took place after the fact relative to the selection of the defined process and defined implementation.

In addition, these discussions of risks tended to be externalized from the selected defined process and defined implementation. In other words, the assumptions used were that the risks of failure to obtain a change did not lie within the processes and implementations selected, but if a change failed to occur, it was due to risks external to those selected processes and implementations.

Fortunately, my life experiences have provided me with some significant exposure to change which, in turn, as you have read in this book, allowed me to continue to explore the subject of change in much greater detail. I came to realized that change was not as mystical as some individuals, organizations, and promoters wanted me to think it was.

More importantly, as I discussed in Chapter 1, I came to discover that change is not strictly something you need to obtain or a strategy to follow but is, in fact, something that you are constantly experiencing. Unlike what many would like you to believe, change, in fact, is not just some method or procedure to execute but an integral, if not a driving, force behind all that exists and all that is happening around us.

Eventually I reached a point where the dilemma I faced was trying to determine the best way to convey to others, such as you, these concepts surrounding change that I had discovered. Fortunately, the solution already existed right in front of me in the definitions, concepts, and principles that had been developed. Change is not just something to execute or implement to obtain. Change is in reality a science.

So after reading this book I hope you are as blown away as I am at:

- How as individuals, organizations, and society we have learned to so routinely handle, adjust, and survive in positive ways to the constant change that is taking place around us.
- How like many other sciences and disciplines, the science of change can be encapsulated in a relatively short list of definitions, concepts, and principles.
- How through viewing change as a science, we have a platform to systematically and scientifically approach all the change that exists in the universe (both known and unknown) in which we live.
- How change can never be guaranteed, but by leveraging off of the science of change, we can improve our ability as individuals, organizations, and society to control, manage, and obtain the change we desire.
- How the subject of change truly does deserve to be a science!

Glossary

Chain of Events Principle. The defined changes that occur because of defined processes that are executed during one time interval on the change/time continuum create the conditions in a given environment, including the triggering event condition (that is, the defined implementations) that implement the next set of defined processes in the subsequent time interval on the change/time continuum in that given environment. This chain of events continues as time progresses along the change/time continuum creating *perpetuating change*.

Change. The transformation or alteration of the current state of being (or *state*) to a different state of being as it relates to a person, place, or thing or as it relates to the interrelationships between persons, places, or things.

Change dispersion. The type, intensity, and direction of energy associated with a defined change emanating outward into its primary and surrounding secondary environments from its epicenter in the primary environment in which it was executed.

Change dynamics. The continuous activities, interactions, and interrelationships that exist between the elements of change, environments, and change science principles.

Change dynamics analysis. An attempt to define all the specific change dynamics <u>that occurred</u> in order to derive a specific defined change that is under consideration. A change dynamics analysis can also be used to try to determine why a specific defined change *did not occur* in a given environment. It includes such items as:

1. A description of the defined change being examined.
2. The environment(s) in which the defined change took place.
3. The starting state of being in the environment(s) under consideration and its specific position on the change/time continuum; in other words, the conditions that existed in the environment(s) in which the defined change took place.
4. The length of the time interval on the change/time continuum associated with progressing from the starting state of being to the ending state of being.
5. The defined process used to obtain the desired defined change and how the associated process factors matched up to the relevant conditions that existed in the environment(s) under consideration at various points in time on the change/time continuum.
6. Implementation strategies used based upon the answers to the above questions.

Change dynamics profile. An outline of all the specific criteria necessary to try to obtain a specific desired defined change. It includes:

1. A description of the defined change we are examining.
2. Environment(s) under consideration.

3. The starting state of being in the environment(s) under consideration and its specific position on the change/time continuum; in other words, conditions that exist in the environment(s) we are considering.
4. The length of the time interval on the change/time continuum (assuming there are restrictions) associated with progressing from the starting state of being to the ending state of being.
5. Possible defined processes under consideration to obtain the desired defined change and the matchup of the associated process factors to the relevant conditions that exist in the environment(s) under consideration.
6. Possible defined implementation strategies based upon the answers to the above questions.

Change effect. Any condition that currently exists in an environment (either a primary or secondary environment) that is the result of a defined change that executed in a different environment at an earlier time interval on the change/time continuum.

Change protectionism. A plan that, if executed, has the potential to counter the impacts of an uncontrollable risk if and when it occurs.

Change science. A perspective of change as a science with definitions, principles, and theories that can be challenged and expanded upon through discussion, experimentation, logic, and mathematics. Change science is a science that is universal, bidirectionally interacting with other sciences.

Change Science Institute. A formal organization whose goal is the promotion of further research, education, and training for the advancement of change as a science.

Change/Time Continuum Principle. A statement that in order to have change in a given environment (that is, progress from one state of being to another state of being), the passage of an interval of time (time interval) must occur. Therefore:

1. Change will not exist in a given environment without the passage of time.
2. Change occurs over a continuum of time or change/time continuum.
3. The greater the length of the interval of time on the change/time continuum (that is, interval of time that passes between one state of being and the next state of being), the greater the potential amount of total change in conditions within that given environment.

Cognitively-influenced change. A defined change that is obtained through the implementation of a process associated with the interaction between the laws of science, the environment, and some cognitive influence that impacts the specific defined change (that is, specific state of being).

Cognitively-influenced conditions. Those conditions derived from change dynamics that would not have occurred in the given environment during a given time interval without cognitive influence.

Cognitively-influenced triggering event. Triggering event conditions derived from change dynamics that would not have occurred in the given environment during a given time interval without cognitive influence.

Complementary relevant conditions. Conditions that support the defined change and/or are directly equal to the required process and/or implementation factors.

Complexity. Certain conditions that are measured in relative terms, can be interrelated, are complicated to understand and manage, and can represent underlying secondary drivers that increase the probability that the primary risk factor of environmental override will exist to negate the ability to obtain a desired defined change or desired overall defined change. Five major underlying conditions of complexity include:

1. Magnitude
2. Disconnect
3. Experience and knowledge
4. Control
5. The degree of unpredictability of future environmental conditions

Conditions. Representations of:

- Actual states of being such as the temperature of the air in a room, a building that exists on a city street, a specific molecular structure, or the existence of a specific star. Conditions can usually be measured and/or defined in some sort of substantive or structural context.
- The end result of a defined change and are directly related to the change dynamics that are occurring along the change/time continuum.

Conflicting relevant conditions. Conditions that are relevant because they in some way do not support the defined change and will obstruct the execution of processes and/or implementations required to obtain the defined change.

Constant conditions. Conditions within an environment that do not tend to change over extended time intervals on the change time continuum. While a constant condition can also be a relevant condition and incorporated into a defined change as a process or implementation factor, it tends to be fixed/constant (that is, stable) in its characteristics over an extended period of time on the change/time continuum.

Control and monitoring points. Stopping points embedded within a defined process/implementation that allow:

1. Evaluation of actual progress status versus expectations
2. Modification of defined process/implementation
3. Update of risk and disconnect analysis
4. Provision of feedback

Controllable risk. Any risk that has the potential to be subject to a direct influence through the action and/or actions (that is, cognitive influence) generated by individuals and/or organizations that in some way have a vested interest in obtaining the given change under consideration.

Defined change. The first element of change that represents an identification/definition of the exact change to obtain or examine.

Defined implementation. The third element of change that represents what conditions must exist in order that the actual execution/implementation of the defined process can take place and how those conditions will be obtained.

Defined process. The second element of change that represents the identification/definition of the exact process that was used or will be used to obtain the defined change under examination. In order to move from one state of being to another state of being, a process must occur. Definition of this process includes an identification of any factors that will be required including the sequence of activities and actions that need to take place in order to move from the beginning state of being to the ending state of being associated with the defined change.

Definitional parameters. Those parameters that define the assumptions and specific characteristics used in determining a defined change and its associated defined process and defined implementation. Definitional parameters include:

1. A clear description of the defined change being examined
2. Environment(s) involved and conditions associated with those environments
3. The length of the time interval on the time continuum (assuming there are restrictions) associated with the defined change under consideration
4. Defined processes under consideration to obtain the desired defined change
5. Defined implementation strategies under consideration.
6. Any other critical considerations associated with the defined change under examination

Desired defined change. A defined change the result of which is desired (wanted) by a specific individual or entity. A desired defined change can be naturally-occurring or can represent an end objective of a cognitively-influenced change.

Direct observation. Observation taking place when someone is located in such a way relative to the defined change that he or she is able to directly experience and/or observe the defined change as it executes during the time/interval on the change/time continuum. This would most likely mean that the person would be in the primary environment, but, depending on how the primary and secondary environments are defined, there is the potential that the person could be located in a secondary environment.

Disconnect analysis. The concept that if a change does not already exist in a given environment, then there is disconnect between the conditions that exist in that environment and the factors required to obtain the change, and, therefore, disconnect analysis attempts to quantify the disconnects in order to reduce risk. These disconnects in essence represent the specifics as to why environmental override exists.

Discrete system. A system that is intended to obtain an overall defined change that is one-off in context. While a discrete system can be duplicated, it has not been specifically constructed to be repeated over time.

Dominant conditions. Conditions within an environment that tend to dominate the change dynamics that are executing over a specific time interval on the change/time continuum. These conditions are characterized by the dominance they have on all the change activity that is occurring over a specified period of time on the change/time continuum.

Dynamics. Something that has continuous activity and interactions.

Effectiveness. The ability to obtain 100 percent of the desired defined change through the execution of a specific defined process.

Efficiency. The ability to obtain a specific defined change with a minimum expenditure of time and other process factors when compared to alternative defined processes.

Effort. All the process factors associated with a defined process other than the time interval process factor, which needs to be analyzed independently. Effort can and should be analyzed from several different perspectives:

- The number of process factors associated with a defined process
- The type of process factors associated with a defined process.
- Situational conditions
- Cost based on the evaluation of effort relative to efficiency

Elements of change. Three basic elements associated with a change:

1. Defined change
2. Defined process
3. Defined implementation

Eliminate and mitigate (controllable and uncontrollable risk). The concept that risk can be viewed in the context of risk factors that are controllable and risk factors that are uncontrollable. A controllable risk factor should be eliminated provided the significance of the risk factor justifies the effort of elimination. However, if the risk factor is uncontrollable, then that risk factor should be mitigated provided the significance of the risk factor justifies the effort of mitigation.

Energy/Effort Hump Theory. The difference in the amount of energy/effort related to a given defined process/implementation compared to the actual amount of free available energy/effort that exists within the pertinent environments associated with the given defined process/implementation representing a disconnect (a Hump Theory disconnect). If the disconnect is negative (that is, the amount of energy/effort related to a given defined process/implementation is greater than the actual amount of free available energy/effort that exists within the pertinent environments), then the defined process/implementation will fail and the desired change will not be obtained. This disconnect exists not just at the macro level of the primary defined process/implementation but also at the micro level of the individual process/implementation factors.

Environment. The context, circumstances, and conditions that exist in a *specific defined space* at a *specific point or period of time* in which the change elements must operate. In theory there can be as few as one environment, which would be represented by the entire known and unknown universe, or there could be countless environments if the space associated with every smallest subatomic particle was treated as an individual environment.

Environmental adjustments. All of the changes (that is, the universe of changes) that occur in a given environment during a given time interval on the change/time continuum.

Environmental dynamics. The continuous activities, interactions, and interrelationships that exist within and between environments. Environmental dynamics focuses not only on the how, why, and what is happening to the conditions within a given environment but also on the interrelationships between environments.

Environmental override principle. A statement that if the conditions contained within a given environment will not support the requirements of a specific defined process or specific defined implementation, the defined change associated with the defined process and/or defined implementation will not be obtained. Therefore, it does not matter if you are using a proven process and/or a proven implementation to obtain a certain defined change. The reality is that the defined change will not be obtained using that defined process and/or defined implementation if the conditions in a given environment are not available to support that specific defined process and/or defined implementation.

Exclusive primary environment. A primary environment that has the distinction of being the ONLY possible environment that is relevant to a specific defined change under examination (for example, your body relative to the defined change of eliminating a headache that you have is an exclusive primary environment).

Experience. The knowledge we have derived of a defined change resulting from a specific "defined process–to-environment relationship."

Experience/Change/Power Equation. Experience = data and information = knowledge = increased ability to select within any given environment superior defined processes and defined implementations = increased probability to obtain a superior effective and successful desired defined change = power.

Expertise. The accumulation of an extensive amount of experiences (either directly experienced or learned from others) in a particular subject matter. In other words, over time, an expert in a particular subject matter is exposed to numerous defined process-to-environment relationships and their resulting defined change. This, in turn, creates a knowledge base that increases the likelihood (that is, reliability) that he or she can predict/select what defined process—compared to others—will execute in the future in a particular environment resulting in a specified defined change.

External environmental adjustments. Environmental adjustments in a primary environment that are partially or completely influenced by the change dynamics that have occurred externally to the selected primary environment (that is, from a secondary environment).

Fixed environment. Any primary or secondary environment that is fixed in location relative to all or certain surrounding environments during a specified time interval on the change/time continuum (for example, your brain can be a primary environment that is fixed in location relative to your body, or a house on a street can represent a fixed environment).

Functionality trade-off. Situations in which a change requires a selection between two alternative functionalities, both of which have a level of desirability but which are interconnected in such a way that you cannot obtain the functionality of one alternative without sacrificing the functionality of the other alternative.

Hierarchy of change or **change hierarchy.** Simultaneous change occurring within the known universe all the way from the subatomic level to the intergalactic level and not only occurring simultaneously at these levels but also interactively between these levels. Based upon the change science principle of simultaneous change.

Implementation factors. The specific factors that must be present, including the activities and actions that must take place, in order to implement the defined process.

Implementation plan. A detailed description of a defined implementation, including not only a definition of all the required implementation factors but also any details related to underlying strategies, assumptions, and potential conflicting relevant conditions associated with the defined implementation.

Implementation system. A specific defined implementation with two or more defined processes embedded in it as implementation factors and the overall defined change would be the creation of the required conditions in the primary environment to support the execution of a specific defined process.

Implementation time interval. The time interval implementation factor associated with the execution of a specific defined implementation.

Internal environmental adjustments. Environmental adjustments that are 100 percent derived from conditions and change dynamics that are internal to a selected primary environment during a given time interval on the change/time continuum.

Intuition. The ability to establish an expected defined process-to-environment relationship and the resulting defined change based upon similar (but not exact) experiences.

Irrelevant conditions. Any condition in the universe of conditions within the relevant environment that is <u>not</u> relevant to the process factors and implementation factors associated with the defined process and defined implementation under examination.

Irrelevant environmental adjustments. Any environmental adjustments out of the universe of all environmental adjustments taking place in a given environment that are not relevant to the change dynamics required to obtain a given defined change under examination.

Magnitude. The degree of change associated with a defined change relative to alternative defined changes that use a common basis of measurement. For example, the defined change of losing 50 pounds of weight is of a greater magnitude than a defined change of losing 20 pounds of weight.

Mobile environment. Any primary or secondary environment that can have movement in its location relative to surrounding environments, thereby having the ability to create a set of new surrounding environments as it moves (for example, the mobility of your body or a cloud in the sky is a primary environment relative to surrounding secondary environments).

Multi-causal system. A system that either utilizes other types of systems or evolves from other types of systems.

Naturally-occurring change. A defined change that is obtained through the naturally-occurring implementation and execution of a process associated with the interactions between the laws of science and the environment. Naturally-occurring change takes place naturally with no cognitive influence or intervention.

Naturally-occurring conditions. Those conditions derived exclusively from the change dynamics associated with the physical laws of science (both known and unknown) in the given environment during a given time interval.

Naturally-occurring triggering event. A triggering event condition derived exclusively from change dynamics associated with physical laws of science in the given environment during a given time interval.

Off-the-shelf/canned systems. Systems developed and promoted by individuals, organizations, and societies to provide products, services, or change methodologies across a diverse base of possible users and/or environments.

Organization and/or society. Two or more individuals combining together to cognitively influence the environment to obtain certain desired defined change that would be difficult if not impossible to obtain at an individual level.

Overall defined change. The output from a system consisting of a specific defined change or set of defined changes.

Perpetuating/perpetual change. The result of a continuous cycle of triggering events (that is, defined implementations) created by the execution of defined processes in one time interval on the change/time continuum, which in turn create conditions that become the triggering events/implementations for the next set of defined processes to execute in the subsequent time interval on the change/time continuum, all of which continues as time progresses along the change/time continuum (as presented in the chain of events principle).

Personal system. A system that is specific to obtaining overall defined change at an individual, organizational, or societal level and is specific to a given individual, organization, or society in a given environment.

Power. The ability of doing or accomplishing something. In change science we equate this to obtaining a desired defined change.

Primary defined change. The ultimate defined change with which the defined implementation is associated. It is the final defined change in the primary environment expected to obtained from the selected associated defined process and defined implementation.

Primary defined process. The ultimate defined process with which the defined implementation is associated. The process factors along with the triggering event condition associated with the primary defined process are the target conditions in the primary environment that the defined implementation is intended to address.

Primary environment. The given defined environment selected for the execution of the defined process associated with the specific defined change under examination.

Primary risk factors. The underlying reasons why the change expected or the change desired will fail to be obtained. Also referred to as fundamental risk factors. They include:

1. Invalid defined change
2. Invalid defined process
3. Invalid defined implementation
4. Invalid primary environment
5. Environmental override

Process factors. The specific variables, elements, activities, or other types of factors necessary for a specific process to occur. Process factors need to be all-inclusive relative to the specific defined process that will be used to obtain the defined change.

Process map. An outline that attempts to map out at a high level the critical characteristics and aspects associated with a specific defined process that is under examination.

Process stacking. The fact that whenever the process factors and/or implementation factors have more than one defined process incorporated in them, the validity, efficiency, effectiveness, and reliability associated with that defined process and/or defined implementation are directly impacted by the validity, efficiency, effectiveness, and reliability associated with each one of the underlying incorporated defined processes. Therefore, the greater the number of defined processes that are incorporated within a primary defined process and/or defined implementation, the greater the potential impact that process stacking has on the validity, efficiency, effectiveness, and reliability associated with the primary defined process and/or overall defined implementation.

Process time interval. The time interval process factor associated with the execution of a specific defined process.

Relativity. Those environmental dynamics that exist relative to the environment under observation and examination at a specific point or during a specific time interval on the change/time continuum.

Relevant conditions. The subset out of the universe of all conditions that exist in a given relevant environment that are relevant to the process factors and implementation factors associated with a defined process and defined implementation under examination.

Relevant environment. An environment that has a defined space, time period, and conditions (or the potential to have conditions) associated with it so as to be relevant to a specific defined change and, therefore, to any defined processes and defined implementations that might be associated with the specific defined change.

Relevant environmental adjustments. The subset out of the universe of all environmental adjustments taking place in a given environment that are relevant to the change dynamics required to obtain a given defined change under examination.

Relevant process factors. Those process factors out of a universe of possible process factors that are relevant to the defined change under examination, taking into consideration such dynamics and characteristics as significance and underlying pragmatic requirements.

Reliability. The extent or expected likelihood that a given defined process will yield the same defined change over multiple executions.

Repeatable change. Change that we would expect to exist on some type of reoccurring basis because of the consistent and repeated implementation and execution of defined processes. Repeatable change can be derived from:

- Individuals or groups (such as organizations or society) that consistently and repeatedly implement and execute defined processes to provide benefit and fulfill the requirements for such change to others
- Individuals through their use of consistent and repeated implementation and execution of defined processes
- Naturally-occurring sources because of the consistent and repeated implementation and execution of processes based upon the physical laws of science

Repeatable system. A system that is intended to recur in a consistent context and with consistent resulting overall defined change at multiple points in time on the change/time continuum.

Risk. The probability that an expected defined change and/or overall defined change will not be obtained. The greater the risk, the greater the probability that a defined change and/or overall defined change will not be obtained (that is, the result will be unsuccessful change).

Risk factors. Characteristics, situations, circumstances, features, aspects, or other factors that increase the risk (or probability) that an expected defined change and/or overall defined change will not be obtained.

Secondary environment. An environment that is external to the primary environment with a first-degree secondary environment representing the secondary environment that directly borders the primary environment.

Secondary observation. Observation by an individual located in such a way relative to a defined change that there is a sufficient time delay on the change/time continuum so that experience and/or observation is related to a change effect condition in the environment resulting from the defined change that took place (that is, from the change dispersion of that defined change).

Secondary risk factors. Risk factors underlying why environmental override can exist. Some of the more prevalent include:

1. Time interval on the change/time continuum
2. Conflicting relevant conditions
3. Complexity

Self-contained environment. Any primary or secondary environment that has a fixed set of boundaries during a specified time interval on the change/time continuum (for example, the self-contained boundary that skin and other body features create or the case of cell phone relative to surrounding secondary environments represents a self-contained environment).

Simultaneous change. Change that occurs simultaneously during any time interval along the change/time continuum across all environments no matter how the environments are defined.

Society and/or organization. Two or more individuals combining together to cognitively influence the environment to obtain certain desired defined change that would be difficult if not impossible to obtain at an individual level.

Subsystem. A set of defined changes and associated defined processes and defined implementations that represents both a system in and of itself and also a part of a larger system.

Successful cognitively-influenced change. A desired defined change obtained in a given environment through the successful implementation of a process associated with the required defined change and for which a cognitive influence exists.

Successful naturally-occurring change. Change obtained when the interaction of the environment and the laws of science naturally produce a defined change (that is, new state of being) that is expected from such an interaction. In technical terms, the environment supports the defined implementation of the defined process required to obtain the expected defined change that has naturally occurred.

System. The amalgamation and combination of two or more defined changes and associated defined processes and defined implementations that are configured and implemented in such a way along the change/time continuum that when they are executed in their totality, they result in a specific overall defined change or set of defined changes. The implementation and execution of the individual defined changes/processes/implementations that are incorporated into a system can occur sequentially and/or simultaneously along the change/time continuum in one or more environments.

System implementation. The methodology associated with the implementation of a specific system.

Tier I defined process. The defined process incorporated into the defined implementation that is expected to execute in the time interval on the change/time continuum immediately prior to the point in time on the change/time continuum in which the triggering event starts the execution of the primary defined process. This time interval must be contiguous to the time interval associated with the execution of the primary defined process. There will always be at least one Tier I defined process.

Tier II defined process. The defined process incorporated into the defined implementation that will execute in the first required time interval (although not necessarily contiguous) prior to the Tier I defined process or processes. There can be situations in which a Tier II defined process or processes are not required. Depending upon how the time interval associated with Tier II defined processes is defined, additional tiers (Tiers III through Tier X+) can be established as needed in order to manage the sequence of the defined processes that are incorporated into a given defined implementation.

Time interval. The amount of time that passes between one state of being and another state of being (for example, a beginning state of being and an ending state of being).

Total time interval. The time interval between the point in time that the defined change/process/implementation is selected and the point in time on the change/time continuum when the desired defined change is expected to be effectively obtained.

Traditional risk factors and/or tactical risk factors. Traditional context to approach the subject of risk associated with change and/or the implementation of change. These factors include:

1. Scope—represents the degree of change and effort to obtain the change that is under consideration
2. Duration—represents the length of time associated with the implementation of an ability to obtain a change, execute a change, and/or any combination thereof
3. Resources—represents the amount of time/effort, human capital, financial capital, and other resources an individual, organization, or society must commit to the implementation of an ability to obtain a change, execute a change, and/or any combination thereof

Triggering event. The first facet of a specific defined implementation that defines the specific condition that must exist in an environment in order for the specified defined process to execute in that environment. It is important to note that a triggering event is the specific condition that exists in the environment that triggers the execution of a specific defined process and is NOT the process or processes that produces that specific condition.

Uncontrollable risk. Any risk for which direct influence is outside of the control of the individuals and/or organizations that in some way have a vested interest in obtaining the given change under consideration.

Unsuccessful cognitively-influenced change. Change occurring when a desired defined change is not obtained from the cognitive influence of the environment or change elements.

Unsuccessful naturally-occurring change. Change occurring when conditions in the environment are such that the laws of science are unable to naturally produce a given defined change. In technical terms, when the defined implementation of the defined process required to obtain a given defined change is restricted by the conditions that exist in the given environment, an expected naturally-occurring change does not take place.

Valid defined process. A defined process that will execute to yield its associated desired defined change if and/or when there are environmental conditions that match all the required process factors and there are no conflicting relevant conditions that exist in that environment. Put simply, there is validity to a defined process if it is known to work in providing a specific defined change, all other things being equal.

Variable relevant conditions. Relevant conditions that at one point in time, or for an interval of time on the change/time continuum, have no direct impact on the change dynamics that are executing but that can become either a complementary and/or conflicting relevant condition at a future point or interval of time on the change/time continuum based upon the results of future change dynamics that execute within the environment.

Index

Pages numbers in boldface type indicate illustrations/figures.

analysis, change dynamics. *See* change dynamics

butterfly effect, 145–148

canned systems. *See* off-the-shelf/canned systems
chain of events principle, 47, 49, **50**, 53, 54, 64, 67, 93, 115, 353, 419, 433
change, cognitively-influenced. *See* cognitively-influenced change
change dispersion, 132–133, 134, 135, 136, 138, 139, 140–142, **144, 145**, 146, 147, 419, 436
change dynamics, 60, 61–87, 119, 256, 420
    analysis, 81, 82, 86–87, 96
    chain of events principle, 93
    and change dispersion, 140–142
    and change effect, 140
    and conditions, 106–115
    and defined implementation, 66, 68, 69
    and defined process, 64
    and environment, 74, 78, 92, 116, 120–122, 123, 125, 131–132, 134, 135, 261
    profile, 80–86, 95, 278–279, 280–283, 284, **285**, 286, **288**, 292, 383, 420
change effect, 128, 129, 130, 131, 134, 136, 191, 261, 421, 436
    and change dispersion, 132–133, 134, 136. 140
    and change dynamics, 140
    and defined change, 137–138
change hierarchy. *See* hierarchy of change
change protectionism, 376, 406, 421
Change Science Institute, 421
change/time continuum principle, 43, **45**, 46, 116, 353, 422
cognitively-influenced change, 31–35, 54, 59, 110, 152, 153, 154, 156, 157, 168, 204, 217, 235, 239, 241, 252, 255, 353, 354, 422, 425
    successful, 437
    unsuccessful, 439
cognitively-influenced conditions, 109, 110, 111, 112, 422
cognitively-influenced triggering event, 109, 422

commitment, lack of, 5–9, 187
complementary relevant conditions, 107, 422
complexity, 11, 347, 353, 357–364, 393, 423, 436
conditions
    change of dynamics, 106–15
    cognitively-influenced, 109, 110, 111, 112, 422
    complementary relevant, 107, 422
    constant, 110–111, 194, 195, 271, 423
    dominant, 111–112, 356, 426
    versus environments, 112–115
    See also conflicting relevant conditions
conflicting relevant conditions, 107, 108–109, 112, 218, 243, 245, 256, **276, 280–283**, 284, 287, 347, 349, 353, 356–357, 423, 430, 436, 440
controllable risk, 373–375, 378, 381, 383, 384, 390, 409, 424, 427
control and monitoring points, **401–404**, 406–407, 424
control, monitoring, and adjustment points, 406–407
defined change, 21–23, 28, 29, 30, 47, 48–49, 59, 64, 65, 67, 69, 71, 74, 75, 76, 137–138, 149–170, 224, 232, 240, 312–314, 347–349, 424
defined implementation, 24–27, 48, 58, 66–71, **72**, 188–192, 198, 202–203, **207, 208**, 249–295, 349–351, 424
defined process, 23–24, 48, 58, 64–65, 67, 70, 171–210, 211–248, 268, 270–275, 349–351, 424, 440
definitional parameters, 81–82, 87, 425
desired defined change, 33, 34, 59, 75, 81, 82, 87, 98, 110, 155–157, 201, 236, 237, 238, 240–242, 278, 302, 330, 349, 425
direct observation, 137–138, 227, 228, 425
disconnect analysis, 368, 378–391, 394, 397, 407, 408, 409, 424, 426
discrete system, 306, 319 320–321, 426
dominant conditions, 111–112, 356, 426
duration
    as traditional risk factor, 344, 345, 354, 439

443

effectiveness, 218, 221–223, 229, 230, 231, 241, 242, 243, 244, 245, 264, 265, 266, 268, 269, 317, 326
efficiency, 218, 219–221, 229, 231, 264, 265, 266, 317, 320, 327
effort, 219, 220, 222–223, 268, 332, 368–369, 392–398, 426, 427
elements of change, 21–24, 27, **28**, 47–48, 152, 427
eliminate and mitigate, 368, 372, 377–378, 381, 390, 407
  See also controllable and uncontrollable risk
Energy/Effort Hump Theory, 368, 392–396, 427
environmental adjustments, 120–121, 124–126, 261, 428
environmental dynamics, 93, 99, 115, 117–148, 185, 200, 215, 256–257, 261, 305, 428
environmental override principle, 40–43, 46, 97, 98, 183, 214, 216, 428
environments, 89–116, 117–148, 428
  and change dynamics, 74, 78, 92, 116, 120–122, 123, 125, 131–132, 134, 135, 261
environments versus conditions, 112–115
exclusive primary environment, 103, 104, 428–429
experience, 232, 429
experience/change/power equation, 234–239, 318, 429
expertise, 232, 233, 429
external environmental adjustments, 120, 121, 125, 261, 429

fixed environment, 105, 127, 429, 430
functionality trade-off, 373–374, 375, 430
hierarchy of change, 187, 192, 203, 353, 430
Hump Theory. *See* Energy/Effort Hump Theory

implementation factors, 26, 27, 40, 59, 66, 70, 107, 188, 191, 201, 217, 253, 256–257, 259, 311, 361, 428, 430
implementation plan, 82, 255–257, 430
implementation system, 310–311, 430
implementation time interval, 200, 257, 354, 398, 408, 430
inter-environmental influence, 128–132

internal environmental adjustments, 120, 125, 431
intuition, 234, 431
irrelevant conditions, 113, 124, 125, 126, 357, 431
irrelevant environment adjustments, 125, 431

magnitude, 217, 359, 31, 363, 423, 431
mobile environment, 105, 127, 431
multi-causal system, 307, 431

naturally-occurring change, 32, 35, 53, 54, 59, 110, 153, 154, 156, 217, 241, 252, 353, 380, 432
naturally-occurring conditions, 109–110, 432
naturally-occurring triggering event, 109, 432

off-the-shelf/canned systems, 274, 307, 432
organization and/or society, 238, 432
overall defined change, **302**, **304**, 305, 306, 308, 309, 310, 311, 312, 320, 322, 323, 325, 326, 328, 329, 334, 335, 342, 361, 423, 426, 430, 432, 437

perpetuating/perpetual change, 432
personal system, 306, 320, 433
power, 234–239, 429, 433
primary defined change, 262, 275, 279, 293, 391, 409, 433
primary defined process, 262, 264, 266, 270, 271, 273, 274–275, 277, 278, 308–309, 311, 393, 408–409, 427, 433, 434, 438
primary environment, 99, 101–102, 113, 120, 121, 123, 124, 125–126, 127, 129, 131, 132, 136, 137, 139, 140, 185, 186, 187, 188, 189, 190, 191, 192, 198, 200, 215–216, 221, 225, 228, 239–240, 243–245, 253, 255, 256, 261, 262, 270, 277–278, 285, 286, 300–301, 309, 310, 311, 348–349, 351, 352, 356, 428, 433
primary risk factors, 346, 347, 351, 352, 433
principles of change science, 37–60
process factors, 23, 64, 67, 70–71, 79, 97, 174, 177, 178–187, 190, 191, 192, 194, 200, 215, 216, 217, 219, 221,

222, 253, 262, 271, 349, 352, 392, 420, 426, 427, 434
process map, 177, 178, 368, 434
process stacking, 264–265, 266–269, 434
process time interval, 196, 200, 354, 388, 434
profile, change dynamics. *See* change dynamics profile

relativity, 113, 126–128, 134, 358, 434
relevancy, 124–0126
relevant conditions, 75, 106–109, 113, 124, 126, 140, 181, 225, 279, 434, 440
    See also complementary relevant conditions and conflicting relevant conditions
relevant environment, 75–77, 95, 96, 97, 107, 434, 435
relevant environmental adjustments, 125, 126, 435
relevant process factors, 181, 271, 277, 435
reliability, 218, 221, 223–229, 230, 231, 243, 244, 245, 264, 265, 266, 269, 284, 317, 326, 327, 329, 435
repeatable change, 159–162, 168, 274, 322, 435
repeatable system, 306–308, 312, 314, 318, 319–320, 322–328, 333, 436
resources, 395, 434
    as traditional risk factor, 344, 345
risk, 201, 316, 337–364, 365–410, 436
risk, controllable. *See* controllable risk
risk dynamics, 337–364, 365–410
risk factors, 342, 343–364, 436
    See also risk
risk, uncontrollable. *See* uncontrollable risk

scope
    as traditional risk factor, 344, 345, 439
secondary environment, 99, 100, 101–102, 103, 104, 105, 114, 121, 123, 124, 125, 129, 131, 132, 137, 139, 140, 141, 142, 143, 191, 261, 436
secondary observation, 137–138, 227, 436

secondary risk factors, 347, 353, 379, 436
self-contained environment, 105, 436
simultaneous change, 55–58, 127, 136, 193, 430, 437
society and/or organization, 437
structural nature of defined processes, 171–210
subsystem, **304**, 305, 321, 437
successful cognitively-influenced change, 34, 437
successful naturally-occurring change, 32, 437
system, 297–336, 437
system implementation, 311–312, 438

tactical risk factors. *See* traditional risk factors
Tier I defined process, 262, 264, 438
Tier II defined process, 264, 438
tiered implementation processes, 260–264
time interval, 44, 47, 49, 50, 53, 57, 82, 98, 438
    See also total time interval
total time interval, 354, 355, 362, 391, 398, 438
traditional risk factors, 344, 346, 439
triggering event, 26, 27, 48, 49, 50, 51, 65, 68, 69, 79, 109, 191, 196–199, 253, 254, 422, 432, 433, 438, 439

uncontrollable risk, 368, 372, 375–377, 378, 381, 383, 384, 390, 405, 406, 409, 421, 427, 439
unsuccessful cognitively-influenced change, 34, 439
unsuccessful naturally-occurring change, 32, 440

valid defined process, 58, 348, 352, 379, 408, 440
validity, 218, 230, 231, 243, 244, 245, 264, 265, 266, 326, 327, 351
variable relevant conditions, 107, 440

Index   445

Tom Somodi is an author, speaker, and consultant on the subject of change applying his extensive business experience, including taking a company public during the difficult financial markets of 2011. His executive management level experience also includes domestic and international reorganizations; acquisitions; and strategic change initiatives in manufacturing, distribution, and service organizations. Tom has been a Certified Public Accountant and has significant public and private sector executive and board level experience including positions as chief executive officer, chief operating officer, chief financial officer, and chief strategy officer.